The Mind and Art of
Giovanni Battista
PIRANESI

Felice Polanzani: portrait of Giovanni Battista Piranesi, 1750, originally used as the frontispiece to the *Opere Varie*

Bust page 118

The Mind and Art of
Giovanni Battista
PIRANESI

with 391 illustrations, including the complete *Vedute di Roma*
and *Carceri d'Invenzione* in full-page reproductions

JOHN WILTON-ELY

THAMES AND HUDSON

For Valerie

Endpapers: (front) G. B. Nolli and Piranesi, *Pianta di Roma* (reduced version, 1748);
(back) part of the *Ichnographia*, from *Il Campo Marzio dell'Antica Roma*, 1762

© 1978 Thames and Hudson Ltd, London

Library of Congress Catalog card number: 77–92272

Filmset in Great Britain by Keyspools Ltd, Golborne, Lancs.
Printed in Switzerland by Imprimeries Réunies, Lausanne

Contents

Acknowledgments

This book was begun and completed in two periods of study leave in Rome and New York respectively granted to me by the University of Nottingham, to whom I am profoundly indebted, particularly for the constant support and encourage ment of Professor Alastair Smart and the Department of Fine Art. The initial leave, financed by a grant from the Italian Institute of London, was largely based at the Bibliotheca Hertziana, Rome, where I was given unrivalled facilities for study by Professor Wolfgang Lotz and his staff. The final stages of this work were undertaken during a British Academy Visiting Fellowship at the Pierpont Morgan Library, New York, with the generous hospitality and encouragement of the Director, Dr Charles Ryskamp, Miss Felice Stampfle and her colleagues in the Department of Drawings, and members of the Library's staff.

I owe special debts of gratitude to Professor Peter Murray, who has greatly advised and encouraged me during the gestation and writing of this work, and to Sir John Pope Hennessy, who provided essential support at critical stages in my research. The progress and final form of this book owe immeasurably to my wife, Valerie, to whom I dedicate it.

Beyond these major obligations, I should like to acknow ledge the invaluable opportunities for examining the European context of Piranesi with colleagues while preparing the Council of Europe exhibition *The Age of Neo-classicism* in London during 1971–2, as well as for the preliminary airing of many ideas in this book at conferences in Naples (*Congresso Vanvitelliano*, 1973), Cambridge (Societies of Architectural Historians of Great Britain and America, 1973), Rome (Colloque de l'Académie de France, *Piranèse et les Français*, 1976) and Los Angeles (Society of Architectural Historians of America, 1977).

The formidable range of activities comprehended by the genius of Piranesi is reflected by the many people who have freely shared their specialist knowledge with me. Although it is not possible to mention all of them here, I should specially like to thank Mr Marcus Binney, Sir Anthony Blunt, M. Georges Brunel, Mr Howard Burns, Conte Carlo Cardelli, the late Anthony M. Clark, Mr Howard Colvin, Monsignor Romeo De Maio, Professor Pierre du Prey, Dr Marianne Fischer, Mr John Fleming, Mr Brinsley Ford, Dr Alain-Charles Gruber, Mr John Harris, Mr Simon Houfe, Mr Hugh Honour, Dr David Irwin, Mr John Kenworthy-Browne, Dr Christian Klemm, Professor Spiro Kostof, Mrs Delia Lennie, Professor Thomas J. McCormick, Mrs Katerina Mayer-Haunton, Mr A. Hyatt Mayor, Dr Robin Middleton, Dr Henry Millon, Mr Herbert Mitchell, Dr Jennifer Montagu, Dr S. Lang, Dr Werner Oechslin, Professor Guido Perocco, Professor Carlo Pietrangeli, Professor Adolf Placzek, Professor Mario Praz, Dr Andrew Robison, Dr Alastair Rowan, Professor Luigi Salerno, Mr Janos Scholz, Professor Damie Stillman, Sir John Summerson, Principe Frà Cyril Toumanoff, Mr Peter Ward-Jackson, Dr John Ward-Perkins, Dr David Watkin, Sir Francis Watson, Mr Ben Weinreb, Mrs Margot Wittkower, Dr Richard Wunder, Professor A. M. Vogt, Dr Ulya Vogt-Göknil and Professor Silla Zamboni.

During the course of my researches I have also received a considerable amount of help from the staff of the following institutions:
In Britain: the Ashmolean Museum, Oxford; the British Library; the British Museum; the Courtauld Institute of Art; the National Gallery of Scotland; the Royal Institute of British Architects; the Society of Antiquaries of London; the Victoria and Albert Museum and the Warburg Institute.
In America: the Avery Library, Columbia University; the Boston Museum of Fine Art; the Cooper-Hewitt Museum of Design, New York; the Fogg Museum of Art, Harvard University; the Metropolitan Museum of Art and the New York Public Library.
In France: the Bibliothèque Nationale and the Ecole Nationale des Beaux-Arts.
In Germany: the Kunstbibliothek, Berlin and the Kunsthalle, Hamburg.
In Italy: the Accademia Nazionale di San Luca; the Biblioteca Vaticana; the British School in Rome; the Calcografia Nazionale; the Gabinetto delle Stampe, Rome and the Galleria degli Uffizi, Florence.
In Holland: the Rijksmuseum, Amsterdam.
In Sweden: the Nationalmuseum, Stockholm.

Finally, I should like to express my appreciation of the typing of the manuscript by Miss Joan Clarke, and of the care and patience with which the book has been seen through the press by the staff of Thames and Hudson.

Preface

AMOUNTING concern with Piranesi over the past two decades, represented by a series of major exhibitions in Europe and North America, testifies to his powerful appeal for our time. Hailed recently as having 'a good claim to be reckoned the first great artist of Romanticism', he is included, along with Blake, Fuseli and Goya, as a symptomatic figure in a changing order.[1] While this proto-Romantic conception is a compelling one, and indeed has respectable ancestry in the writings of De Quincey and Baudelaire among others, there is a real danger of our failing to understand the artist within his own time; equally so, of confining his versatile and complex personality within artificial categories of styles and movements. As the bicentenary of Piranesi's death approaches, it is the aim of this work to offer the basis for a reappraisal of this protean figure.

Since Henri Focillon's major study of the artist published in 1918, no one is likely to underestimate Piranesi's achievement in transforming the European vision of antiquity to such an extent that his view continues to affect us today.[2] Considerable study has subsequently been devoted to Piranesi as a graphic artist of technical brilliance and of great expressive range, on a par with Rembrandt and Goya. In addition to more recent work on the artist's graphic history, connoisseurs and collectors will remain indebted to the pioneering studies of Albert Giesecke and Arthur Hind, as also to Hylton Thomas's monograph on the drawings of Piranesi. Extensive analysis has also been devoted to Piranesi's themes of fantasy and their intimate connections with his training in the world of the Baroque theatre. The celebrated *Carceri d'Invenzione*, in particular, have prompted more studies than any other group of his works, ranging from the psychological interpretations of Aldous Huxley to Ulya Vogt-Göknil's investigation into the ancestry and formal complexity of this potent imagery.

These major aspects of Piranesi, essential as they are for an appreciation of his visual significance, have tended, with certain exceptions, to neglect the Enlightenment world of his ideas and the sources of his motivation as revealed by his substantial writings which cover virtually his entire career. They have overshadowed, too, Piranesi's practical activities as a pioneer in Roman archaeology, which were universally acknowledged at the time and recognized by his election to the Society of Antiquaries of London. Insufficient attention has also been given to his creation of a range of technical illustrations of far-reaching importance in the history of antiquarian publications.

Moreover, apart from the seminal studies of Werner Körte and Rudolf Wittkower, it is only comparatively recently that sufficient consideration has been given to Piranesi's chosen profession as architect. A new impetus to this particular study has been the acquisition by Columbia University of the complete building accounts of Piranesi's reconstruction of S. Maria del Priorato, and, more recently, the magnificent presentation drawings for the projected tribune of St John Lateran. As a result of current developments in furniture history studies, fresh light is being thrown on Piranesi's highly original, if often bizarre, furniture and decorative schemes, as well as on their influence on a succession of designers from Robert Adam to Percier and Fontaine. Also receiving fresh study is Piranesi's idiosyncratic use of the past as reflected in the imaginative restoration and sale of antiquities during his later years, involving British patrons and collectors particularly.

Through all these multifarious activities runs a common theme – the interpretation and transposition of Classical antiquity by imaginative acts of an increasing originality. Due to the over-emphasis of Piranesi's Romanticism, it has rarely been appreciated how deeply involved are his roots and his mode of composition in the stylistic language of the Baroque, and, more distantly, in Mannerism. It is only by going back to figures such as Borromini or Pirro Ligorio – artists whom Piranesi particularly admired – that one encounters a comparably inventive use of antique forms, a phenomenon revived in the Rococo idiom of Piranesi's formative years.

At the same time, within the era of the Rococo were developing the revolutionary forms and ideas of a movement which can be seen to inaugurate in so many respects the modern era – Neo-Classicism. The life and work of Piranesi are fundamentally bound up with the early and most important phase of this intellectual ferment which reflects the Enlightenment in its radical questioning of established concepts in all branches of knowledge. Like any period of transition, that of Neo-Classicism was shot through with conflicts and paradoxes as new modes of expression emerged from traditional patterns. In this disturbing process the activities and attitudes of Piranesi help us to understand the intricate character of Neo-Classicism as the preliminary phase of the Romantic movement.

The central phenomenon behind Neo-Classicism, common to all its diverse aspects, was a profound change in attitude towards the nature and uses of the past. As is well known, the latter half of the eighteenth century witnessed an unprecedented burst of antiquarian activity, symbolically heralded by the discoveries at Herculaneum and Pompeii. Besides the various expeditions made to the unfamiliar fringes of the Roman Empire at Baalbek and Palmyra, the rediscovery of Greece and Egypt, even the serious revaluation of the Gothic, all in their separate ways served to promote a relative view of the past. The static view of a Golden Age with immutable standards of art and design was no longer tenable in an age inspired by Rousseau's image of 'natural man' and taught by Winckelmann to see cultural achievements as related to the dynamic growth of society in all its aspects.

Two results with particular relevance to Piranesi emerged from this phenomenon of historicism. As the perspective of the past grew wider, the more strongly emerged an awareness of the unique character of the present, as well as of the need for an appropriately modern form of expression. This in turn was related to a growing self-consciousness in the artist and a conviction of the superiority of inventive genius over the limited authority of ancient wisdom such as was enshrined in the writings of Pliny or Vitruvius. In this respect the career of Piranesi can be shown as one of artistic self-discovery through the study of antiquity – a creative dialogue in which the roles of scholar and visionary were fruitfully engaged.

The other product of historicism was a growing belief in the evolutionary nature of civilizations and the cultural destiny of nations, in which the artist plays a determining function. Piranesi, as he became increasingly embroiled in the Graeco-Roman debate in the 1760s, became heir to the historic belief in the indigenous characteristics of Italic civilization, as founded by the Etruscans and perfected by the Romans. This faith in the capacity of the Italic races for cultural rejuvenation – *rinnovo* – and in their inexhaustible fertility of invention can be traced to the writings of Vasari and had received fresh vitality early in the eighteenth century through the historical studies of the Neapolitan philosopher Vico. By Piranesi's later years these themes – the artist's right to creative originality and the cultural destiny of Rome – had become fused in his fervent dedication to reinterpreting the past for his own time.

Significantly, these two motivating forces can be seen to originate in the dual origins of Piranesi himself. His characteristically Venetian creative independence and capacity for flights of imaginative originality were to be combined with an overriding sense of mission acquired among the heroic remains of the Eternal City. It is to a consideration of his formative experiences in these two environments that we must now turn.

A Note on the Illustrations
The complete series of *Vedute di Roma* (137 plates) and of *Carceri d'Invenzione*, second state (16 plates) are reproduced full-page at the back of the book. In the chapters dealing with the first of these works, therefore, marginal numbers refer the reader to this section for fuller illustration of the text; in the second the original plate numbers are themselves a sufficient reference.

Titles of the topographical etchings are translated where there are accepted English equivalents, but generally left in Italian where proper names are involved. Where an ancient site is now known to have been inaccurately identified by Piranesi it has been given its correct designation, even though the result is an occasional discrepancy between Piranesi's inscription and the modern caption. Titles of series and of books are given in the original languages: in full on first mention, abbreviated later.

1 Michele Marieschi: the Grand Canal, Venice, with SS. Simeone e Giuda on the left, from *Magnificentiores selectioresque Urbis Venetiorum Prospectus*, 1741

I

Apprenticeship: Venice and Rome, 1720–1750

PARADOXICALLY, the key to understanding the complex personality of Piranesi, among the most Roman of artists, consists in his origins and training as a Venetian. His first twenty years – over a third of his life – were spent in that city, one of the most vital artistic centres in Europe, and the continual interaction between the respective contributions of Rome and Venice to his character constituted an essential driving force in his career.

Venice in the early eighteenth century was entering the final phase of its brilliant artistic history as a republic. After a century of what has been described as 'active mediocrity', a new creative era had emerged with the achievements of such painters as the Ricci and Piazzetta, reaching its apogee in Piranesi's lifetime with the internationally recognized figures of Canaletto, Rosalba Carriera and, pre-eminently, the Tiepolos.[1] Despite the moribund nature of the Republic's rigid social structure, characterized by an aristocracy holding on to the last vestiges of privilege and a notoriously oppressive censorship, Venice revived its role as a leading centre of international exchange through the Grand Tour. Traces of the dawning Enlightenment found expression in writers and theorists such as Francesco Algarotti and Andrea Memmo, and Venetian artists travelled throughout the courts of Europe serving such diverse centres as Paris, Dresden, London and Warsaw.[2] Meanwhile, a long tradition of artistic individuality was expressed in new art forms such as the *veduta*, or topographical view, and the *capriccio*, or architectural fantasy – works produced in response to the demands of visitors, even if their full potential was only reached outside the somewhat restrictive atmosphere of the city.

Giovanni Battista Piranesi, born 4 October 1720 at Mogliano, near Mestre, was destined at the outset for an architectural career. His father was a stonemason whose family had originated from Piran in Istria, the source of the fine white limestone of which monumental Venice is built. Something of this artisan background is later to be seen in the strongly practical and independent cast of mind which lies behind his more unconventional achievements, as well as in his intransigent behaviour in the face of opposition. On a higher social plane, however, his mother's brother, Matteo Lucchesi, was a leading architect in the Magistrato delle Acque, the state organization actively responsible for maintaining the vital sea defences of the city and regulating the hydraulic system of the Venetian lagoon and its local rivers.

According to his early biographers, Bianconi and Legrand, after working under his uncle Piranesi was apprenticed to Lucchesi's senior colleague in the Magistrato, Giovanni Scalfarotto.[3] This architect was noted for his engineering works as well as for his sympathetic skill in renovating and restoring historic buildings in Venice, such as the fourteenth-century church of S. Rocco. Piranesi probably assisted in the final stages of Scalfarotto's chief building, the church of SS. Simeone e Giuda, constructed overlooking the Grand Canal between 1718 and 1738. The striking simplicity of this reticent design, with its plain surfaces and clearly defined volumes, was among the earliest revivals of the Pantheon formula favoured by the architects of Neo-Classicism. Moreover, its even closer debts to the small chapel of Villa Barbaro at Maser testifies to the cardinal inspiration of Palladio's works in the first reaction against the Baroque in Venice: less a matter of revival, as in contemporary England, than the survival of a deep-rooted tradition, as demonstrated by Longhena's S. Maria della Salute, erected at the other end of the Canal in the previous century.[4]

Among the most influential figures in Scalfarotto's circle was his nephew Tommaso Temanza, a designer of an even more radical persuasion, as later shown by his church of the Maddalena in 1753.[5] Besides his extensive works for the Magistrato delle Acque, Temanza was deeply involved with theory as well as the history of Venetian art, publishing in 1778 a collection of biographies of leading sixteenth-century Venetian sculptors and architects. His practical involvement with the remains of Classical antiquity, moreover, may have initiated the young Piranesi's sense of vocation. In 1735 Temanza assisted Scalfarotto in surveying and restoring the Roman bridge and Arch of Augustus at Rimini, later to be featured in his book *Le Antichità di Rimini*, published in 1741.

The importance of antiquarian studies to the practising architect is also demonstrated in the career of Lucchesi. Besides concerning himself with the harbour works of the ancient Romans while carrying out installations for the Magistrato, Lucchesi, like Temanza, was involved in protracted antiquarian disputes such as that provoked by the Veronese scholar Scipione Maffei over his claim to have discovered an Etruscan entablature.[6] Such intermingling of practical and theoretical concerns is also characteristic of the elusive if seminal teachings of the Dominican priest Pietro Lodoli, in general

2 Ferdinando Bibiena: stage design showing a *scena per angolo*, from *Architettura Civile*, 1711

3 Marco Ricci: *Capriccio* from *Experimenta*, 1730

currency in Venice during Piranesi's youth. Apart from questioning the entire validity of the Classical principles of architectural design, Lodoli based his arguments upon the criteria of function and the direct expression of materials which he found exemplified in the stone construction of the Etruscans.[7]

Equally fundamental to Piranesi's later development, if in considerable contrast to these utilitarian experiences, was his training in stage design. By the early eighteenth century the prolific activities of the Bibiena family in particular had perfected a science of illusion in which the exercise of linear perspective offered an ever-expanding world of fantasy. Inevitably many of the most imaginative architects of the Baroque, from Bernini to Juvarra, were involved in this field which offered a richly experimental medium for new ideas. Venice, with its traditions of spectacle going back to Tintoretto and Veronese, reborn in the art of Tiepolo, was particularly sympathetic to the world of the stage. With its many opera houses and theatres, it offered exceptional opportunities for the imaginative designer, and despite the vagueness of the early biographers it is clear that Piranesi underwent a formal training in this discipline. He was schooled in perspective theory by Carlo Zucchi, and at some time in these early years is said to have worked with members of the Valeriani family of stage designers. Although it is unlikely that he was trained by the great Ferdinando Bibiena, as claimed by certain sources, he would certainly have studied this master's treatise *Architettura Civile*, of 1711, with its exposition of the principle of *scena per angolo* – a revolutionary concept whereby the traditional centre viewpoint was abandoned in favour of several diagonal axes, each of which enabled further vistas to open, creating a spatial structure of the richest complexity.[8]

The intensely urban character of Venice itself provided a theatre of continually changing perspectives, amplified by varying effects of light and colour. The tradition of self-scrutiny in Venetian art, extending back to the detailed canvases of Carpaccio and the Bellini, had been reborn in Piranesi's youth with the *veduta*. This art form was pioneered by foreigners such as Heintz and Van Wittel, subsequently developed by Carlevaris, and brought to perfection by Canaletto from the mid-1720s onwards. As one of the leading European centres of engraving and finely printed books, Venice saw the development of the engraved view, notably in Visentini's suite of engravings of Canaletto's views of the Grand Canal, issued in 1735, and the etchings of Marieschi of 1741.

Appropriately, it was in Venice that the combination of the topographical view and the imaginary world of the Baroque stage reached perfection in the architectural *capriccio*. The origins of this particular genre can be traced to visions of a lapsed Arcadia and the mysterious melancholy of ruins in the antiquarian fantasies of Mantegna and the esoteric woodcuts of the late fifteenth-century work *Hypnerotomachia Poliphili*. The mature expression of this theme was achieved by Marco Ricci, particularly through the etched compositions of his posthumous *Experimenta* of 1730, and the theme was to be carried on into the next decade by Canaletto's etched *vedute ideate*.

The lack of contact with any substantial quantity of Roman monuments during these years, apart from those in Rimini and Verona, and the imaginative scope offered by theatre design and the *capriccio*, may well account for the early formation of Piranesi's heroic visions of the past. Moreover, we are told that much of his early love of antiquity was due to his brother Angelo, a Carthusian monk, who instructed Piranesi in Latin and fired his imagination with descriptions of the stirring history and legendary exploits of ancient Rome. Something of the importance of this literary foundation to Piranesi's imagination is suggested by Legrand's account of the artist's last hours, when he called for a copy of Livy instead of the traditional consolation of the scriptures.

In 1740 the young architect received his first opportunity to experience Rome at first hand when he was appointed draughtsman in the retinue of Marco Foscarini, Venetian ambassador at the court of the new Pope Benedict XIV. Foscarini, a patrician of the highest rank with pronounced intellectual interests, had travelled widely in Europe, particularly while ambassador in Vienna. His main interests being literary and historical (he was official historiographer to the Republic), he had commissioned various works for his Venetian palace celebrating great men of the past. Foscarini's interest in Piranesi marks the beginning of an important strain of Venetian patronage throughout his career, and may have been connected with the ambassador's employment of artists to carry out learned programmes, as in the case of Pompeo Batoni's painting *The Triumph of Venice*.[9]

Rome was then developing as the main centre of the European Grand Tour.[10] As a city dominated by its monumental past, however, it lacked the spirit of artistic individuality and unorthodoxy possessed by Venice. Still very largely medieval in form, the dense network of its narrow streets was traversed by a system of grand processional routes. Like Venice, this environment possessed certain properties of the theatre, if of a totally different scale, with axial vistas terminated by ancient basilicas and punctuated by splendid fountains or considerable fragments of ruin. The remains of the Classical past, where they were not isolated like the Colosseum or half buried as the Arch of Septimius Severus, were surrounded by a conglomeration of modest structures, as in the case of the Pantheon, or transformed almost beyond recognition, like the Theatre of Marcellus. For the receptive artist such as Piranesi, a wealth of new experiences arose from the contrasts between the monumental and the modest structures fortuitously juxtaposed, as well as from the constant reminder of the relentless passage of time – the rhythm of growth and decay producing an architectural palimpsest.

Rome was on the threshold of a new epoch of achievements, becoming the intellectual capital of Europe by mid-century, and the meeting-ground for the leaders of a new movement of reform in the arts. Besides the increasing numbers of Grand Tourists and the attendant *ciceroni*, dealers and antiquarians, the city was also attracting an ever growing quantity of young artists and architects. Many came through official institutions such as the French Academy, established in Rome since 1666, others were attracted by the sensational discoveries at Herculaneum.

At the time of Piranesi's arrival the future lay more with painting and sculpture than in architecture, since the city was then nearing the end of a particularly important period of building, initiated by De Sanctis's Spanish Steps, Galilei's Lateran façade and the start of work on Salvi's Fontana di Trevi. The 1740s were to see Fuga's façade to S. Maria Maggiore under construction and Vanvitelli's remodelling of S. Maria degli Angeli, before the latter's departure for Naples to begin the vast palace at Caserta in 1750.[11]

During his first years in Rome, apart from Foscarini's support, Piranesi was given firm encouragement by the Venetian builder Nicola Giobbe, who offered him the use of his books and engravings and showed him all the principal monuments.[12] It was Giobbe also who introduced his young compatriot to the leading architects in Rome, Salvi and Vanvitelli, although it is improbable that Piranesi was contemplating a conventional architectural career even at this stage. In the course of time Vanvitelli was to represent the contrary pole to Piranesi's attitude towards architectural design, and was to be attacked by the Venetian's other early patron, Bottari, for his cavalier treatment of Michelangelo's work at the Angeli.[13]

Monsignor Giovanni Bottari, who was librarian to the Corsini family and later at the Vatican, was the leading member of a group of antiquarians and scholars who strongly disapproved of contemporary art and architecture on theoretical grounds. In their criticism of late Baroque expression they pioneered the way for Neo-Classical reform a generation before the arrival of Winckelmann and the painter Mengs.[14] Bottari possessed an outstanding knowledge of engravings as keeper of the celebrated Corsini collection. Being in regular contact with such international figures as Mariette and Algarotti, he was instrumental in extending the intellectual foundations of Piranesi's attitude to the Classical past, already begun by Temanza and Lucchesi in Venice.

From his arrival in Rome, however, it was the visual impact of the Classical remains, rather than the practice or theory of architecture, which appears to have absorbed Piranesi's attention. Legrand's description of his assiduous exploration of the various ruins in the company of the sculptor Corradini, another protégé of Foscarini, is reminiscent of Vasari's account of the first encounter of Brunelleschi and Donatello with the Roman past in the early fifteenth century. In the intervening three centuries the sheer inaccessibility of the antique remains was even greater if anything, and only comparatively recently had the papal authorities begun to check the devastation and abuse of the ruins as well as the export of the more valuable antiquities.[15] The means of locating and identifying the ruins was in an equally rudimentary state. In addition to early guide books to Rome with their credulous blend of myth and conjecture, a series of attempts to record and classify the physical character of Roman architecture may be traced from the sixteenth-century publications of Marliani and Palladio to more recent works such as Desgodetz's *Edifices antiques* of 1682.[16] But apart from an increasing accuracy, the illustrations in themselves provided little beyond the basic information of surface appearance and dimensions.

Piranesi's Venetian training had already provided him with a basic knowledge of the methods of ancient building science as well as a sense of the poetic appeal of the ruined past as seen in the etchings of Ricci. But in the latter's compositions the ruins

4 Frontispiece of the *Prima Parte di Architetture e Prospettive*

An indication of Piranesi's early progress can be gained from a group of small views produced in company with students at the French Academy such as Jean Barbault, Laurent Le Geay and François Duflos. By 1745, when some ninety of these were published as *Varie Vedute di Roma Antica e Moderna . . .,* forty-seven were signed by Piranesi. However, at least six of the latter were already in existence by 1741 when published by G. L. Barbielli, including the view of St John Lateran.[18] Compared with the plate in Vasi's first volume of collected views, his *Magnificenza di Roma Antica e Moderna* of 1747, with its prosaic regularity of line, Piranesi's etching, for all its immaturity, already reveals his sensitivity to the qualities of mass and volume as well as a more painterly technique. It is hardly surprising that Piranesi quarrelled with his master who, according to Legrand, once observed: 'You are too much of a painter, my friend, to be an engraver.'[19]

The remarkable speed with which Piranesi acquired a skill in the medium may be connected with his friendship with the Venetian Felice Polanzani, also working with Vasi. Polanzani's memorable portrait of Piranesi, published at the end of the decade, shows the more subtle qualities of his swollen line technique as compared to the even line of Vasi's approach, or the more delicate style of artists such as Duflos, who derived their inspiration from the seventeenth-century artist Stefano della Bella.

In retrospect it can be seen that the production of these engraved views merely served to provide a precarious living while Piranesi was involved in a more creative relationship with antiquity, culminating in his first independent publication, the *Prima Parte di Architetture e Prospettive . . .* of 1743. As a synthesis of the artist's early years in Venice and Rome, this collection of imaginary compositions, which included a frontispiece and twelve plates, was dedicated to Giobbe and appeared as a valedictory act before Piranesi left Rome through lack of financial support.[20] Many of these architectural compositions are closely inspired by Giuseppe Bibiena's recent work *Architetture e Prospettive* of 1740, a demonstration of mastery over elaborate systems of perspective and the virtuoso manipulation of the elements of monumental Classical design.

Piranesi's intention, however, as expressed in the dedication, suggests a more specific as well as a more visionary approach. In this work, clearly intended to be followed by a sequel, he undertook an act of creative reconstruction using the remains of the past as a point of departure – a purpose which owes less to the striking rhetoric of Pannini than to the seriousness of the professional architect. In Piranesi's words:

These speaking ruins have filled my spirit with images that accurate drawings, even such as those of the immortal Palladio, could never have succeeded in conveying, though I always kept them before my eyes. Therefore, having the idea of presenting to the world some of these images, but not hoping for an architect of these times who could effectively execute some of them . . . there seems to be no recourse than for me or some other modern architect to explain his ideas through his drawings and so to take away from sculpture and painting the advantage, as the great Juvarra has said, they now have here over architecture. . . .[21]

In the *Prima Parte* the tangible ruins of antiquity, as represented by the frontispiece and the *Ruins of ancient buildings,* provided the basic material for Piranesi's excursions into

were subordinated to a picturesque landscape, possessing little independence in themselves. It was the works of the greatest living exponent of the ruin fantasy, Giovanni Paolo Pannini, then at the height of his powers, which undoubtedly opened Piranesi's eyes to the portrayal of more architectonic values. Pannini, who had worked on stage designs for Juvarra in the 1720s, had become attached to the French Academy as Professor of Perspective. During this time he had developed a number of different types of *veduta*, especially the *veduta ideata*, in which various accurately rendered monuments of ancient Rome were assembled in imaginary compositions.[17] Piranesi, who became involved with the Academy students at this time, found himself in a situation where the *pensionnaires* were being drawn away from their hitherto traditional tasks of executing measured drawings of recognized exemplars in favour of the more imaginatively stimulating compositions *al capriccio*.

The necessity of finding some means of regular employment, patently lacking in the architectural field, may also partly account for Piranesi's decision to enter the field of topographical engraving. Within a year of his arrival in Rome he entered the studio of the Sicilian Giuseppe Vasi, a former pupil of Juvarra and the foremost engraver of *vedute* in the city. There he appears to have learnt the technical rudiments of etching and the procedure for producing the engraved views of the city and its monuments then in great demand.

Ruine di Sepolcro antico posto dinanzi ad altre ruine d' un Acquedotto pure antico; sopra gli archi del medesimo si è il canale, per cui si conduceva l'acqua in Roma.

5 *Ruins of ancient buildings*, from the *Prima Parte*

6 *Ancient burial chamber*, from the *Prima Parte*

7 *Great gallery*, from the *Prima Parte*

fantasy. The composition of these ruin scenes is more indebted
to the *capricci* of Marco Ricci than to those of Pannini. On closer
examination, however, particularly of the latter plate, it can be
seen that the artist already has a far greater knowledge of and
concern with antique construction than either of them. This is
true even in the specific process of deterioration in masonry. On
the other hand, Piranesi's Venetian training is also manifest in
such visionary compositions as the *Monumental bridge* where the
inspiration of Palladio is seen not only in the subject (derived
from the projected Rialto bridge as published in the *Quattro
Libri*), but also in the Classical orthodoxy of the individual
components. Largely Venetian also is the manipulation of light
to amplify the Bibienesque effects of *scena per angolo* and inflated
scale. Signs of an awakening originality, moreover, can also be
seen in the confident rearrangement of Classical motifs and the
total plausibility of the result as a fully coherent structure.

Even closer to the Bibiena traditions of stage spectacle is the
composition of the *Great gallery*, incorporating references to
antique sculptures such as the Dioscuri, and possibly even
allusions to Borromini's Lateran aedicules. Similarly the
Ancient Campidoglio originates from several Bibiena sources,
especially in the use of motifs such as the obelisk supported by
slaves.[22] But again, in both these works, the assurance with
which spatial relationships, plans and structures are organized
sets the designs apart from the ephemeral world of the Baroque

Ponte magnifico con Logge, ed Archi eretto da un Imperatore Romano, nel mezzo si vede la Statua Equestre del medesimo. Questo ponte viene veduto fuori di un arco d'un lato del Ponte che si unisce al sudetto, come si vede pure nel fondo un medesimo arco attaccato al principal Ponte.

8 *Monumental bridge*, from the *Prima Parte*

9 *Ancient Campidoglio*, from the *Prima Parte*

Campidoglio antico a cui si ascendeva per circa cento gradini. Nel mezzo di questi gradini vi è una piazza sopra la quale vi stanno Collonne rostrate, miliarie, Trofei, ed altri ornamenti. Vassi al Tempio fabbricato da Ottaviano Augusto nella Guerra Cantabrica per voto fatto a Giove Tonante. Sopra il Frontispizio di questo Tempio vi sta il medesimo Ottaviano in Cocchio tirato da quattro Cavalli. E appiè del medesimo vi stanno le Statue inalzate dal Senato per le imprese riportate dagli Uomini Illustri. Lungo da gradini suddetti vi si scuoprono in lontano Archi trionfali, colonne attorniate di bassi-rilievi, ed iscrizioni degli Uomini Illustri, Tempj, Fontane, ed il Pubblico Erario, come pure il Palazzo Capitolino. Appiè de' gradini suddetti vi stanno Guglie trionfali colli Statua Equestre del Grande Augusto con Vasi, Statue, e trofei portati in trionfo.

10 Preparatory drawing for the *Ancient mausoleum* (National Gallery of Scotland, Edinburgh)

11 *Ancient mausoleum*, from the *Prima Parte*

stage and architectural *capriccio*. In the *Campidoglio* considerable passages of antique ornament and sculpture, as well as the form of a large domed temple, reflect a serious concern with the intrinsic values of the antique which are notably absent in the fantasies of Ricci, and even of Pannini.

Unquestionably the most striking of all the plates is the *Ancient mausoleum*; the preparatory drawing for it survives at Edinburgh. Indeed, the maturity of its conception caused it to be dated to later in Piranesi's career until it was discovered in rare copies of the *Prima Parte* in the Princeton and Avery Libraries.[23] Here all the qualities of imaginative breadth and scholarship found in the other plates are developed to an unparalleled pitch of monumentality. After certain specific sources have been identified in the Imperial mausolea, not to mention Borromini's highly idiosyncratic S. Ivo della Sapienza, the inspiration behind the scope of Piranesi's imagination is hard to attribute to any preceding essays at imaginative reconstruction in Italy. An important key to the problem, however, is suggested in two surviving pages of sketches made by Piranesi from Fischer von Erlach's *Entwurf einer historischen Architektur* of 1721. The life-cycle of this particular concept of the mausoleum does not end here, for within the decade Piranesi's funerary vision was to play an important role in the genesis of radical architectural ideas originating in the French Academy.

Before returning to Venice in 1744, Piranesi appears to have journeyed south to Naples. The fluent elegance of late seventeenth- and early eighteenth-century Neapolitan painters, led by Luca Giordano, which had already exerted a decisive influence on Venetians like Sebastiano Ricci, may also have contributed to a marked change in Piranesi's expression, fully complete by the latter half of the decade. The only recorded paintings by Piranesi appear to have been executed in Naples.[24] These studies of street figures, *bambochades*, subsequently owned by a later patron, Senator Abbondio Rezzonico, were the ancestors of the gesticulating humanity which was to play such an enlivening role in Piranesi's future compositions.

The main incentive for the journey was unquestionably the growing fame of the discoveries made at Herculaneum in excavations undertaken systematically from 1738 onwards. The resulting atmosphere of excitement and expectation was heightened by the general air of secrecy surrounding the finds, assembled in the Royal Museum at Portici, as well as by the severe restrictions on sketching and recording the material imposed by the Bourbon King of Naples, Charles III. In fact, despite various clandestine publications through the 1740s and early 1750s, extensive evidence was not made officially available until the eight folio volumes of the *Antichità di Ercolano esposti* were issued from 1757 onwards. What Piranesi actually saw, however, among the recovered frescoes, sculptures and miscellaneous fragments of domestic life, probably mattered less than his introduction to the exciting possibilities opening up through excavation, in the revelation of fresh dimensions to the knowledge and inspiration of antiquity. Equally evident was

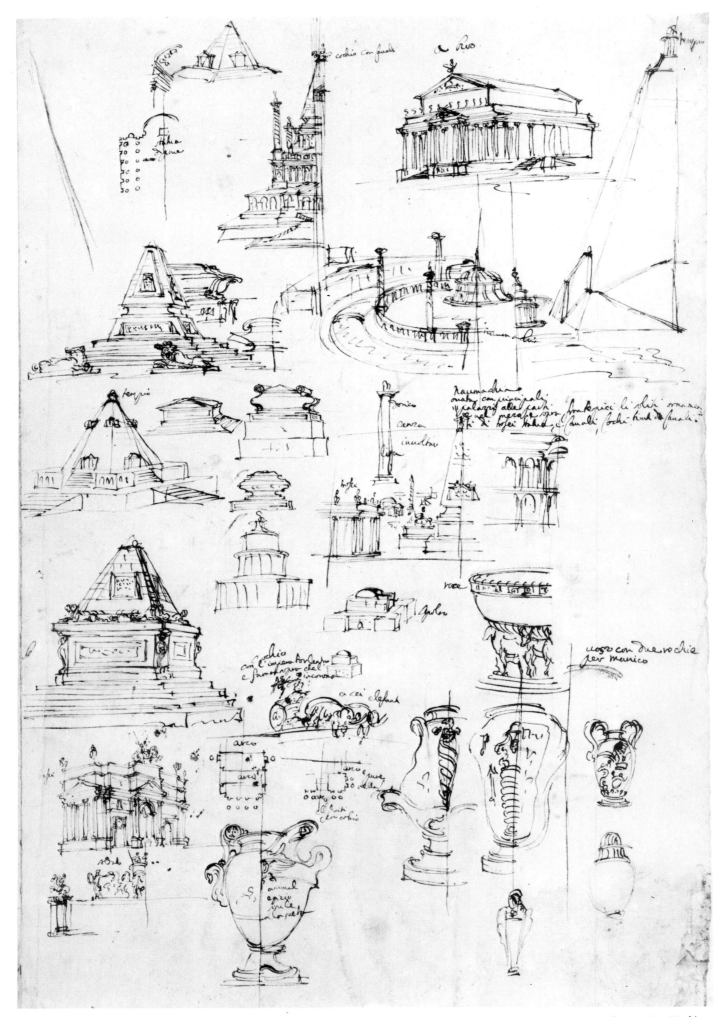

12 Page of sketches made by Piranesi from Fischer von Erlach's *Entwurf einer historischen Architektur*, 1721 (Pierpont Morgan Library, New York)

13 Antonio Canaletto: imaginary view of Venice, from *Vedute altre prese dai luoghi, altre ideate, c.* 1744

the pressing need to disseminate this remarkable wealth of information through meaningful and arresting images. Such, indeed, seems to have been the vocation recommended to him there by Camillo Paderni. This artist had been among the first to recognize the potential importance of the discoveries, as well as the inefficient and destructive nature of the earlier excavations. His concern ultimately led to his appointment as Director of the Portici Museum in 1751.

By May 1744 Piranesi, hampered by inadequate funds, was back in Venice, where he wrote a brief letter of appreciation to Bottari.[25] Exactly how he spent the next couple of years is still conjectural, but the remarkable transformation in his range of expression in terms of draughtsmanship, etching technique and expression by the later 1740s undoubtedly stems from this fresh contact with his native environment.

The Venetian development of engraved views and *capricci* had made a striking advance in the years since Piranesi first left for Rome. Visentini's engravings of Canaletto's *vedute*, first issued in 1735, reappeared with further plates in 1742. Of greater significance, however, was the suite of twenty-one views 1 of the Grand Canal by the painter Marieschi, issued in the previous year, which opened the way towards a new richness of effect as compared with the dull scenic formulae of Visentini. From 1741 onwards an even greater contribution came from Canaletto himself, who took up etching then for the first time. 13 The resulting collection of his actual and fanciful views, *Vedute prese dai luoghi, altre inventate*, probably appeared in 1744, the year

in which the dedicatee, Joseph Smith, became British Consul. Although these etchings were executed with the use of even lines, avoiding cross-hatching and with only two strengths of tone obtained through double biting, they possess an unparalleled freshness and immediacy comparable to the same artist's preparatory pen sketches.

While this idiosyncratic style of handling the etching needle is found in Piranesi's later works, a far more crucial influence was that of Giovanni Battista Tiepolo, in whose studio Piranesi is said to have worked at this time. By now Tiepolo had become the leading artist in Venice and was painting the *Banquet of Cleopatra*, later sent to Dresden, and working on the Scalzi frescoes. Like Canaletto, moreover, he had also taken up creative etching with a series of fanciful compositions posthumously entitled the *Capricci.* 15

The striking change which now comes over the meticulous and somewhat tightly organized nature of the majority of Piranesi's early topographical etchings was already anticipated in certain plates of the *Prima Parte*, such as the frontispiece and 4 the *Ruins of ancient buildings*. The delicate, vibrant and painterly 5 lines of the latter are now given a new fluency and elegance of expression. Added to this is a new confidence in the manipulation of tonal contrasts with an economy and power nearer to the breadth of Tiepolo than to the brittleness of Marco Ricci. In brief, it is the point where Piranesi becomes master of a personal style of draughtsmanship peculiarly suited to his own temperament. Something of these new qualities is evident in the

14 Design for a ceremonial gondola (Pierpont Morgan Library, New York)

group of drawings in the Pierpont Morgan Library, which include compositions for wall decorations, book ornaments, and even for a highly elaborate ceremonial gondola or *bissona*.[26] These exquisite drawings, couched in the current idiom of Venetian Rococo, with their play of sinuous line and elaborate passages of fantasy, lend support to Legrand's statement that Piranesi carried out decorative work in certain palaces.[27]

Both style and subject-matter of Tiepolo's etchings had a direct bearing on Piranesi's graphic works. The imagery as well as the dating of Tiepolo's *Capricci*, as of the related group, the *Scherzi di Fantasia*, is controversial, but the former are known to have been in existence by 1743, when published in a larger work by Anton Maria Zanetti.[28] This print dealer and engraver was a key figure in Venice as a leading centre of printmaking, particularly in bringing together the work of past and contemporary engravers through his outstanding collection and discerning patronage.

Tiepolo's *Capricci* and, even more, his *Scherzi* owe much to the ideas and style of earlier engravers like Stefano della Bella, Salvator Rosa, Benedetto Castiglione and Marco Ricci. Beyond the recurring themes of mortality and the relentless passage of time, expressed by crumbling ruins and symbols of death, their strain of fantasy in itself provided a liberating effect from the restrictive conventions of reproductive, topographical and antiquarian engraving. Through this means Piranesi began to discover within himself a form of subject-matter which was neither Venetian nor Roman but, like the comparable development in his style, was peculiarly suited to his own inventive nature.

After his Roman initiation it is unlikely that Piranesi could ever have reconciled himself to working in Venice for long. The dedicated passion with which he addressed the visions of the *Prima Parte* to Giobbe is sufficient proof of this. At some point in 1744 he was offered the chance to return to Rome as agent for the print dealer Giuseppe Wagner, and shortly set up business there in the Via del Corso, opposite to Palazzo Mancini, headquarters of the French Academy.

The effect of his recent experiences in Venice may be seen in the two groups of plates in which his capacity for fantasy and his new-found freedom of expression in technique are pushed to new heights – the *Grotteschi* and the *Invenzioni capric di Carceri* (later reissued as *Carceri d'Invenzione*). In neither instance is the initial dating certain, but the consummate balance between the characteristics of his two prime centres of inspiration suggests a time close to his renewed contact with Roman antiquity while Venice was still fresh in his mind.

In the four plates of the *Grotteschi*, Piranesi returns to a theme originally explored in certain plates of the *Prima Parte*. While, as has been noticed, the theme of antique ruins in melancholy decay derives from Ricci in particular, the exquisite sense of fantasy in Piranesi's arrangement of objects and textures reflects the decorative language of contemporary Venice. A new fluency of expression, suggesting rather than defining forms, and the built-in luminescence achieved by leaving substantial areas of the paper blank, are owed particularly to Tiepolo. But even more to this master belongs a new level of intensity of feeling which conveys an underlying sense of mystery, if not actual fear, far beyond the brittle elegance of the Venetian Rococo.

Like Tiepolo's *Capricci* and *Scherzi*, Piranesi's plates belong to a complex visual and literary tradition which had become interwoven, by the early eighteenth century, into fanciful *invenzioni*, devised to appeal to the erudite connoisseur. But unlike Tiepolo's works, Piranesi's plates suggest an intentional coherence of meaning, both as a group and as individual compositions, each with its specific identity. A wealth of clues, such as the appearance of the signs of the zodiac, the masonic handshake, half-legible inscriptions and a number of tantalizingly indistinct symbols, have prompted various attempts at elucidation. Maurizio Calvesi, for instance, has suggested the representation of groups involving four themes – the seasons, humours, times of day, and even the phases of historical change propounded in the influential writings of Vico.[29]

Whatever the underlying message of these enthralling designs, it is certain that never before had the *capriccio* been endowed with such profundity. It is as if the spectator were involved in a series of acts of contemplation, comparable to the stark confrontations between life and death in the *Melancholia* of Dürer or in the Arcadian compositions of Guercino and Poussin. Piranesi appears to continue the theme of the *Prima Parte* – heroic visions inspired by the contemplation of ruined antiquity. In the four *Grotteschi* the intense proximity of and relationship between living and dead forms, human and inanimate, imply the presence of new creative forces arising from the process of decay. In discerning the message of revival, it is possible to distinguish the first tentative signs of a theme which emerges with obsessive force in the later career of Piranesi – the theme of *rinnovo*, the inherent property of rejuvenation in Roman civilization.

The potent blend of Venetian fantasy and Roman grandeur is equally manifest, if at a more complex level, in the *Carceri*, also produced in the years following Piranesi's return to Rome. The precise date of these fourteen plates is still uncertain, and while the only point of reference yet established is their reissue in 1751, at least two earlier editions were distributed by the publisher Bouchard (spelt by Piranesi in Venetian dialect as 'Buzard' in the first state of the frontispiece).

No other works of Piranesi have generated more discussion or elicited greater claims to significance than these, dramatically reappearing in a further state around 1760.[30] Again the artist elaborates a theme first introduced in the *Prima Parte*, in this case
140 that of the *Dark prison*, and, impelled by the Venetian spirit of working *al capriccio*, pushes the concept to new levels of significance and expression. It has often been pointed out that the origin of the prison motif is to be found in the common heritage of Baroque stage design. It does not occur only in the
139 work of the Bibiena family; far closer versions to Piranesi's compositions are to be found in surviving designs by Marco
138 Ricci and, more significantly, in Juvarra's sets for Cardinal Ottoboni's theatre in the Cancelleria, Rome, executed between 1708 and 1712. That Piranesi was familiar with these designs is proved by his drawings, now in the British Museum, based on engravings of the stage sets for the opera *Teodosio il Giovane*.[31] In these sketches Piranesi's rapid and broadly handled pen
9, 150 technique, also found in surviving preparatory drawings for the *Carceri*, is equally close to Juvarra's style of draughtsmanship. This would suggest that the new facility of drawing technique, which also finds its way on to the etched plate, derives from Juvarra as much as from Tiepolo and, perhaps, the more elusive Francesco Guardi.

As with the *Grotteschi*, the treatment of subject-matter is intimately bound up with Piranesi's technical advance in these plates. Through a brilliant and highly idiosyncratic mesh of lines, the solidly constructed masonry arches, piers, vaults and
140 stairs of the *Dark prison* are transformed into a series of
141 insubstantial visions. As in the *Grotteschi* also, where tangible objects appear to evaporate, the creeping sense of fear in the *Carceri* is heightened by suggestion. In their vaulted halls the limits of material confinement are no longer distinct, but extend
156 through the imagination of the spectator into infinity. Moreover, each attempt to adjust to the spatial code established in our perception by conventions of perspective is quickly frustrated by

15 Giovanni Battista Tiepolo: *Capriccio*, 174?

deliberate ambiguities, obscured points of connection or irrational relationships between neighbouring planes and 148 surfaces.

The meaning of this work, too, is subtly elusive, and even more involved than that of the *Grotteschi* with the artist's personality. Considering various contemporary accounts of Piranesi's volatile temperament and frenetic mode of activity, the art historian is justified in discerning in the *Carceri* reflections of a deeply engaged and creatively unbalanced temperament. The way in which a highly personal style of engraving can, like calligraphy, reflect personality is demonstrated in the work of other experimental artists such as Rembrandt, Goya or Daumier. However, the myth of an opium-stimulated imagination in Piranesi, cultivated by the Romantics and revived predictably in our own time, disregards the degree of control throughout as well as this graphic expression of the artist's basic character.[32] More importantly, it misunderstands the nature of the *capriccio* as a creative outlet for personal fantasies in an age still dominated by restrictions of patronage and conventions of subject-matter.

This swift maturing of Piranesi's language of expression in the later 1740s is nowhere better demonstrated than in his work as a *vedutista*. While in Venice he appears to have produced a plate for a collection of views of the environs of Florence by Giuseppe Zocchi, published in 1744. Back in Rome, however, the stimulus of the past, strongly evident in the *Grotteschi* and *Carceri*, caused him to transform the conventional form of the engraved *veduta* out of all recognition.

Although Piranesi continued to contribute to the series of the *Varie Vedute*, published in 1744 and again in 1748, he was by now thinking in terms of a publication of his own. In 1748 appeared a collection of thirty small views of various Roman monuments seen not only in Rome itself but during his travels around Italy in 1743–5, entitled *Antichità Romane de' Tempi della Repubblica e de' Primi Imperatori*. This work was subdivided into two groups, the plates featuring ruins within and outside Rome, and was dedicated to Bottari. It was reissued after 1765 as *Alcune Vedute di Archi Trionfali*, and is normally known by this title to distinguish it from the treatise *Antichità Romane* of 1756.

16 *Ancient altar*, from the *Prima Parte*

17 Plate from the *Grotteschi*

These plates, which are among the most exquisite and sensitive works that Piranesi ever produced, show a marked advance on the *Varie Vedute* in almost every respect.[33] Their debt to his recent Venetian experiences, especially to the works and style of Tiepolo, is seen in the subtle effects of light, the skilful treatment of various materials and textures, and an elusive sense of fantasy which continues from the *Grotteschi*. More striking still is the daring and experimental way the monuments are no longer viewed from a distance but made to dominate the composition. In certain cases, such as the *Pyramid of Cestius*, they are dramatically silhouetted against bold areas of sky. In others, such as the *Arch of Janus* (or *Temple of Diana* as Piranesi regarded it), their massiveness dominates the composition to a point of exceeding the narrow limits of the plate. Indeed, in certain instances the composition actually overflows the margin – a device exploited to greater effect in later works. Spatial relationships with adjacent buildings are stated with great economy of means, as in the *Arch of Constantine*, where this monument is framed by an arch of the nearby Colosseum.

As in the *Grotteschi*, with which these plates have close affinities in both content and style, the expression of Rococo forms in the shape of luxuriant foliage or predatory creeper amplifies rather than merely decorates the subject. In contrast to the treatment of picturesque ruins in the *capricci* of Ricci, the transient phenomena of foliage and sky serve to emphasize the majestic durability of the past, less in a spirit of melancholy than in celebration of the power of antiquity to survive as an eternal source of inspiration.

Despite Piranesi's unrivalled skill in conveying the awesome scale of antiquity in these modest plates, even greater opportunities were offered by folio-sized plates for his accumulating knowledge and dramatic vision. Towards the end of the decade he began to produce the large *Vedute di Roma*, which were to appear individually or in groups until his death in 1778, establishing his fame and spreading his unique vision of Rome throughout Europe. According to his son Francesco, the series was begun in 1748, but recent research suggests that certain of these plates may well be earlier than the small *vedute* of the *Archi Trionfali*.[34] This fact apart, the decisive change in dimension is almost certainly connected with Piranesi's financial association with Giovanni Bouchard, publisher of his

early works such as the *Carceri*, before the artist set up his own business in 1761. The remarkable development in technique and expression plotted by 135 plates over some thirty years, to be discussed later, takes its departure from certain basic principles established in the smaller plates of the *Archi Trionfali*.

Piranesi's swift mastery of the new plate size is amply demonstrated by the first thirty-four plates included as part of the composite publication *Le Magnificenze di Roma*, issued by Bouchard in 1751. (Some nineteen of these actually appear to have been published earlier, according to a rare edition without a title page at Princeton.) For example, between the small *veduta* of Galilei's recently completed Lateran façade, first issued in 1741, and the large view of the same subject appearing in 1751, the hesitant style and awkward relationships have been completely resolved by a technique involving the subtle gradation of tone and sensitively etched lines of great vitality. Apart from the compositional device of the theatrical *scena per angolo* in the larger *veduta*, an effect of swift recession into depth is also enhanced by the boldly assertive parapet in the foreground. This is occupied by an arresting group of figures, themselves abruptly juxtaposed against the specks of humanity punctuating the view at intervals almost as far as the horizon.

Towards the end of the decade Piranesi's increasing concern with archaeological matters is reflected by a growing emphasis on ancient monuments, as compared to the proportion of modern subjects opening the series. At first the dramatic treatment perfected in miniature with the small *Archi Trionfali* views is applied hesitantly. For instance, although the device of a commanding silhouette set against an expanse of sky is used in the *veduta* of the *Pyramid of Cestius*, Piranesi avoids the effect of close proximity and a boldly simplified form as employed in the smaller version. Now the main subject is set well back, as if to include the maximum of information about its setting near Porta S. Paolo in the Aurelian Wall.

The *vedute* of the *Magnificenze di Roma* were accompanied by a handsome title page and frontispiece. Both plates continue the dominant theme of the *Grotteschi* in depicting a dense conglomeration of antique fragments and ruined buildings overgrown by the agents of their destruction, luxuriant foliage and vegetation. While they continue to celebrate the eternal spirit of Rome in the midst of decay, there is a greater preoccupation with archaeological detail than before: our attention is brought into sharper focus on inscriptions and bas-reliefs as well as on the specific nature of ornamental detail. The decorative skills of the Rococo designer of the *Grotteschi* are overlaid by the enquiring and didactic attitude of the antiquary, without loss of fluency or any diminution of imaginative powers. Fantasy is more developed than ever, but it is now directed to specific goals. In the frontispiece certain features, such as the unorthodox spiral reliefs of the distant Corinthian colonnade, the seeming animation of the statuary, and the sheer ambiguity between visionary and conventional space, point to new directions in the artist's development.

Piranesi's inclination for bending the rules of Vitruvian and Palladian design closely follows and grows from his developing powers of expression. Although this tendency is already discerned in the *Prima Parte*, his personal vision had become more developed by the second half of the same decade, with far-reaching consequences for contemporary architectural design.

By the time of Piranesi's return from Venice, Rome had already entered an important new era in its history. Looking back over the later course of European Neo-Classicism, it might seem almost inevitable that the city was to attract some of the most original minds of the age to study antiquity and to exchange ideas during the second half of the century. In the field of architectural design a particularly remarkable series of innovatory concepts originated from a group of student *pensionnaires* at the French Academy. Among the first to arrive was Laurent Le Geay, who won the Prix de Rome in 1732 and who, during his residence at Palazzo Mancini between 1737 and 1742, established a reputation for ideas of brilliance and great originality. The acknowledgment of these powers by such authorities as Mariette and Natoire, Director of the Academy from 1751, has encouraged certain scholars to make strong claims for the decisive influence of Le Geay on Piranesi as well as on the other members of the group concerned.[35] Le Geay was followed by Le Lorrain and Challe in 1742, Jardin in 1744 and Dumont and Petitot in 1746.

Piranesi had already made contact with students at the Academy during his first years in Rome, possibly through his collaboration with some of them, such as Le Geay, on the plates of the *Varie Vedute*. He also shared with these students the stimulating approach embodied in the *vedute ideate* of Pannini, their Professor of Perspective. Following the publication of the visionary compositions of the *Prima Parte* in 1743, however, the influence began to flow in the opposite direction, and on Piranesi's return from Venice his involvement with the Academy was to become of increasing importance, socially as well as artistically. This is indicated by regular references to the appearance of his works in the correspondence between the Director of the Academy and the Marquis de Marigny, *Directeur des bâtiments royaux* in Paris; also by the fact that in 1746 Piranesi designed a festival decoration involving fireworks to celebrate the recovery from illness of the student sculptor Saly.[36]

This latter commission highlights one of the most important outlets for Piranesi's architectural training – the production of temporary structures and decorative schemes for ceremonies and public entertainment. As elsewhere in Europe, the improvised nature of these commissions enabled progressive designers to experiment freely with original forms and concepts, uninhibited by the practical limits of permanent works.[37] The *pensionnaires* in Rome, reacting against the lax guidance of the Director, De Troy, had already begun to move in this direction. Their paintings and designs of fantasy compositions, inspired by Pannini and subsequently encouraged by Natoire, inevitably led to their entering competitions for festival architecture and decorations.[38] Recent research has begun to reveal the considerable significance of these designs, rarely recorded except in engravings.

Significantly the leader of the group concerned at Palazzo Mancini, Le Lorrain, was trained as a painter. Having swiftly built up a reputation with his various festival designs, he was commissioned in four successive years, beginning in 1744, to devise the setting for the important *Festa della Chinea*.[39] This event, held twice yearly in Rome and involving a token offering from the King of Naples to the Pope, required temporary structures or a painted backcloth to be displayed in front of Palazzo Colonna and, later, in Piazza Farnese. Although Le Lorrain's initial designs were only mildly adventurous, he produced in 1746 a work of striking originality – a Temple of Minerva, richly colonnaded and surmounted by a large pedestal of monumental severity, capped by a continuous frieze. Equally dramatic was the design for 1747, in the form of a circular open-colonnaded temple between obelisks with smoking altars and robed figures. Although the influence of Le Geay may have contributed to these designs, the overall mood and individual motifs, especially in the 1747 design, owe much more to Piranesi, particularly to his *Mausoleum* and *Campidoglio* compositions.

Michel-Ange Challe, who initially trained as an architect, changed to painting and finally won the Prix de Rome in 1741, subsequently establishing himself in the field of festival design like Le Lorrain. During Challe's eight years in Rome, Piranesi was working on the *Prima Parte*, and the architectural fantasies preserved among Challe's surviving drawings show

18 Louis-Joseph Le Lorrain: design for the *Festa della Chinea*

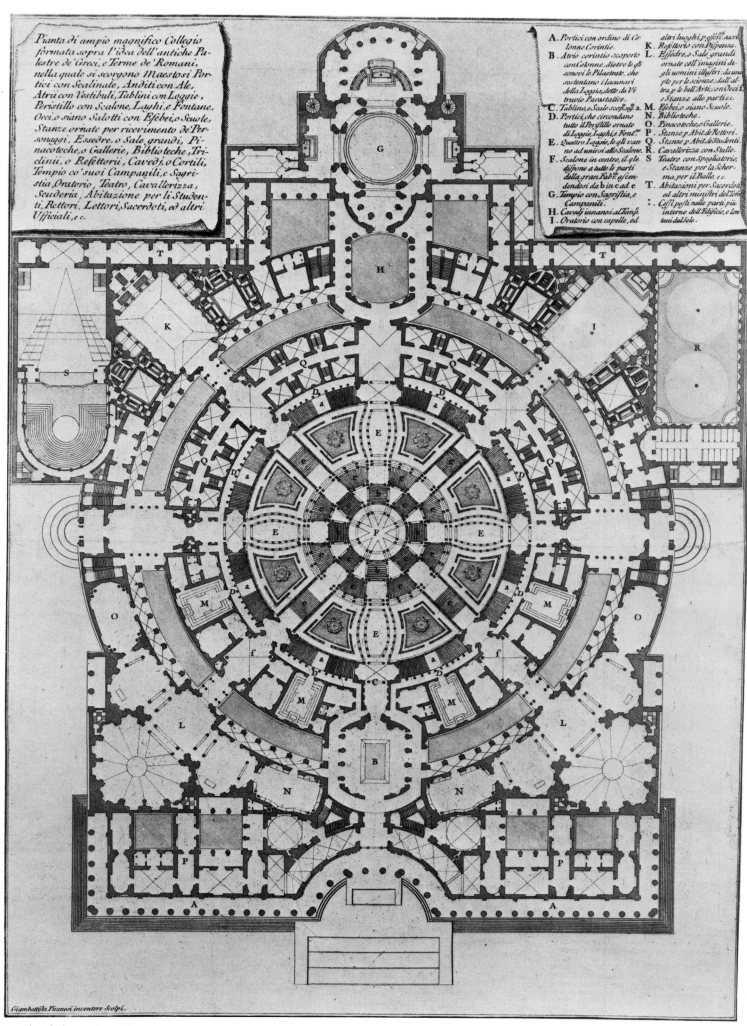

19 *Plan of a large and magnificent college*, from *Opere Varie*

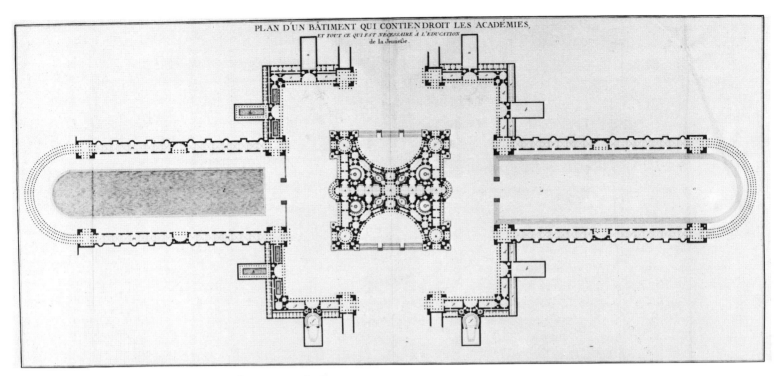

20 Marie-Joseph Peyre: design for academies, from *Oeuvres d'architecture*, 1765

how closely he assimilated both the concepts and the tempestuous lines of Piranesi's later style of draughtsmanship.[40] The closely involved nature of the group, and the interaction of similar schemes, can also be seen in the work of Jardin and Dumont. By 1751 all of the group were back in Paris where, in the course of the following two decades, their new ideas entered the mainstream of French progressive architecture. And the influence spread further, for Le Lorrain shortly went to St Petersburg, via Potsdam and Berlin, Jardin to Copenhagen and Petitot to Parma.

Clearly the ideas and concepts of the *Prima Parte* plates were by no means the only source of Piranesi's influence upon the student *pensionnaires* and those of other nationalities. During the later 1740s, he was developing more ambitious designs which subsequently appeared in the *Opere Varie . . .*, published by Bouchard in or around 1750. Included in this composite volume were eleven of the original twelve plates of the *Prima Parte*, certain additional plates produced at about the same time, the four *Grotteschi*, and the frontispiece to the *Vedute di Roma*. To these works Piranesi now added two fantasies of 19 unparalleled brilliance, the *Plan of a large and magnificent college* 22 and the *Part of a great harbour*.

The fact that these latter works were developed in contact with the *pensionnaires* is later testified by the British architect William Chambers, who refers disparagingly in his *Treatise on Civil Architecture* to the *College* plan as being produced after an argument between the artist and the French students.[41] The coherence of this vast design of the utmost complexity shows that Piranesi, despite his inclination for pictorial fantasy, continued to think as an architect. One of the sources for the plan of this Utopian academy, with its fully detailed key in the margin, can be traced to the scenographic nature of Venetian church design, especially Longhena's Salute with its octagonal 'nave' and radiating vistas. On the other hand, the elaborate modulation of spatial forms reflects a close study of the Imperial thermae, significantly the prime inspiration for the next

generation of *pensionnaires*, especially Marie-Joseph Peyre and Charles de Wailly.

Peyre, shortly after arriving in Rome in 1753, produced designs for a group of academies and a large cathedral complex. 20 These works, not published until 1765 in his *Oeuvre*, were to prove of far-reaching importance for the ideal planning of Boullée and Ledoux in the 1790s, and were to remain a basic exercise in French architectural education for over a century after that.[42]

The *Harbour* remains among the most extravagant visions 22 ever created by Piranesi. The relatively bold rearrangement of Vitruvian elements in the *Prima Parte* designs is now taken to its utmost limits, reflecting Piranesi's greater range of technical skills as an etcher and his expanding archaeological knowledge. Despite the spatial ambiguity of the vast curving façades, the sheer precision with which the foreground structures are executed, and the learned display of ornament, demonstrate the combination of Mannerist and Baroque principles of design with a new austerity of surface and breadth of composition, soon to become the hallmark of early Neo-Classical architecture in France.

As frontispiece to the remarkably diverse group of works in the *Opere Varie*, executed within his first decade in Rome, is set the most arresting image ever created of Piranesi himself. Polanzani's etching, based almost certainly upon a self-portrait *frontis* drawing, reflects the fruitful ambivalence of the artist's personality. Part modern man, part antique fragment, Piranesi's formidable features are revealed as if an exhalation from the remains of a visionary past. Emphasis is also given through the classical inscription to his proud origins and to his guiding profession as Venetian architect, while the folio volume indicates his chosen medium of communication, the etched illustration. Within the next decade this unique fusion of visionary designer and committed antiquarian was to transform his generation's conception of the Roman past and to initiate a revolution in the field of classical archaeology.

21 Michel-Ange Challe: architectural fantasy, 1746 (Collection Phyllis Lambert, Montreal)

Parte di ampio magnifico Porto all'uso degli antichi Romani, ove si scuopre l'interno della gran Piazza pel Comercio superbam.te decorata di colonne rostrali, che dinotano le più segnalate vittorie maritime. Le Pareti che sono d'interno alla gran Piazza vanno formando molti Archi tronfali ornati parim.ti di troffei navali, quali Archi si uniscono dalla parte opposta al Tempio della Fortuna, sopra la cui cima sta collocato il gran Fanale per guida de' naviganti. Le dette Pareti sono dirise ed alternate da Contraforti, che gli fanno argine e nel medesimo tempo gli servono di solido maestoso ornam.to. Sopra di queste forti in qualche distanza sono distribuiti, e posti di guardia per le sentinelle con a piedi de' mascheroni per espurgo delle immondizie. Le grandi Scalinate che veggonsi, portano alla gran Piazza ornata di Portici, Basilica, e d'altre nobili edifizi con l'ara di Profumi insignabili dedicata a Nettuno Dio del mare. Si vedono ancora sepolcri ed urne colle ceneri de' benemeriti Capitani, estinti ne' conflati navali situate a miglior vista del Porto per eccitamento di gloriosa emulazione. Questa vasta Fabrica tutta di sola architettura compresa la nobilistà di Statue, Fontane, Trofei, Bassirilievi e di tutto ciò che può servire non meno d'ornamento, che di comodo per la navigazione, resta molto bene difesa dagl'insulti del mare per mezzo del Mole, de' Lazzaretti e Magazzini, che la circondano.

22 *Part of a great harbour,* from *Opere Varie*

II

The Vedutista

ROME by 1740, when Piranesi first set eyes on the city, offered the richest theatre of visual experiences in Europe. Since the fall of the Empire, a complex series of both calculated and fortuitous changes had affected the surviving monuments and structure of the ancient capital.

The early Church had added the impressive basilicas such as the Lateran, S. Paolo fuori le Mura and S. Maria Maggiore. As a result of the Goths' destruction of the aqueduct system, the legendary hills of the city were abandoned in favour of low-lying areas along the banks of the Tiber, such as the Campus Martius. Here an intricate network of medieval townscape spread round, over and even through the vestiges of the ancient monuments, notably in the areas of the Pantheon and Piazza Navona, where antiquity maintained a dominant role. The remains of monuments which had survived centuries of indifference and quarrying for building materials became incorporated into churches, as with the Forum of Augustus or the Curia Hostilia. Others, by their sheer magnitude, remained commanding features, like the Basilica of Maxentius rising starkly from the grazing land of the Campo Vaccino, once the Forum Romanum. Meanwhile the Columns of Trajan and Antoninus, together with the Arches of Constantine, Janus, Septimius Severus and Titus, were reduced to the level of curiosities in the itinerary of pilgrims.

The Renaissance, with its conscious revival of antique symbolism, enhanced the city with further monumental structures: not only the new St Peter's and the Vatican Palace, but the first of the great dynastic palaces and villas. The papacy created the first major civic space since antiquity in Michelangelo's Piazza del Campidoglio on the Capitoline Hill, and also made the first hesitant steps towards protecting the ancient monuments from further spoliation. In the closing decade of the sixteenth century, Sixtus V began the process of transformation into the Baroque city, laying out the sweeping perspectives of giant processional roads which were focused on the basilicas and ancient monuments, such as the Colosseum, and punctuated by obelisks or enriched by fountains. The lasting imprint of this magnificent act of scenic planning can readily be appreciated in the miniature version of G. B. Nolli's map, produced in collaboration with Piranesi in 1748.[1] Existing monumental spaces such as Piazza del Quirinale and Piazza del Popolo now began to receive their modern form.

Subsequently, the age of Bernini witnessed the completion of Bramante's and Michelangelo's St Peter's with its spectacular piazza; also of the largest palaces of the pontifical families such as the Borghese, Barberini and Pamphili, accompanied by their villas outside the city walls.

The final act of the drama came in the eighteenth century with the addition of monumental façades to the Lateran and S. Maria Maggiore, great palaces such as Fuga's Palazzo della Consulta and Palazzo Corsini, and pieces of urban exuberance such as the Spanish Steps, the water-stairs of the Ripetta on the Tiber, and the Fontana de Trevi.[2] Even then a good two-thirds of the area within the Aurelian Walls remained largely undeveloped architecturally, as may also be seen from Nolli's map. The richly natural setting of gardens, orchards and vineyards round gaunt remains such as the Baths of Caracalla or the Pyramid of Cestius adjoining Porta S. Paolo was extended into the outlying countryside, as immortalized in the paintings of Claude Lorrain and his followers. Here were to be found in a wilder setting such structures as Ponte Salario and the stark fragments of aqueducts. Further afield, in the Alban Hills and at Tivoli, lay a more violent cast of scenery in which the remains of antiquity, attacked by nature as much as man, provided the romantic imagery found in the canvases of Salvator Rosa. Given this plentiful and varied range of subject-matter, it is noteworthy that, while painting had already begun to exploit its visual potential by the seventeenth century, topographical engraving had barely entered into competition even at the outset of the next century.

During the later Renaissance engraved views had begun to be produced extensively in order to meet the demands of visitors to Rome, the more sophisticated being provided by the French artists Dupérac and Lafréry together with their collaborators. Similarly, the topographical achievements of the seventeenth century were recorded by Stefano della Bella and Israel Silvestre, while at the turn of the century the first sizeable line engravings were issued by Alessandro Specchi and Giambattista Falda.[3] Inevitably, the advent of the Grand Tour provided a powerful incentive in the early eighteenth century, and on Piranesi's arrival in the city the leading purveyor of engraved *vedute* was his future master, Giuseppe Vasi. Between 1747 and 1761, Vasi was to publish the principal sights of the city in a sequence of 250 plates, gathered together in the ten books of his *Magnificenze di Roma Antica e Moderna.*[4]

23 *Piazza del Quirinale*, from *Varie Vedute*

24 Laurent Le Geay: *Piazza del Quirinale*, 1741, from *Varie Vedute*

25 *Façade of St John Lateran*, from *Varie Vedute*

26 Giuseppe Vasi: *Façade of St John Lateran*, 1753, from *Magnificenze di Roma Antica e Moderna*

Vasi's etchings provided a methodical account of the city,
26 recording such fresh additions to the townscape as Galilei's
30 Lateran façade, and notable antiquities such as the Pyramid of
48 Cestius or Ponte Salario, with the same prosaic attention. In
these plates the principal subject is placed within the
compositional frame with the same monotonous impartiality
that included adjacent structures, regardless of significance, in
an identical focus. Technically, this style of etching emulated
the properties of intaglio engraving, allowing the acid to bite the
copper plate with a series of even, parallel lines similar to those
produced manually with the burin. Even the textures of ground
and sky were reduced to a series of stock formulae, as
inconsequential as the mechanical inclusion of figures and genre
detail. Nothing whatever had survived of that alternative
development in etching technique extending from Parmigi-
anino to Callot and, pre-eminently, Rembrandt, whereby the
freedom of the needle on the wax or resin ground placed over
the copper plate allowed limitless possibilities to the biting acid
for creating irregular or varied lines and strongly defined tonal
contrasts.[5]

Even during his brief apprenticeship under Vasi in the early
1740s, Piranesi's resistance to this graphic monotony is already
discernible in those small plates produced in collaboration with
pensionnaires of the French Academy such as Duflos, Bellicard

and Le Geay – works which were subsequently used to
illustrate various editions of guide books published by Barbielli,
Amidei and Venuti.[6]

A comparison between Piranesi's view of *Piazza del* 23
Quirinale of 1741 and the almost identical subject by Le Geay 24
from the same edition of Barbielli shows the former tentatively
feeling his way towards a revolution in the engraved *veduta*. For
instance, Piranesi has begun to sense the possibilities of
exploiting various thicknesses of line as well as breaking or
undulating their course in order to register differences in
materials or the effects of recession. Properties of lighting, almost
instinctive for a Venetian, are used not only to emphasize the
main building, the Pontifical Palace, and its relationship to the
distant secondary mass of Fuga's Palazzo della Consulta; they
also direct our attention to the darkly hatched form of the
Dioscuri as a pivotal feature in the intervening space, whereas
Le Geay loses the force of this sculpture, even in silhouette.
Piranesi's inherent sense of theatre and feel for the irregular
shape of the space between the surrounding buildings,
completed by the Pontifical Stables to the left, leads him to select
a viewpoint with the greatest topographical potential. Within
the area defined by the receding orthogonals of the perspective,
he completes his composition with the aid of the sky (merely a
negative area for Le Geay) to give a series of descriptive roof-

Chiesa di S. Paolo fuori delle Mura

Piranesi fe.

27 *S. Paolo fuori le Mura*, from *Varie Vedute*

lines. The animation of tiny energetic figures serves to articulate the sloping nature of the ground. In brief, where Le Geay simply assembles a collection of given buildings, Piranesi already manipulates them to create an image of three-dimensional fact with pictorial coherence.

Piranesi's developing skill in extracting the maximum from the small *veduta* is also seen in a comparison with Vasi himself when depicting the new Lateran façade. Where Vasi includes for good measure a conscientious inventory of the adjacent buildings, Piranesi immediately directs our attention to Galilei's building while adopting an almost identical diagonal viewpoint. He brings this commanding feature close to the picture plane – even to the point of truncating the pedimental statue of Christ – by means of a deeper biting of this area of the plate. Meanwhile his lighter etching of the adjacent Lateran Palace diminishes its importance and leads the eye effortlessly into the far distance where the buildings of a hospital and the ruins of Nero's aqueduct are reduced to patterns of delicately suggested form. The Triclinio façade, opposite the basilica, is foreshortened radically to act as a strong counterbalance to the principal mass. Markedly pronounced in Piranesi's plate, also from the 1741 edition of Barbielli, is the increasingly 'painterly' technique which registers the subtle passage of light across, and even within, the main façade. This same feeling for aerial

perspective and for forms modelled rather than defined by strong sunlight is shown by a fusion of architecture and nature in the contemporary *veduta* of the gardens of *Villa Ludovisi*.

During these years, with Bottari's encouragement and the resources of the celebrated Corsini print collection at his disposal, Piranesi studied and absorbed the achievements of earlier artists in his chosen medium. The influence of the style as well as the subject-matter of Marco Ricci's ruin fantasies is found in certain plates of the *Prima Parte*, such as the frontispiece or the *Ruins of ancient buildings*. In the *Ancient altar*, however, the expression is closer to the stippled, feathery technique of Benedetto Castiglione, also strongly reflected in the exquisite *S. Paolo fuori le Mura*. In this particular *veduta*, with its freer and more atmospheric treatment of forms almost reaching the effect of a heat-haze, the last traces of Vasi's manner are disappearing. Within the same composition the artist introduces a favourite device which is used throughout his later works: an intricate system of compensating lines and masses. According to this device the main subject is shown in pronounced recession, its volume emphasized by strong shadow to one side, with a counter-diagonal in the immediate foreground, also deeply etched. To one side and close to the picture plane is a powerfully defined column, related spatially as well as compositionally to the distant mass of the basilica.

Circo di Caracalla

28 *Circus of Caracalla*, from *Varie Vedute*

29 *Pyramid of Cestius*, from *Varie Vedute*

30 Giuseppe Vasi: *Pyramid of Cestius*, 1747, from
Magnificenze di Roma Antica e Moderna

Piramide di Caio Cestio vicino alla Porta S. Paolo

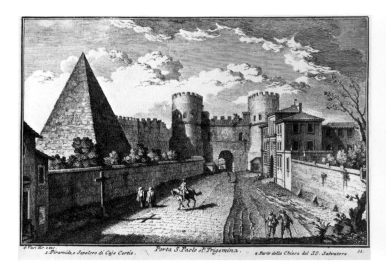

Piramide, e Sepolcro di Cajo Cestio .   Porta S. Paolo et Trigemina .   a Parte della Chiesa del SS. Salvatore .

Between these initial plates and Piranesi's completion of forty-seven of them by 1745, published by Fausto Amidei in the *Varie Vedute di Roma Antica e Moderna . . .*, occurred the decisive return to Venice where the influence of Tiepolo and Canaletto in particular consolidated these tentative beginnings.[7] The new freedom of technique and an increased sense of fantasy, already reflected on Piranesi's return to Rome around 1744 in the four *Grotteschi* and the early *Carceri*, are accompanied by a greater degree of tonal contrast, essentially foreign to the Venetians. Although the influence of Rembrandt's actual etching technique on Piranesi was negligible, his dramatic effects of tone were swiftly assimilated, and few other etchers were to compare with Piranesi in this bold and dramatic use of the medium. It is also possible that his brief but first-hand encounter with Neapolitan painting in the mid-1740s may further have impelled his development in this direction.

Whatever the prime source of influence in this respect, a later plate in the *Varie Vedute*, such as the *Circus of Caracalla*, combines within it a new range of contrasting tones with a greater amplitude of form, not to be reached by Piranesi on a larger scale until appreciably later in his career. A monumental portion of the ruined stadium, placed close to the picture plane, is built up through a series of hints and suggestions in broken lines, deep shadows and luminescent surfaces. An effect of space is aided by the omission of the conventional margin to the plate, while an abundance of foliage softens the main fragment

and unites it to its natural setting. Also in this plate can be seen maturing a method of presenting information about visually unpromising material unavailable to the restricted technique of Vasi. The foreground arch, providing a strong *repoussoir* effect, is set against the faintest traces of the oblong arena, with its *spina* or central reservation, to which this fragment is clearly related.

The same boldness in descriptive means can be seen in the *Pyramid of Cestius* – a monument to which Piranesi was to return in three later *vedute*. Compared with Vasi's relatively objective if unimaginative statement, Piranesi's interpretation must have appeared disturbingly summary to contemporaries, especially in the illusionistic effect of clipping off the apex of the pyramid with the plate edge. Despite the symmetrical placing of the tomb at the centre of the compositional surface, its full volume is effectively described by the play of light enlivening the ascending planes of the two visible faces. Nothing of significance in the setting is omitted, whether the battlements of the adjacent Porta S. Paolo or the two solitary Doric columns, but the careful placing of a delicately foliate tree to the right completes the design and reinforces the stern dignity of this funereal geometry.

Within these same years Piranesi was also preparing the twenty-eight small *vedute* of the *Antichità Romane de' Tempi della Repubblica e de' Primi Imperatori*, published in 1748 and reissued around 1765 under the more familiar title *Alcune Vedute di Archi Trionfali*.[8] Their unity of style suggests that these plates were mainly produced within a short period of time, although many of the second section, featuring monuments in Istria and in central Italy, were probably based on sketches made during the recent return to Venice. While several of the later *Varie Vedute* already discussed anticipate something of the striking force of the *Archi Trionfali*, in this latter publication is to be found a complete mastery of many techniques of composition and presentation employed by Piranesi throughout the remainder of his career.

In the *Archi Trionfali* Piranesi brings to topographical engraving not only the architect's eye for structural and spatial information but also the artist's capacity to convey these facts through striking images with the greatest economy of effect. For instance, in the *Forum of Augustus* (or Nerva) he outdistances a contemporary like Duflos in transforming the inconsequential jumble of antique and medieval buildings into a coherent and formidable expression of grandeur.[9] Boldly compressing the principal elements of the site close to the picture plane and lowering the viewpoint, Piranesi causes these structures to tower above and to envelop the spectator's field of vision. A skilful placing of the masses to either side of the central arch, framing a tiny group of humanity, gives the delicately touched area of the sky a remarkable potency. Space is described by light, even to the extent of implying the adjacent buildings on the right through a broadly cast shadow.

As its later title suggests, the various monumental arches of Rome dominate the first part of the collection. In each etching Piranesi attempts an unexpected approach without ever jeopardizing the basic function of the *veduta*, the communication of fact. For example, the view of the *Arch of Constantine* immediately states the building's relationship to the neighbouring Colosseum as framed by one of the stadium's arches. Densely as the plate is worked, with a wealth of decaying masonry and Rococo foliage, the small but telling areas of light, together with a subtle tonal recession achieved through repeated bitings of the plate, avoid any effect of excess or restriction.

Another such masterpiece, where Piranesi utilizes almost the entire plate surface without confusion or a sense of claustrophobia, is the view of the *Arch of Janus*. Here the principal structure, seen from below as if from a nearby excavation, is portrayed with the greatest accuracy, both in its unique form as a four-sided arch and in its relationship to the neighbouring Arco degli Argentari. Piranesi's familiar device of expanding the principal subject beyond the plate area to suggest immediacy is nowhere more effectively exploited than here. Significantly, it was at this time that he began to explore the potential of far larger plates.

It was probably shortly before 1748 that Piranesi started to etch the first plates of the large *Vedute di Roma* – the sequence of 135 views which extend over his remaining thirty years of activity, marking each phase in his stylistic evolution and intimately reflecting his current intellectual concerns.[10] Although the larger plates were to develop many of the ideas first explored in the *Archi Trionfali*, the process of adapting such potent images to the larger format was to take well over a decade to achieve a comparable expression.

While the earliest fixed date for this series is 1751, when thirty-four of the plates were published by Giovanni Bouchard in *Le Magnificenze di Roma*, it is certain that at least nineteen of

31 François Duflos: *Forum of Augustus*, from *Varie Vedute*

32 *Forum of Augustus*, from *Archi Trionfali*

33 *Arch of Constantine*, from *Archi Trionfali*

34 *Arch of Janus*, from *Archi Trionfali*

35 *Piazza di S. Pietro*, from *Vedute di Roma* (see *Vedute di Roma*, pl. 3)

36 Preparatory drawing for the *Piazza di S. Pietro* (from the Gorhambury Collection, by permission of the Earl of Verulam)

them were available in a definable set a good deal earlier, probably indeed before 1748, the traditional date of inception given by Francesco Piranesi.[11] Moreover, the possibility that a business liaison with Bouchard enabled the artist to afford the larger plates in the mid-1740s may be confirmed by the fact that fourteen of this early set are similar in dimension to three of the *Carceri* and another two are close in size to the *Grotteschi*.[12]

The area of the new plate size enabled Piranesi to tackle the monumental public spaces of the city which, understandably, were beyond the scope of the smaller *vedute*. No piazza provided

35 a greater challenge than that of St Peter's, and the resulting view, although by no means the first large plate executed, provides a fitting overture to the series.

Piranesi's approach in this plate is somewhat schizoid: on the one hand dryly topographical, on the other richly pictorial. The strictly architectural portions are rendered with the meticulously hatched and evenly bitten lines of Vasi, as found in the early plates of the *Prima Parte* such as the *Ancient*

9 *Campidoglio*. The perspectival scheme is organized symmetrically from a viewpoint well above ground level. This construction, common to several others among the early *Vedute di Roma* featuring public spaces, is analogous to the calculated view from the royal box in a Bibiena theatre. Recession plotted by clusters of minute figures and vehicles is uneasily managed, and the visual jump from the main piazza to the foreground is disconcertingly abrupt.

The foreground area, in strong contrast to the architectural rendering, is heavily indebted to Piranesi's recent Venetian experiences. It is composed of a mesh of broken lines and vigorously worked forms, as already developed in the small *Archi Trionfali*. A wealth of minutely observed genre, from the refined to the crude in subject, is concentrated along a piece of rough ground which inexplicably appears to slope up towards

37 the spectator. A group of senatorial coaches provides an effective symmetry, one of them being embellished with the

14 same exotic frenzy as Piranesi's design for a ceremonial gondola now in the Pierpont Morgan Collection.

Light, although carefully distributed over the entire plate, is not yet a successful unifying agent, as can be seen from its differing action in the two 'styles' contained within this plate. It is evident, though, that Piranesi during these years was beginning to explore the possibilities of depicting this piazza from a strongly oblique viewpoint, using light to a more concentrated and expressive degree. An exploratory pen sketch in Lord Verulam's collection, executed in the brown ferrous 36 gallnut ink of these years, isolates the problem with a striking economy of notation.[13] It was to be another twenty years, however, before Piranesi's mastery of this unifying pheno-menon allowed Domenico Fontana's great obelisk to fulfil its *Ved* role as the visual fulcrum of this majestic composition.

37 Coach, detail from pl. 35

38 Giovanni Paolo Pannini: *Interior of S. Paolo fuori le Mura* (Fitzwilliam Museum, Cambridge)

39 *Interior of S. Paolo fuori le Mura*, from *Vedute di Roma* (see *Vedute di Roma*, pl. 5)

40 Giovanni Paolo Pannini: *Capriccio of Roman Ruins and Sculpture*, 1741 (Yale University Art Gallery)

This ambivalence in style is also found in one of the earliest interior views, *S. Paolo fuori le Mura*. Here a carefully delineated architectural perspective is activated by a variety of foreground figures, ranging from aristocratic ladies and their followers to beggar women and children, squabbling mongrels and a pathetic group of cripples. The early *Vedute di Roma* contain a veritable anthology of Roman life, and Legrand describes how the artist filled his sketchbook with rapid studies such as those surviving in the Basle Kunstmuseum. Like Leonardo, Piranesi appears to have sought out the strange, the grotesque and the deformed with the same passion that others showed in recording the discovery of a new Apollo or Venus.[14] In Piranesi's figure studies we are also reminded of Hogarth's keen eye for idiosyncrasy, and of a similar visual memory the English artist used to populate his contemporary views of London life. Although based on fact, the delicately hatched forms of these wiry, energetic characters seem to have been derived by Piranesi from earlier engravers such as Jacques Callot and Stefano della Bella.

The presiding influence of Giovanni Paolo Pannini upon Piranesi's development, already evident in the visionary compositions of the *Prima Parte*, is otherwise of minor importance until the advent of the *Vedute di Roma*. The new size of plate enabled Piranesi to compete with the painted *veduta* for the first time, and a close comparison is offered by Pannini's preparatory study in the Fitzwilliam Museum for *The Cardinal of York visiting S. Paolo fuori le Mura* of 1741–3. Where the painter records with the same decorative elegance the architectural setting, its wall-paintings and the courtly humanity below, Piranesi's concern is already more selective, if perhaps less sophisticated. By choosing a slightly more oblique viewpoint and by registering the different strengths and fall of light through the apertures, he demonstrates structure as well as spatial character. For example, he indicates the principal and subordinate arcading to the aisles, and by resorting to the unique device of an architectural section through the nave wall reveals a lower clerestory over the latter aisle. While both artists adopt a common distance from the ciborium over the high altar, Piranesi's view is surprisingly accurate, while it is Pannini who exaggerates the length of the vast nave.

41 *Piazza del Campidoglio*, from *Vedute di Roma* (see *Vedute di Roma*, pl. 14)

42 Antonio Canaletto: *Piazza del Campidoglio*, 1755 (Leger Galleries Ltd, London)

Another such comparison can be made with the other great topographical painter of the age, Canaletto, through a portrayal of the Campidoglio in two works separated only by a matter of years. In the painting, executed for Thomas Hollis while Canaletto was in England in 1755, the Venetian painter adopts a central viewpoint of Michelangelo's composition.[15] Eliminating the neighbouring S. Maria in Aracoeli with its staircase, he imposes a deadening symmetry by repeating the carriage ramp on the left-hand side. The Cordonata, or main flight of steps, thus seen straight ahead, loses its dynamic energy through foreshortening, while the parading *milordi* merely serve to trivialize rather than to animate this sublime setting. On the other hand, Piranesi's unerring sense of the dramatic offered by an oblique angle of vision invests the scene with architectural energy while at the same time supplying the maximum degree of information (assisted by a numbered key in the margin). His use of descriptive lighting, and the careful placing of the moving figures in response to the varied inclinations of the two staircases and their related buildings, confers on this urban masterpiece both vitality and dignity.

The manipulation of light, one of the essential properties of pure etching, became increasingly important to Piranesi in the plates of the *Magnificenze*. The choice of an oblique viewpoint, moreover, offered far greater scope for the dynamic play of perspective, especially in those heterogeneous areas of townscape where the banality of Vasi's approach often resulted in confusion and incoherence. In several of the early *Vedute di Roma* can be found an attempt to combine these two approaches, opening up dramatic possibilities as yet unknown for the engraved view.

In *Piazza Navona* the artist found a ready-made piece of urban theatre, where monumental buildings of outstanding calibre are embedded in an irregular townscape of the greatest vitality and variation in scale and texture. The play of light over the piazza not only modulates the recession with a far greater success than in the *veduta* of Piazza di S. Pietro; it also adds a powerful emphasis to the steep orthogonals of the left-hand

façade in contrast to the gentler diagonal of Sant' Agnese and its flanking palaces bathed in strong sunlight.

The sky begins to play an increasingly important part as the surface of Piranesi's townscapes is articulated by flickering shadows and pools of light. As seen in this particular plate, the stereotyped cloud patterns of conventional engravers are replaced by a far more painterly treatment, heightening the emotional temperature of the scene with atmospheric effects. Legrand describes how attentive Piranesi was to the changing patterns of light, and the facility with which the artist recalled the fleeting passages of the sun when etching salient features of a particular façade as he worked on the plate from a rapid pen or chalk sketch.[16]

This growing co-ordination of light and perspective applies equally to Piranesi's concern with a monumental façade such as the Lateran. Here he selects a similar view to that of the early small *veduta* of 1741, but draws back further to take in virtually the entire basilica, the complex system of entrance ramps and the neighbouring spaces. The use of a strongly accentuated counter-diagonal in the foreground wall recalls the initial appearance of this device in his small view of *S. Paolo fuori le Mura*. From the strong shadow of the nearby wall the eye is led by a series of tonal gradations across a group of classical fragments (a favourite motif in the *Magnificenze*) towards the main façade. Here light articulates Galilei's giant columns while describing the internal spaces of the arcading. High above the gesturing statuary on the parapet glowers a sky of the utmost drama. This tonal journey, without losing momentum, carries us across the adjoining palace façade to the furthermost limits of the piazza, where the distant domes and spire of S. Maria Maggiore are glimpsed with a marked respect for the directional accuracy of Roman topography (see Nolli's map, front endpaper).

Given the far more uneven and variegated site of *Piazza del Quirinale*, the subject of one of his earliest essays, Piranesi's exploitation of directional lighting now reaches an almost visionary intensity. The rays of the sun setting over the Janiculum emphasize with Baroque drama, and seem to

Ved 10
35
42
41
Ved 6
25
27
Ved 9
23

animate, the colossal figures of the Dioscuri, set against a sky of great luminescence. This same source of energy brings sparkling life into the cascades of the fountain below and throws into bold relief a deeply etched heap of classical fragments in the foreground. By this act of lighting, a diagonal emphasis is produced across the intervening space between the darkly projecting angle of Palazzo Rospigliosi and the steeply foreshortened façade of the Pontifical Palace. The unity of the plate surface is completed by a series of genre incidents extending from the parading soldiery across to a meandering procession of ceremonial carriages. Placed at ground level and hemmed in by the flanking buildings, the spectator is no longer a remote witness to a theatrical act, but is now firmly involved within the picture space itself.

This development of expressive qualities in line and tone in the etching process offered a new descriptive tool to Piranesi as an antiquarian. While the timid, even technique of the earlier *Vedute di Roma* was efficient enough to record the complete buildings of recent centuries, it was clearly unable to cope satisfactorily with an accurate portrayal of the ruined past, of increasing concern to Piranesi by 1750. The small plates of the *Archi Trionfali* had already begun to suggest certain fruitful directions of approach, but it was only through the gradual process already described that the entire surface of the larger plates was invested with a comparable power to portray and to describe.

Ved 19 The extent of the progress made in this direction by the early 1750s is summed up in the *veduta* of the *Arch of Constantine and the Colosseum*. Significantly, Piranesi avoids the conventional vista of the seemingly complete façade of the giant amphitheatre towards the Esquiline in favour of the more didactic view from the higher ground of the Palatine. From here is obtained an instructive panorama in which almost the entire structural system of the stadium is exposed by a series of fortuitous sections resulting from destructive man and nature.

33 As for the Arch of Constantine itself, the mirage-like image of the small plate of the *Archi Trionfali* is exchanged for a more sombre and weighty treatment, emphasizing ornament and individual reliefs as well as the building's precise location within the contours of the site. Even the picturesque mass of foundations in the foreground of the plate, on which a group of *43* antiquarians are standing in heated discussion, is examined and depicted by Piranesi's etching needle with the closest attention to its structural components of brick, stone and concrete. The brittle Rococo foliage of the *Archi Trionfali* is replaced by a more substantial vegetation actually encountered by the artist, then beginning his painstaking examination of antiquity with spade and hatchet.

As Piranesi's archaeological activities gained momentum, his concentration upon individual monuments of antiquity became of overriding concern in the *Vedute di Roma*. Certain buildings were to possess such an obsessive attraction that he returned on several occasions to redefine their character as his conception of antiquity altered. Such was the Pyramid of Cestius, etched on at least four separate occasions within fifteen years. While many of the initial *Vedute* show evidence of later reworking, mainly in terms of lighting and the clarification of minor details, none show such striking evidence of revision as the plate of the Pyramid belonging to the *Magnificenze*.

43 Group of antiquarians, detail of the *Arch of Constantine and the Colosseum*, from *Vedute di Roma* (see *Vedute di Roma*, pl. 19)

In the first state, Piranesi adopts a similar viewpoint to that *Ved 13* used in the small plates of the *Varie Vedute*, although the angle of *29* the Pyramid's apex is less acute, being in fact close to the 60° of the actual monument. Generous space is given to registering the wildness of the natural setting, as well as the buildings connected with the nearby Porta S. Paolo. Sometime before 1760, however, Piranesi was to recut this plate radically, *44* bringing the image of the Pyramid far closer to that of the small plate by raising the apex to within a few centimetres of the margin and altering its angle to 55°. Much of the monument's surface is now cleared of foliage to produce a cleaner profile and, more importantly, to allow the inscriptions to be visible. Changes are also made to the fortifications of the Porta, and the blank area close to the right-hand margin of the plate is worked over in greater detail. In particular, a prominent tree is inserted to achieve a compositional result extremely close to the small initial view of the Pyramid. The strongly etched foreground is *29* balanced in the revised plate by a more dramatic reworking of the sky, while the play of shadow is intensified at the centre of the composition. The final result is a factual statement of exaggerated force, if lacking something of the scholarly directness of the plate published in the *Antichità Romane* in 1756, *46* against which the revised plate appears self-consciously theatrical.

From the appearance of the *Magnificenze di Roma* in 1751 until after his publication of the *Antichità Romane* in 1756, setting the seal on his international reputation as an archaeologist, Piranesi's antiquarian tasks appear to have allowed him no time to produce more than a handful of the *Vedute di Roma*. It is true, nevertheless, that a considerable number of the larger plates of the *Antichità*, like the *Pyramid of Cestius*, might be classified as such except for their somewhat dryly informative manner. It would be surprising if the intensive examination of so many of the structural and ornamental achievements of the Romans had not affected the later course of the *Vedute*. Indeed, we already see the beginnings of an important change in certain plates of the *Magnificenze*, such

44 *Pyramid of Cestius*, from *Vedute di Roma* (3rd state of *Vedute di Roma*, pl. 13)

45 *Pyramid of Cestius*, from *Vedute di Roma* (see *Vedute di Roma*, pl. 57)

VEDUTA della Piramide di Caio Cestio, situata sopra l'antica Via Ostiense, oggi detta di S. Paolo. Il Lato, che guarda sopra la strada verso Levante è la Facciata principale. 1 Mura di Roma, le quali sono congiunte ai lati della Piramide. Furono esse dilatate sino a quello Sepolcro dall'Imperatore Aureliano; e poscia quivi ristabilite ne' tempi posteriori. 2 Porta Ostiense detta oggi di S. Paolo.

Piranesi Archit. dis. e inc.

46 *Pyramid of Cestius*, from *Antichità Romane*

see page 92
plate 57

Ved 27 as the so-called *Curia Hostilia* (actually the substructure of the Temple of the Divine Claudius). Here, in addition to a new breadth of expression, there is also a greater sharpness of focus in the way Piranesi registers the individual blocks of masonry in this massive structure, incorporated into the medieval fabric of SS. Giovanni e Paolo. One senses here the result of that early training in engineering and stone construction, gained in the Venetian circle of Lucchesi and Scalfarotto, now having its full effect upon Piranesi's technical understanding of the past.

It was just at this point in his career that the enlarged vision produced by Piranesi's antiquarian researches, together with the remarkable advances made in his etching technique and compositional powers, were activated by a new force – nothing less than an awakening sense of artistic destiny. Although it has been customary to date Piranesi's violent entry into the Graeco-Roman controversy to the publication of his controversial treatise, *Della Magnificenza ed Architettura de' Romani*, in 1761, the beginnings of the story belong to the previous decade. As he grew more familiar with the extent of the destruction of ancient monuments around him, so developed a resolution to preserve and celebrate the heroic achievements of Rome through his works. As he expressed it in the preface to the *Antichità*:

When I first saw the remains of the ancient buildings of Rome lying as they do in cultivated fields or gardens and wasting away under the ravages of time, or being destroyed by greedy owners who sell them as materials for modern buildings, I determined to preserve them for ever by means of my engravings.[17]

A growing sense of identification with his material is more explicit still in a letter addressed to a wayward patron, Lord Charlemont, published in 1757, in which he asserted that:

I believe I have completed a work which will pass on to posterity and which will endure so long as there are men curious to know the ruins which remain of the most famous city in the universe.[18]

Accordingly, as the first provocative claims in favour of Greek originality by Laugier, Le Roy and others began to appear within this decade, so Piranesi's sense of personal involvement grew more intense, finding reflection in a dramatic change which overtakes the *Vedute*.

This new pitch of expression appears in a *veduta* which was produced in the mid-1750s, probably intended originally for use in the *Antichità*.[19] Castel S. Angelo, formerly the *Ved 37* mausoleum of Hadrian, like the Pyramid of Cestius, was of particular concern in the *Antichità*, and several plates were 95 devoted to it in Volume IV, including the most dramatic plate 96 in the entire work. In the *veduta* the artist no longer attempts to restrain his sense of the dramatic within the boundaries of fact, as compared say to the relatively objective treatment of the Curia Hostilia. Although much of the specifically topographical detail is of the same impeccable standard as that of the latter plate, it is now expressed in a compositional language dormant since its first appearance in certain plates of the *Archi Trionfali*. The forbidding bulk of the papal fortress occupies the larger part of the plate area and is set against an extremely histrionic

47 Street scene, detail of *Palazzo Mancini*, from *Vedute di Roma* (see *Vedute di Roma*, pl. 44)

sky. By skilfully arranged patterns of light and shadow, the outworks of the modern fortifications, distinguished from the antique masonry, loom menacingly over the minute figures carrying out duties in their shadow. With such a plate Piranesi crosses the narrow boundary between the amplified truth of the previous *vedute* and the rhetorical language of polemical debate.

In the renewed burst of topographical activity following the publication of the *Antichità*, Piranesi's succeeding group of the *Vedute di Roma*, published by Bouchard and Gravier in the late 1750s, includes many of his finest plates, in technical as well as formal terms. These works, particularly outstanding for their variety of tones achieved through repeated bitings, as well as for their fine, clean printing in a darker black ink, show the growing effect of Piranesi's heroic vision even in the interpretation of modern buildings. For instance, an imposing *Ved 44* façade such as that of *Palazzo Mancini*, headquarters of the French Academy where the artist was actively involved during this decade, shows the bold recession of the Corso as far as the distant obelisk of Piazza del Popolo. Piranesi, with an appetite *47* for detail sustained along the entire street frontage, also employs this recession to provide his composition with a strong tonal diagonal across the whole plate. His keen observation of authentic street activities in the earlier *Vedute* continues undiminished, ranging here from the group of workmen

dragging a colossal antique statue towards the Academy to the merchandise of a swordsmith's stall set against its wall. The artist's figure style is now even more assured, and serves to amplify the emotional tone of the plate with a greater intensity of movement and individual gesture. Technically, this aspect of Piranesi's development is closely allied to a richer working of the plate surface, ranging from the flickering specks in the extreme distance to the vigorously defined personalities around the bollards in the left foreground.

While a large basilican façade, such as *S. Paolo fuori le Mura*, *Ved 38* is given a dramatic force hardly suspected in the earlier *veduta* of the Lateran, the transforming power of Piranesi's heroic *Ved 6* diagonal is nowhere more effectively demonstrated than in the view of *Ponte Salario*. At a first glance Vasi's etching of the *48* subject, taken from a comparable angle, promises to be a more faithful if pedestrian record. Setting aside Piranesi's proclivity for the melodramatic silhouette, however, the informative scope of his plate proves incomparably superior on a closer *49* examination. By the late 1750s his command over the medium enabled his needle to register a range of textures with much subtlety, allowing us to distinguish the various stages of the structure's history, outlined in the detailed text below. Where Vasi's building is a picturesque encounter of little consequence on one of the consular roads to Rome, Piranesi's has become an eloquent symbol of Roman engineering genius.

48 Giuseppe Vasi: *Ponte Salario*, 1754 from *Magnificenze di Roma*

49 *Ponte Salario*, from *Vedute di Roma* (see *Vedute di Roma*, pl. 47)

50 *Arch of Titus*, detail, from *Vedute di Roma* (see *Vedute di Roma*, pl. 52)

Towards the close of the 1750s the artist's portrayal of the imagery of decay in the large *vedute* reaches a level of power attained a decade earlier by certain plates of the *Archi Trionfali*. In the *Arch of Titus*, the closest possible viewpoint is contrived without sacrificing a feel for the whole fragment, to be restored to completeness by Valadier in the following century. The last trace of Piranesi's Rococo expression has disappeared from this plate with its wide range of contrasting tones and fiercely hatched foreground. Antique masonry is under attack from a violent nature, and the stunted forms of a pair of vigorously etched trees become as much the subject as the arch itself. The plate contains a veritable anthology of deterioration – decaying stonework, peeling stucco, crumbling brick, chipped marble, cracked tiles and weathered timber. Further pathos is added through the indifference implied by the mundane activities centred around a powder mill adjacent to the noble bas-relief of an Imperial triumph.

Returning for the last time to the Pyramid of Cestius, Piranesi created his most striking interpretation, developing to its maximum possibilities the compositional formula first outlined tentatively in his earliest version. As in the view published in the *Antichità*, he extends the apex of the Pyramid to touch the upper margin of the plate. In the new version, however, he seeks the lowest viewpoint possible in order to throw into vertiginous contrast the open sky on one side and the

crumbling escarpment of the Aurelian Wall on the other. The sheer violence of the tomb's perspective is echoed by the apparent assault of the gnarled trees on the antique masonry, and both throw into pitiful insignificance the minute forms of the human beings scratching about in the shadow. The unprecedented step of introducing the caption on a giant scroll illusionistically placed within the picture space (a device used increasingly in the later *Vedute*) serves also to minimalize human identity in the gesturing figure placed in front of it.

Piranesi now proceeds to achieve in townscape what he had accomplished with individual monuments: a bold act of compression involving the spectator within the picture area. The beginnings of the process in the large *Vedute* have already been demonstrated by the *Piazza del Quirinale* with its choice of a low viewpoint and the close proximity of the principal buildings concerned. An even earlier expression of this concept was found in the small plate of the *Forum of Augustus*, and now, in the late 1750s, it was to be applied on a larger scale with the *Campidoglio*.

As with the *veduta* of the *Arch of Augustus*, the spectator's familiarity with the general context and character of the main subject is assumed, since a panoramic view of the Campidoglio already exists among the previous plates to serve as reference. With an impressive degree of topographical accuracy (borne out by Nolli's map), Piranesi succeeds in discovering a *endpaper*

Ved 52
50
45
29
46
Ved 9
32
51
Ved 14

51 *Piazza del Campidoglio*, from *Vedute di Roma* (see *Vedute di Roma*, pl. 56)

52 Preparatory drawing for *Piazza del Campidoglio* (British Museum)

53 Preparatory drawing for *Piazza di S. Pietro* (British Museum)

viewpoint which not only includes parts or the whole of all the chief components of Michelangelo's design, but shows all the chief pieces of antique sculpture incorporated in the piazza – the Dioscuri, the Trophies of Marius (subject of Piranesi's full-scale antiquarian folio, *I Trofei di Ottaviano Augusto*, in 1753), two imperial statues, the equestrian Marcus Aurelius and the river gods flanking the central staircase to Palazzo Senatorio.

A preparatory drawing in the British Museum, from the same direction and to the same scale, allows us a rare opportunity to see the structure of this composition in final preparation. Although a number of Piranesi's drawings survive in the form of presentation works signed and mounted by the artist, the majority of his preparatory studies appear to have been done on the backs of trial proofs of his prints (often a useful means of dating them) or on any available scraps of paper. In this particular instance – one of a mere handful of final drawings for the large *Vedute* which survive (see also pls 53 and 62) – his vigorous use of red chalk over a light initial sketch in black chalk emphasizes the tonal colour, especially the areas to be strongly etched. Touches of sepia define the zones of greatest shadow. Significantly, areas of the greatest detail, such as that to the left of the scroll where he was to etch an outstanding group of tense figures in heated debate, are indicated in the briefest manner. The absence of more finished drawings than this is confirmed by Legrand's account of Piranesi's insistence on resolving his detail while working the plate:

Piranesi never produced finished sketches, a rough study in red chalk, reworked with pen or brush and even then only in parts, being sufficient to secure his ideas. It is almost impossible to distinguish his thoughts on paper because it is nothing but a chaos from which he only extracted a few elements for his plate with consummate skill.[20]

According to the same source, Piranesi himself is reported to have said:

Can't you see that if my drawing were finished my plate would become nothing more than a copy while, on the contrary, I create the impression straight on to the copper making an original work.[21]

Legrand reports a similar comment by Piranesi's friend Hubert Robert, and describes the way the artist spoke to his plate as his needle covered its surface with the details that flowed from his remarkably retentive memory. It was this peculiarly intimate relationship with the etching process that prompted Piranesi to retouch his plates frequently, as in this plate of the Campidoglio where he eventually decided to remove the ragged outline of the building projecting from the right-hand margin.

The opening of the 1760s marks the climacteric period in Piranesi's career. His growing fame, established internationally with the *Antichità Romane* and the first fifty-nine of the *Vedute di Roma*, brought him new sources of patronage from the ever increasing numbers of professional artists as well as the *dilettanti* visiting Rome. Recognition had begun to come his way with his election to an Honorary Fellowship of the Society of Antiquaries in 1757 and to the Accademia di San Luca in 1761. His fiery commitment to celebrating the Eternal City now brought him into a prominent position in the Graeco-Roman debate, equalled only by his rival Winckelmann. Socially no longer the recluse of eccentric habits described by Hubert Robert, Piranesi was bringing up a family after his marriage with Angela Pasquini, daughter of the Corsinis' gardener, in 1752. His daughter Laura was born in 1755 and his first son, Francesco, around 1758–9, both of them to be trained as collaborators with the intention that they should carry on the family business.

By 1 March 1761 Piranesi had moved to new premises in Palazzo Tomati in the Strada Felice (now Via Sistina), close to the Trinità de' Monti at the top of the Spanish Steps. This was the area inhabited by the British, French and German artists and architects studying in Rome as well as by many visiting

Grand Tourists. Already, by the mid-1750s, Piranesi's contact with Robert Adam, William Chambers, George Dance and Robert Mylne among others had initiated a strong influence on the future course of British architecture. Indeed, in certain respects Piranesi's move from his previous headquarters on the Corso symbolized a gradual shift of ambience away from the closely knit world of the French Academy to a widening circle of colleagues and patrons.

Most important of all, however, Piranesi was no longer dependent on Bouchard and Gravier, now signing his plates *presso l'autore nel Palazzo Tomati*. He established his own printing business, with a far closer contact than ever with the vital process of producing his plates. At about this time also he issued the first state of the invaluable *Catalogo inciso* – a copy of which he presented on election to the Accademia di San Luca – setting out his achievements to date in unprecedented detail, including the first fifty-nine *Vedute di Roma*.[22]

Ved 60 The combination of commited scholarship and emotive imagery in the *Vedute*, evolving simultaneously over the 1750s, is summed up in Piranesi's magisterial plate of the *Pantheon*. This work, produced in Piranesi's new establishment, was the first view to be added to the original *Catalogo*, and among the first plates to have the new address as well as the price of three *paoli*.[23] The size of the plate is the largest yet used – 465 × 685 mm, as compared to the 385 × 620 mm of the *Arch of Titus*. The weak definition and often poor inking of early impressions from Piranesi's own edition of the *Vedute* suggest a certain inexperience in printing which was rapidly overcome within the next few years.

Ved 11 A decade earlier the Pantheon had first appeared in a plate of the *Magnificenze* as a background feature to an energetic panorama of Roman street life. The building now appears as the greatest exemplar of antiquity's triumphant powers of survival through the vicissitudes of sixteen centuries of historical change. A telling viewpoint, a wide range of directed lighting and the fullest deployment of etching techniques are directed towards scholarly ends. We are placed at a sufficient distance to receive an instructive glimpse into the heart of the temple's interior, yet close enough not only to feel the overpowering grandeur of its massive shade but to read the smallest details of its complex history in the richly worked surface of the plate. Dramatic recession and a skilful definition of materials are co-ordinated within a range of etching extending from the rough striations of the giant monolithic columns to the wispy foliage attacking the further flank of the building.

In one of the most detailed captions yet appearing under a *veduta*, Piranesi the antiquarian summarizes the building history while Piranesi the artist illustrates the visual results. We are shown the portico added by Agrippa, still revealing channels for its bronze inscription later replaced by the bold lettering of Septimius Severus. The missing portion of the subordinate pediment is explained by the addition of Urban VIII's bell-turrets, and attention is drawn to the renewal of the stonework of the main entablature under Alexander VIII. No detail is too small for comment or definition.[24]

The supporting role of humanity diminishes as the *Vedute* assume greater rhetoric. Although Piranesi contrives to pack a wealth of observation into the passages of townscape to either side of the Pantheon, such material is becoming increasingly

54 Detail of *Temple of the Sybil, Tivoli*, from *Vedute di Roma* (see *Vedute di Roma*, pl. 61)

irrelevant except as a visual foil to the main statement. In certain parts of this plate mankind is reduced still further to the functions of indicating the stepped curve of the Pantheon's dome or marking the diameter of the hidden oculus against the skyline.

The new decade of the 1760s saw the broadening of Piranesi's antiquarian concerns to include a detailed investigation of Roman and supposedly Etruscan engineering – a key theme of *Della Magnificenza*. A profoundly important source of patronage from the new Pope, Clement XIII Rezzonico, and his family gave the artist financial backing for several major publications in this field. Piranesi's expeditions into the remoter areas of the Campagna to gather material relating to the Roman water supply and the draining of Lake Albano brought him into contact with the wilder and more sublime settings of antiquity. A particular field of operation in this decade was Tivoli and the ruins of the nearby Hadrian's Villa, which were to provide him with subjects for several of his finest views of this period.

Whereas nature had appeared in a subordinate, if increasingly assertive role in the earlier *Vedute*, it now began to assume an even more forceful and intrusive aspect. As seen in the *Temple of the Sibyl, Tivoli*, the undisciplined forms and *Ved 61* destructive forces of trees, plants and creepers are pitted against a noble work of human intelligence. The evolution of Piranesi's graphic technique from a linear architechtonic style towards the registering of pictorial values in tone finds expression in the romantic anarchy of the foreground. Here, emerging out of the deep shadows, are human figures and animals, obeying the *54* same jagged rhythms as the wild forms around them, and directing the spectator's attention to the ruins by a chain of kinetic gestures.

55 Figure studies (Private Collection, Switzerland)

56 Studies of trees (Ecole des Beaux-Arts, Paris)

The treatment of the human figure in the *Vedute* by the mid-1750s had begun to alter from the particularized and carefully hatched definition of the early plates to more broadly handled forms, executed by a stronger biting of the plate. Towards the close of the decade, however, a new type of figure becomes increasingly prominent, as first found in the *Pyramid of Cestius*. In the superhuman conflict portrayed in Piranesi's art between antiquity and nature, mankind is gradually reduced to an energetic cipher, assuming the tense rhythms of the gnarled trees and broken masonry. The few sheets of figure studies surviving from Piranesi's studio suggest that they were drawn from life to provide an anthology of pictorial motifs, similar in function to the material of Watteau's sketchbooks. Making certain allowances for the difference in handling of chalk and pen, the two sets illustrated here from the early 1750s and early 1760s respectively represent a change of interest from the description of particular incidents in human behaviour to the registering of dynamic forces in general.

This system of pictorial contrasts and tensions is found in Piranesi's approach to interior space in the *Villa of Maecenas, Tivoli*. Imposed upon the geometrical system of recession, derived from his Bibienesque training, is an alternative and occasionally conflicting system of pictorial organization involving powerful areas of tonal contrast, violent textures and jagged lines of energy. In this particular plate a comparatively mediocre structure, impervious to the regimented lines of Vasi, is transformed into a work of arresting majesty. Unprecedented areas of the deepest shadow, executed through a fierce biting of the plate, introduce into the *veduta* a new language of the irrational and the ambiguous, currently being exploited by Piranesi in the reworked *Carceri*. Conflicting with the

conventional orthogonals are contrary thrusts of directional energy, marked by passages of light introduced through the apertures from above and to the side, and picked up by the irregular patterns of the ground, by the decaying masonry and by diagonally related moving figures.

Legrand describes Piranesi's method of building up such compositions while in the process of working the plate:

He used to engrave on the hardened varnish and never crossed the lines since one alone was sufficient for him, varying the thickness for each detail. . . . He covered the whole of his plate with these lines, intelligently arranging them with regard to the design, and varying their thickness according to tone without losing the most brilliant lighting effects. Only after this preliminary work were these effects put in with a brush dipped in varnish rather as a drawing is touched up with white. In this way the highlights gained an infinite freedom and vitality of inspiration. This breadth of execution replaced the mechanical precision sometimes found in conventional engraving. . . . He then applied the acid with a care and patience that one would have thought him incapable of, covering those areas to be shaded one by one and repeating the process in certain plates as much as ten or twelve times. . . .[25]

The range of dense blacks which had begun to replace the sepia-coloured inks in the late 1750s, as well as Piranesi's closer supervision of the actual printing process, raised new technical problems as well as formal advantages. There is evidence that the artist was experimenting with new and unorthodox methods of inking his plates. Certain of the plates of the 1760s involved a marked degree of failure as Piranesi pushed the medium to fresh extremes in his search for more arresting effects. The assured balance between tonal gradation on the plate and the separation of hatched lines was particularly affected by these

57 Figure study (Kunstmuseum, Basle)   58 Figure studies of two men, detail (Ecole des Beaux-Arts, Paris)

Ved 75 new developments. This is noticeably the case in one of the rare views of almost pure landscape, the *Grand Cascade, Tivoli* of 1766 – the only dated plate of the entire series, with a signature celebrating the Knighthood of the Golden Spur, conferred on the artist by Clement XIII that October and confirmed by papal brief the following January.

By the second half of the eighteenth century, the dramatic landscape around Tivoli was attracting an ever increasing quantity of artists to depict this *locus classicus* of the Sublime. In the way that art feeds on art, Piranesi's search for a suitable mode of expression led him to Salvator Rosa – several of whose paintings he owned – as shown in the vigorous treatment of water, vegetation and, in particular, trees.[26] An extremely rare

57 pen study for two ragged trees from this period of activity reflects the violent hatching and broad areas of shadow in the etching technique which caused the darker parts of the plate to print in an unrelieved and lifeless black.

During the later 1760s the extensive remains of Hadrian's Villa began to absorb a great deal of Piranesi's energies. A number of preparatory drawings for unexecuted plates appear to be connected with a projected publication, and the large map of the site published by Francesco Piranesi in 1781 was almost certainly based on his father's earlier researches.[27] Piranesi's close familiarity with the Villa dates back at least to the 1750s, when there are accounts of sketching expeditions made in the company of Robert Adam, Clérisseau and Allan Ramsay.[28] However, the actual publication of the ten *Vedute* devoted to the Villa belongs to the succeeding two decades. It is almost as if the fusion of ruined structures and the wild forms of nature offered an attractive new field of pictorial effects in keeping with the artist's aesthetic development. It may also be of some

significance that Piranesi's fresh interest in Hadrian's Villa occurred at a time when he had finally abandoned Vitruvian canons of design with the controversial *Parere su l'Architettura* of 1765. He may have begun to find here a greater imaginative stimulus in the incomplete works of antiquity with their suggestion of infinite dimensions, amplified by the limitless effects of their natural setting.

Piranesi's view of the interior of the Baths presents a record *Ved 93* of structural decay in which the agents of destruction share an equal importance with the architecture. The broader treatment of detail, subtly registered by light rather than by line, contrasts 59 with the more specific account of decomposing materials some ten years earlier in the *Arch of Titus*. Something of the potency 50 obtained in this earlier work by leaving considerable areas of the paper blank is exchanged in the Tivoli plate for a complex system of diffused lighting, registered by extensive working over virtually the entire plate.

The painterly qualities of Tivoli are captured in a superb chalk study of the *Marine Theatre*, now in the Ashmolean 60 Museum, which was never finally etched. In marked distinction to the carefully devised perspective of a preparatory drawing such as that for the *Campidoglio*, the broader use of the 52 medium here relates to new preoccupations. With a striking economy of technique, Piranesi's understanding of structure is conveyed with the most summary strokes of chalk and shading. The hastily sketched passages of foliage are clearly based on fact although utilized as a means of uniting the irregular fragments into the overall composition. The energizing role of light, however, memorized rather than specifically recorded, is reserved for inclusion in the creative act of etching the plate. As Legrand puts it:

59 Vegetation, detail of *Hadrian's Villa, Tivoli, interior of the Baths* from *Vedute di Roma* (see *Vedute di Roma*, pl. 93)

60 Sketch of the Marine Theatre, Tivoli (Ashmolean Museum, Oxford)

The truthfulness and vigour of his effects, the precise projection of his shadows and their transparency along with certain liberties taken in this respect, even indications of colour, were all based on exact daily observation. This was equally true whether in normal conditions, or under the full glare of the sun, or by moonlight when the masses of the architecture seemed to increase their effects of strength and solidity as well as a softness and harmony often far superior to the brilliance of daylight. He learnt these effects by heart from studying them both close at hand and from afar and at all times.[29]

By the final decade of his life, Piranesi's activities had expanded into a prosperous business concern, satisfying the requirements of visitors to Rome as well as various foreign collectors, numbering among them the Empress of Russia. This became increasingly the case with the decline of Rezzonico support after the death of his single greatest patron, Clement XIII, in 1769. In addition to a brief début as a practising architect in the mid-1760s, Piranesi had begun to design suites of furniture and schemes of interior decoration, the subject of his internationally directed publication, the *Diverse Maniere d'adornare i Cammini*, of 1769. The principles of a highly imaginative system of eclectic design, outlined in this work, were applied to the production of elaborate chimneypieces and a wide range of substantially restored antiquities. Considering these commitments, the resulting need to employ assistants in the production of his various graphic works accounts for an uneven quality in certain of the later *Vedute*. This is particularly true, for instance, in routine passages of architectural detail, carried out to the artist's design but lacking the intensity of his personal touch, so essential to the etched plate. What, on occasion, is less explicable is Piranesi's seeming indifference to the definition of the principal figures in certain plates, in contrast to areas of superb detail elsewhere which retain much of his former vitality of observation.

In these last years Piranesi returned to a reappraisal of several of the major spaces and monuments of Rome, first portrayed in the *Magnificenze* in 1751. The increased plate size and perfected mode of expression, uniting tonal gradation and dramatic perspective, now superseded the earlier versions, which possessed the highest vitality of detail but without anything like the same cohesion.

Piranesi's new plate of *Piazza di S. Pietro* now fully engages the spectator in an urban experience. The viewpoint is lowered almost to ground level and brought close to the point of entry between the arms of Bernini's massive colonnades. A preparatory drawing in the British Museum allows us to see the structure of the design nearing its solution. Characteristically omitted, however, is the orchestration of dramatic lighting, added during the etching process, which unites the foreground activity with the densely worked area of the main piazza. Unlike the earlier version, moreover, the entire composition now revolves round the dominant shape of the obelisk which leads the eye back to the basilica, in terms both of the picture plane and three-dimensional space. Piranesi's control over nuances of delicate etching is undiminished, as can be seen in the exquisitely rendered cascades of water accentuating the twin fountains against the distant colonnades. Equally assured is the asymmetrically placed area of dramatic sky, lending strength to the Vatican buildings below and providing a lateral emphasis to the composition.

However, the Piazza di S. Pietro, with its dominant symmetry and almost inescapable perspective, still did not offer Piranesi the greatest scope for the play of dramatic forces. As already seen in the *Magnificenze*, the distinctive shape of Piazza Navona was eminently suitable, with its vitality provided by greater contrasts in scale and far more varied urban functions than were presented by Bernini's pontifical site. Piranesi's fresh interpretation, with its greater breadth of tonal effects and unequalled panoramic sweep, is a triumph of selective emphasis. The time is nearing midday and the view is taken from an upper window of Palazzo Lancelotti, whence we are taken in a variety of visual journeys through Domitian's arena. One of these leads the eye over the strongly *repoussoir* form of Bernini's Fontana del Moro to an area of sunlit ground before

Ved 10

53

Ved 10

Ved 10

the façade of Borromini's Sant'Agnese. Another *passeggiata* leads us the full length of the amphitheatre – site of the *Circo Agonale*, as the inscribed scroll reminds us. Moving into depth by means of a recession plotted by strongly etched lines of shading and intermittent bands of light from three side streets, we are guided past Bernini's theatrical fantasy, the Fontana dei Quattro Fiumi, followed by the distant Fontana del Nettuno, to leave the piazza by a further street bathed in vibrant light. In addition to these directional journeys there is a wealth of alternative experiences, not only dependent on the main orthogonals but arising from lateral movement from areas of light to deep shadow wherever the eye alights on the plate surface.

Where required, however, Piranesi's language of directional emphasis could be concentrated upon a single act of movement, evoking the immensity of a monumental piece of architecture such as the *Basilica of Maxentius*. Compared to the relatively objective study of antique masonry in the *Curia Hostilia*, Piranesi's later work is a masterpiece of overstatement, extending the possibilities of plate area, tonal recession and plunging perspective to their fullest extent. With the selective power of an arc light, the artist searches out the structural patterns of concrete and the brick reinforcement, as well as the incidence of decay, which makes this plate a demonstration of ancient building science. But far more than this, the *veduta* has been fashioned into a weapon of polemical force against which the austere line engravings of Greek architecture by Le Roy, Stuart and Revett must pale into insignificance.

The same property of emphatic movement had been applied some four years earlier to the vast basilican interior of *S. Maria Maggiore*. In comparison to the early plate of *S. Paolo fuori le Mura*, values of mass and volume are expressed with the greatest assurance without sacrificing any topographical detail. Using accurately located light sources from aisle and clerestory windows, Piranesi articulates the receding perspective of the north colonnade with a solemn tonal march towards the ciborium. The distractions of ebullient Rococo genre in the earlier plate are now replaced by decorous groups of broadly hatched figures which, by means of the low viewpoint, become party to the spectator's presence in this awesome vista.

The final group of the *Vedute* added to the *Catalogo inciso* in 1778 contains as broad and varied a repertoire of compositional variations as ever. Among these eighteen plates are a number of closely observed groups of ruins, aerial vistas of the greatest amplitude and further portraits of the outstanding buildings of modern Rome such as Galilei's Lateran façade. The definitive version of the latter comes at the end of a development emerging from the modest plate of the *Varie Vedute* and the growing powers of manipulated light and perspective of the *Magnificenze di Roma*.

The placid walks and terraces of the Baroque formal garden at *Villa Pamphili* are transformed by Piranesi into an image of potency, almost inconceivable when compared to the small plate of *Villa Ludovisi* from the *Varie Vedute* thirty years earlier. The composition, resting on an armature of intersecting diagonals, as revealed in the preparatory drawing in the Uffizi, becomes, through vigorous etching, a network of turbulent shadows and menacing foliage.[30] The artist, by reversing the conventional priorities with Mannerist skill, converts the Villa

itself into a mere garden pavilion overlooking an arena of dramatic encounters. The fulcrum of the design is supplied by the jagged silhouette of a Salvatoresque tree. The strong shadows cast by the raking sunlight, especially in the left-hand walk, reduce the numerous visitors to the importance of scuttling ants.

61 *Villa Pamphili*, from *Vedute di Roma* (see *Vedute di Roma*, pl. 124)

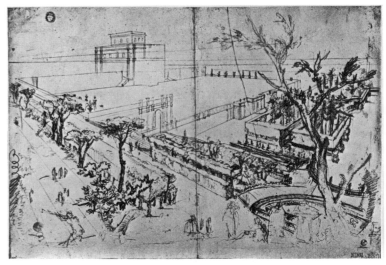

62 Preparatory drawing for *Villa Pamphili* (Uffizi)

63 *Villa Ludovisi*, from *Varie Vedute*

Of all the great ruined monuments of antiquity, the Colosseum continued to challenge the powers of the single *veduta*, not only because of its sheer immensity but owing also to the wide range of its visual aspects. In the early years of his antiquarian activity, while preparing the *Antichità Romane*, Piranesi had attempted to demonstrate the Colosseum's skeletal *Ved 19* structure within the context of its urban environment. A *Ved 58* subsequent *veduta* of the complete façade in the 1760s was *Ved 78* followed in the next decade by an interior view exploiting the savage decay of the auditorium. Now, in his last years, with two *Ved 126* decades of experiment behind him, Piranesi took to the air for a final look at this heroic skeleton – likened by Focillon to one of the circles of Dante's Hell. With the aid of preparatory draw- *64* ings like that in Berlin, he succeeded in combining elevation, section and plan in a single act of breathtaking vision.[31]

Humanity within and around the circumference of this vast shell is reduced to a series of scratches and marks of the etching needle. Of little wonder that the generation of the early Romantics such as Goethe, brought up on such images, underwent a profound disillusionment on their initial encounter with the reality. In some thirty years of continual experiment, cross-fertilized by the many other activities of his protean genius, Piranesi had transformed the conventional *veduta* from a mere topographical souvenir into an image of the greatest expressive power – an image which has continued to haunt the European imagination to this day.

> While stands the Coliseum, Rome shall stand;
> When falls the Coliseum, Rome shall fall;
> And when Rome falls – the World.[32]

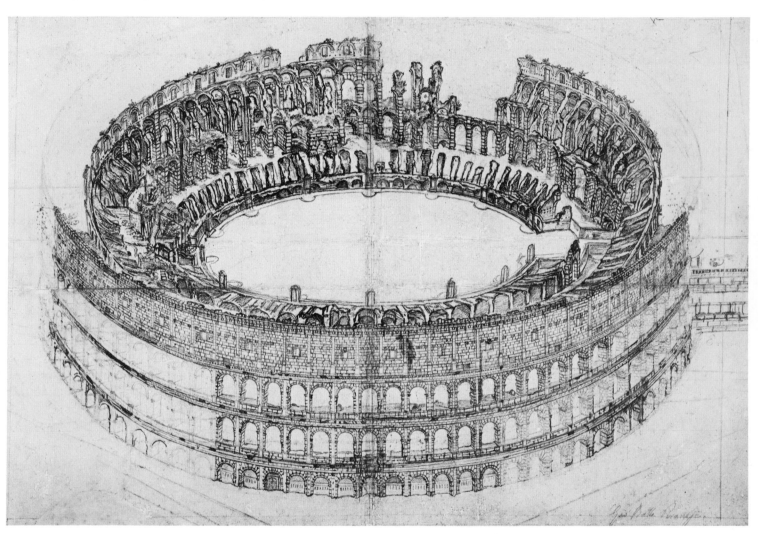

64 Preparatory drawing for the *Colosseum* (Kunstbibliothek, Berlin)

III

The Artist as Archaeologist

'ROME in ruins is a symbol of a lost world – the emotional impact is intense.'[1] From its infancy in the early Renaissance right up until Piranesi's time, Classical archaeology had been impelled by the idea of recovering a Golden Age. Each generation in turn projected its aspirations and values into the study of mute fragments and fresh discoveries. The ruins, inscriptions and texts which had inspired the ephemeral Roman republic of Cola di Rienzo in the mid-fourteenth century were to furnish Poggio Bracciolini and Cyriac of Ancona in the next century with the guiding ideals of the humanist life.[2] Facts and visions were inextricably bound up in Cyriac's revolutionary studies, for all their critical examination of evidence and the conflation of texts with coins, gems and inscriptions. It was Cyriac's aim to 'wake the dead' and by 'potent and divine art to revive the glorious things which were alive to the living in antiquity but had become buried and defunct through the lapse of ages and persistent injury at the hands of the half-dead; to bring them from the dark tomb to light, to live once more among living men'.[3]

This same visionary impulse passed from humanists to contemporary artists and architects whose superior powers of visualization developed the pictorial reconstruction as a necessary aid to the scholar. From Brunelleschi and Alberti to Sangallo, Raphael and Palladio, the act of reconstructing antiquity was a major influence upon contemporary design. The most sophisticated form of this activity was reached in the work of Mannerist architects such as Giulio Romano and Pirro 65 Ligorio, where the historical reconstruction merged into fantasy and became a medium for creative experiment in itself.[4]

During the seventeenth century fresh advances were made in the critical methods and range of antiquarian studies, as exemplified by Bellori's publication of the incomplete fragments of the Severan Marble Plan of Rome (*Forma Urbis Romae*), Santi Bartoli's books on the contents and decoration of Roman tombs, Montfauçon's monumental compendium of 79 Classical iconography and Desgodetz's more accurate delineation of the chief monuments.[5] Closely connected with this specialist research and documentation was a rapidly increasing literature of guide books and topographical surveys which replaced the indiscriminate farrago of the medieval *Mirabilia* by systematic itineraries following the exemplars of surviving classical texts such as the *Regionaries*.[6]

The visionary tradition, meanwhile, persisted as an invaluable instrument of archaeological enquiry in the works of G. B. Montano and of Athanasius Kircher, continuing into 66 Piranesi's youth with the reconstructions of Fischer von Erlach 12 and Francesco Bianchini.[7] In turn, the stimulus of Fischer's 102 methods in particular conditioned Piranesi's earliest fantasies in the *Prima Parte*, where he was to acknowledge that the 'speaking 11 ruins have filled my spirit with images that accurate drawings could never have succeeded in conveying'.[8] Some seven years later, the mature realization of this development in Piranesi's work was achieved in the supplementary plates of the *Opere Varie*, notably in the *Great harbour* and in the plan of the *College*. 22, 19

Running counter to this imaginative process in eighteenth-century archaeology, however, was the keener critical attitude and far broader outlook of the European Enlightenment, especially in the growing concern with the phenomenon of historical change and the social context of antiquities. Vico's seminal treatise *Scienza Nuova* (1725), while obscure for the greater part and of delayed impact in its time, is indicative of new preoccupations with cultural history, as derived from the study of language and custom in relation to tangible remains. Within this discipline an incipient nationalism gave fresh edge to the otherwise objective study of antiquity, as manifested in Italian scholarship by a revived interest in the indigenous civilization of the Etruscans.[9] The pioneering work of the seventeenth-century Scot Thomas Dempster, in *De Etruria Regali* (first published in 1723–4), was soon followed by excavations at Volterra (1728) and Palestrina (1738), together with the setting up of an Etruscan Academy at Cortona in 1726 and a museum at Volterra in 1750. The new discoveries were recorded and evaluated in a growing body of publications by specialists such as Gori, Passeri and Guarnacci.[10]

More far-reaching still for the European conception of antiquity, however, was the disorienting effect of the discoveries at Herculaneum from 1738 onwards and at Pompeii ten years later. Conventional attitudes towards the Classical achievement, largely based upon literary authorities rather than upon physical evidence, were replaced almost overnight by a new awareness of the richness and sheer diversity of the past. The seemingly limitless possibilities suggested by the haphazard excavations in southern Italy were increasingly confirmed during the middle decades of the century by expeditions to

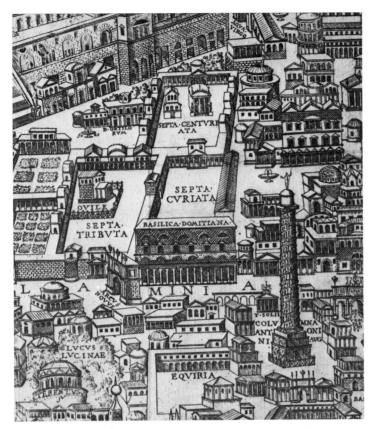

65 Detail from Pirro Ligorio's map of ancient Rome showing the Column of the Antonines, 1561

66 Giovanni Battista Montano: *Ancient temple in the Roman campagna*, from *Raccolta de' Tempii et Sepolcrali*, 1638

Greece and to Asia Minor, with their subsequent publications.[11] By the 1760s, the inevitable polarization of the respective achievements of Greece and Rome was to develop into an acrimonious debate with wild distortions in scholarship on both sides but highly productive side-effects for architecture and the applied arts.[12]

Some of Piranesi's most formative experiences in the field of archaeology had occurred in the Venetian circle of Lucchesi and Scalfarotto before his arrival in Rome in 1740 and his adoption into the similarly progressive ambience of Giovanni Bottari. The overriding concern of the engineers of the Magistrato delle Acque lay in the utilitarian achievements of Roman marine and hydraulic works. These impressions would have been reinforced in Piranesi's mind by his likely involvement in Temanza's expedition to Rimini to measure and record the bridge and Arch of Augustus for publication in his *Antichità di Rimini* of 1741.

During his early years in Rome, Piranesi would have come across the latest antiquarian guide book of the ancient city, Francesco de' Ficoroni's *Vestigie di Roma* of 1744. With a few 84 exceptions this work was mainly concerned, both in plates and in text, with the articulation of surfaces by the orders and the ornamental character of the remains, an attitude largely reflected in the competent if uninspired character of much contemporary architecture which Piranesi had scathingly dismissed in his dedicatory remarks to the *Prima Parte* in the previous year.[13] The same insensitivity prevailed in the excavations themselves, where the search for treasures, marbles and curiosities was conducted with a marked indifference to the value of recording the character of the containing structures, let alone their immediate environment.[14] Indeed, the situation had barely changed a century later when the uncovering of the Columbarium of Pomponius Hylas in 1831 was depicted in an 67 engraving.

The medium of the *veduta*, which largely occupied Piranesi's first ten years in Rome, provided the means through which he perfected a fresh mode of seeing as well as of documenting the past. The three plates added to the *Magnificenze di Roma* after 1751, particularly the *Curia Hostilia*, show a new concern with *Ved* the specific nature of construction and of architectural space, and with the way the etching needle might record more effectively individual materials and their functions.

It was by aid of the *veduta*, in fact, that Piranesi made his first specific contribution to archaeology when around 1750 he published a modest collection of eleven plates, *Camere Sepolcrali degli Antichi Romani le quali esistono dentro e di fuori di Roma*. In this volume he included six of his own works – one plan and five views – together with five plates from Francesco Bianchini's publication on the tomb of the household of Augustus, of 1727. In the inescapable comparison between the perspective view in Bianchini's book and Piranesi's *Tomb of L.* 68 *Arrunzio*, we immediately sense that a boundary has been 69 crossed between the recording and the interpretation of the past; between the merely informative diagram and the portrait of a particular historical situation. Quite apart from Piranesi's feel for the structure and the third dimension of the tomb chamber, the impression is produced by his ability to convey the actual passage of time through the various degrees of decomposition. As with his *vedute* of townscape, the combination of perspective

67 *Uncovering the Columbarium of Pomponius Hylas*, engraving of 1852

68 Francesco Bianchini: *Tomb of the household of Augustus*, 1727

69 *Tomb of L. Arrunzio*, from *Camere Sepolcrali*

and directed lighting provides a visual journey for the spectator. Developing further the compositional features of his sepulchral fantasy in the *Prima Parte*, his asymmetrical viewpoint gives an oppressive sense of the enclosing space, with glimpses into adjoining rooms and cavities indicated in a preceding plan. The use of light is not simply dramatic, but also acts as a powerful torch-beam to penetrate the gloom, isolating details of the vault's stucco reliefs and emphasizing the basic volumes of the load-bearing elements. The vibration of light and shadow over the entire plate surface is augmented by the movement of various figures who search or engage in discussion, providing an intangible air of pathos by their very animation amid this decay.

A new phase of antiquarian publication opened with the Comte de Caylus's *Recueil d'antiquités*, which began to appear from 1752.[15] Not only did the text stress *la plus noble simplicité* of Greece at the expense of Rome, but the plates of comparative material, despite their mediocre quality, revealed the range of decorative material available from Etruscan and Egyptian as well as Greek and Roman art. Almost as if in reply, in 1753 Piranesi produced his first detailed treatment of Roman decorative art, *I Trofei di Ottaviano Augusto*. Specifically intended for painters, sculptors and architects, these ten plates show Piranesi's graphic powers, which had already been applied to architectural themes, now concentrated upon the minutest detail of relief. Each motif of the two marble trophies,

70 *Trophy of Augustus*, from *I Trofei di Ottaviano Augusto*

known popularly as the Trophies of Marius but thought by Piranesi to commemorate Augustus's victory at Actium, and transferred from the *mostra* or principal fountain of the Acqua Giulia to Michelangelo's Campidoglio in 1590, is carefully depicted to convey the impression of the original material symbolized, metal or fabric, with a consummate balance between dramatic and informative emphasis.[16]

Along with these early studies of tombs and monumental ornament, Piranesi began to intensify his examination of the vast structures of the civic and utilitarian buildings of Rome, 19 already reflected in the complexity of the *College* plan which had opened the decade. Through his continuing association with the French Academy, a new generation of *pensionnaires* followed his guidance in surveying the formidable mesh of structures of the Imperial thermae. It was the stimulus of Piranesi's personal interpretation of Roman planning, rather than the cool facts of a methodical site plan, which ultimately influenced the course of French architectural design through the 20 medium of Peyre's *Academy* project of 1753.

From the early 1750s onwards a succession of young British designers and artists began to replace the French in Piranesi's attentions, in particular William Chambers, Robert Mylne and Robert Adam. It was also at this time that Piranesi first made contact with the young Irish peer James Caulfield, 1st Earl of

Charlemont, who had established in 1749 an informal and short-lived academy for British artists under the painter John Parker.[17] In 1753 Charlemont's patronage was secured for an expanded version of the *Camere Sepolcrali*, and before he finally left Rome in the following year frontispiece designs had been submitted by Piranesi in accordance with the dedicatory text supplied by the patron himself. As Piranesi's archaeological enquiries expanded, however, it became increasingly clear that a far more ambitious work was justified, especially in the light of new publications appearing, such as that planned in Naples by the new Accademia Ercolanese.[18] Accordingly, in 1755, Piranesi proposed a four-volume work, the *Antichità Romane*, 71 for which he eventually obtained his new patron's approval, together with a revised dedicatory inscription and an extremely grudging advance payment.

The appearance of the *Antichità* in May 1756 represented a turning-point in the history of Roman archaeology, of which Piranesi himself was fully aware. Moreover, while the preface outlining the principal objectives of the enquiry was particularly addressed to scholars, the work as a whole was directed towards a far wider audience than any previous antiquarian publication, not least to architects, who came in for some harsh criticism. It is only within these explicit terms of reference that certain exaggerated features of Piranesi's reconstructions in the plates of the *Antichità* can be properly understood and something of the general distrust of later scholarship shown to be misdirected.

Piranesi's unique achievement in this work rests on the application of a fresh mind to a hitherto restricted world of study, a mind which unusually combined a specialist understanding of engineering and architectural design with imaginative faculties of the highest order. In his preface, after expressing the traditional concern at the rapidly vanishing remains of antiquity and the desire to perpetuate the Roman achievement for posterity, Piranesi sets out the principal guidelines of his approach. Firstly, the recording of mere external features was no longer enough. Only by combining this information with plans, sections and internal views could structures be adequately described, together with the nature of the materials and the constructional techniques employed. Secondly, the problem of partially surviving or vanished buildings must be faced with the aid of conjectural plans, based on the possibilities inherent in the site concerned and the materials available. Thirdly, all such investigations would be fruitless without continual reference to antique sources, notably the Marble Plan, and their relation to the topographical character of the modern city, which would enable later buildings and accretions to be distinguished from the original structures. Finally, the sum total of these enquiries should contribute to a complete reconstruction of ancient Rome, which, as Piranesi informs us, was due for future publication.

Considering these comprehensive terms of reference, Volume I appropriately opens with a master-plan setting out 72 the theatre of Piranesi's principal activities within the Aurelian Walls – a *tabula rasa* in which medieval and modern Rome have been erased to reveal all the surviving fragments of the ancient city in relation to the geographical context of the Seven Hills and River Tiber. Some of the principal pieces of the Marble Plan – a constant source of inspiration throughout the *Antichità*

NOBILISSIMO·VIRO
VTILITATI·PVBLICAE·NATO
IACOBO·CAVLFIELD
VICECOMITE·DE·CHARLEMONT
REGNI·HIBERNIAE·PATRICIO
QVOD
ROMAE·DVM·DEGERET
INGENIIS·FAVEBAT
ARTES·PROMOVEBAT
IOANNES·BAPTISTA·PIRANESIVS
ARCHITECTVS·VENETVS
ANTIQVORVM·ROMAE·AEDIFICIORVM·VESTIGIA
PROVT·SVPERSVNT·TOPOGRAPHICE·DISPOSITA
VETERIBVS·VRBIS·ICHNOGRAPHIAE·FRAGMENTIS
ET·PLVRIBVS·TVM·IPSORVM·AEDIFICIORVM
CVM·ALIORVMQ·QVAE·DESIDERANTVR
SVPPLEMENTIS·ET·ADDITIONIBVS·ILLVSTRATA
MONVMENTA·SEPVLCRALIA·ANTIQVAE
ROMAE·ROMANVMQ·PER·AGRVM·SPARSA
ET·ANTIQVOS·VRBIS·FONTES
OMNIA·AERI·MANV·SVA·INCISA
LVBENS·DEVOTVSQVE
DEDICAVIT

71 Frontispiece of *Antichità Romane*

72 Master-plan of Rome, with fragments of the Marble Plan, from *Antichità Romane*

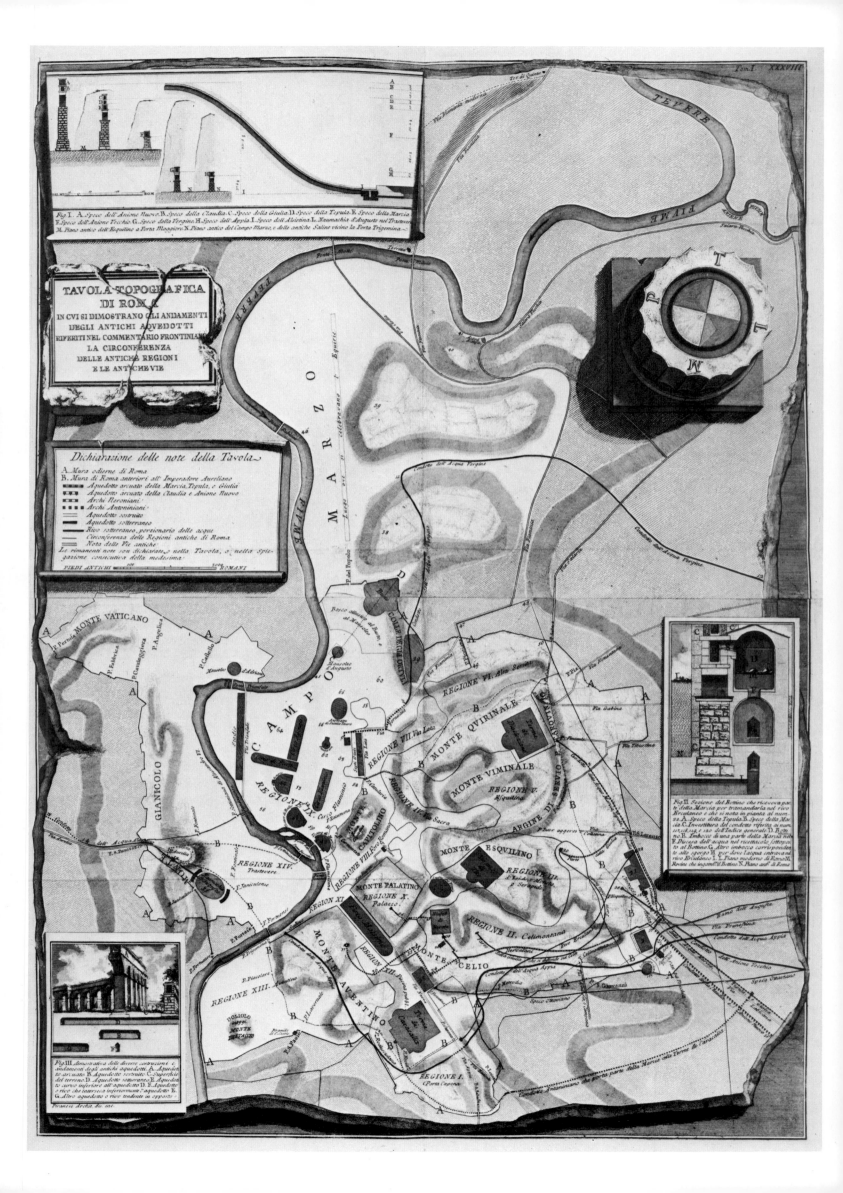

Fig. I. A. Speco dell'Aniene Nuovo. B. Speco della Claudia. C. Speco della Giulia. D. Speco della Tepula. E. Speco della Marcia
F. Speco dell'Aniene Vecchio. G. Speco della Tergine. H. Speco dell'Appia. I. Speco dell'Alsietina. L. Naumachia d'Augusto nel Trastevere
M. Piano antico dell'Esquilino a Porta Maggiore. N. Piano antico del Campo Marzo, e delle antiche Saline vicino la Porta Trigemina.

TAVOLA TOPOGRAFICA
DI ROMA
IN CVI SI DIMOSTRANO GLI ANDAMENTI
DEGLI ANTICHI AQVEDOTTI
RIFERITI NEL COMMENTARIO FRONTINIANO
LA CIRCONFERENZA
DELLE ANTICHE REGIONI
E LE ANTICHE VIE

Dichiarazione delle note della Tavola.

A. Mura odierne di Roma
B. Mura di Roma anteriori all' Imperatore Aureliano
Aquedotto arcuato della Marcia, Tepula, e Giulia
Aquedotto arcuato della Claudia e Aniene Nuovo
Archi Neroniani
Archi Antoniniani
Aquedotto sovruito
Aquedotto sotterraneo
Rivo sotterraneo, partionario delle acque
Circonferenza delle Regioni antiche di Roma
Nota delle Vie antiche
Le rimanenti note son dichiarate o nella Tavola, o nella Spiegazione consecutiva della medesima.

PIEDI ANTICHI   ROMANI

Fig. II. Sezione del Bottino che riceve a parte della Marcia per tramandarla nel rivo Ercolaneo e che si nota in pianta al num. 33. A. Speco della Tepula. B. Speco della Marcia C. Invertitura del condotto riferita a num. 31 nella 64. e 51. dell'Indice generale D. Bottino B. Imboco di una parte della Marcia nel F. Bottino dell'acqua nel ricettacolo sottoposto al Bottino G. Altro imboco corrispondente allo spogo H. per dove l'acqua entrava al rivo Ercolaneo I. L. Piano moderno di Roma M. Rovine che ingombra il Bottino N. Piano antico di Roma.

Fig. III. dimostrativa delle diverse costruzioni e andamenti degli antichi aquedotti. A. Aquedotto arcuato B. Aquedotto sovruito C. Superficie del terreno D. Aquedotto sotterraneo E. Aquedotto arcuato inferiore all'aquedotto D. E. Aquedotto o rivo che interseca inferiormente l'aquedotto E. G. Altro aquedotto o rivo ondante in opposto.

Piranesi Archit. dis. inc.

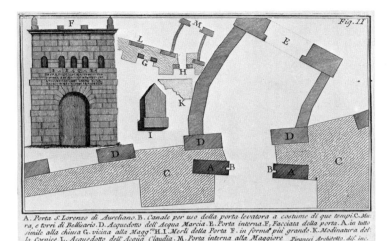

74 Plan and elevation of the Porta S. Lorenzo in its original form, from *Antichità Romane*

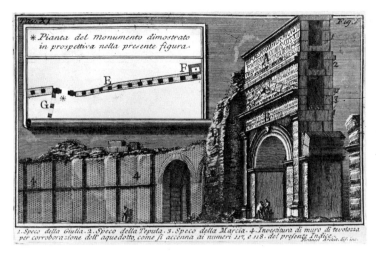

75 Final form of the Porta S. Lorenzo, stripped of later buildings, from *Antichità Romane*

76 The Porta S. Lorenzo today

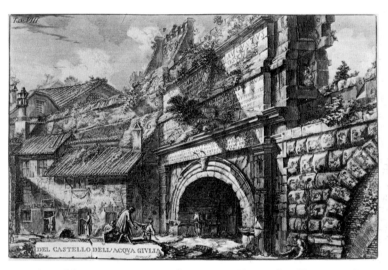

77 View of the Porta S. Lorenzo, from *Rovine del Castello dell'Acqua Giulia*

– are arranged prominently round the borders of this map, itself, like all others in the volume, rendered illusionistically as if a fragment of a similar work of authority.[19]

With nearly fifteen years of topographical activity already behind him, Piranesi was eminently equipped for the task of revealing the structure of ancient Rome through its impact upon the growth of the modern city. This is equally true of his innovatory study of the historic water system, reinstituted by the Baroque Popes as an essential part of the townscape as much as a necessary amenity.[20] With his understanding of hydraulic engineering gained with the Magistrato delle Acque, and a study of the first-century treatise by Frontinus on the subject, Piranesi attempted the first comprehensive map of the eleven major aqueducts in relation to the urban plan.[21] Sense is now made of amorphous ruins, largely ignored by antiquarians for lack of an inscription or ornamental features, and of the elaborate integration of defensive and water systems along the perimeter of the Aurelian Walls.

The index of 315 subjects, which follows the master-plan and subsidiary plates representing the other fragments of the Marble Plan, summarizes the history of each individual structure numbered accordingly on the plan. It also quotes from relevant authorities, transcribes existing inscriptions and comments upon current interpretations in recent scholarship. By means of this index, not only is the sequence of some sixty

small plates which follow, two to a page, readily placed within a larger context, but by a comprehensive system of cross-referencing the maze of isolated fragments are explained in relation one to another.

To take a specific example, Porta S. Lorenzo, the ancient Porta Tiburtina (no. 23 on the opening map), is shown in plan in plate X, figure ii, with reference to the superimposed water system. A comparative plan, in miniature, of the similarly constructed Porta Maggiore nearby (no. 28 in the master-plan) helps to reconstruct missing elements. Also included in the plate is a reconstruction of the entire outer façade of the original Porta Tiburtina, together with details of a merlin and the profile of the cornice. In the index, the paragraph relating to no. 23 discusses the structure in the context of the Aurelian defences to Rome, and supplies the various inscriptions on the inner face of the arch, shown in the *veduta* of plate XI, figure i, which refers to restorations to the conduits made by Augustus, Titus and Caracalla. In this latter plate the arch and adjoining elements of the aqueduct are stripped of later buildings (the structure thus disclosed is strikingly confirmed by a modern photograph), and shown at an angle which reveals in section the three superimposed conduits of the Acque Marcia, Tepula and Giulia, in ascending order. Some six years later Piranesi was to return to this subject, with a greater monumental expression but no less fidelity, in his treatise on the Acqua Giulia.[22]

◁ 73 Plan of the aqueducts of Rome, from *Antichità Romane*

78 *Arch of Gallienus*, from *Antichità Romane*

79 Antoine Desgodetz: *Basilica of Maxentius*, from *Edifices antiques de Rome*, 1682

In the index entries for nos. 117 and 118 on the master-plan, the text considers the gate as an integral part of the water system in describing the traces of the aqueduct's subsequent passage towards the Esquiline. Mention is also made of a separate branch of the Acqua Giulia which terminates in its *mostra* (no. 230 on the general plan). Finally, all these related structures are shown in dramatic isolation in plate XXVI, figure ii, with intervening gardens and vineyards removed and the whole scene dominated by the Arch of Gallienus (no. 232) in the foreground. 78

After discussing the walls and water system which provided the armature of the Imperial city, Piranesi passes on to deal with many familiar monuments such as the temples, triumphal arches, stadia and thermae. Despite a century of detailed enquiry before him, he was still able to make many fresh contributions, as with the Basilica of Maxentius, then 80 considered as the Templum Pacis. Compared with the relevant plate in Desgodetz's *Edifices antiques* of 1682, Piranesi's 79 illustration not only indicates the volume and weight of the fragmentary basilica, but by including certain related structures in the immediate foreground demonstrates the particular building techniques involved and the relationship of the major work to its setting. Moreover, in attempting to identify this structure he arrives at a wrong conclusion, but by a sound method, providing his evidence through one of the series of maps of urban reconstructions at the end of the first volume. In the map devoted to the densely built area of the Forum 81 Romanum, where existing fragments are distinguished from conjectural elements by differentiations in hatching, the Basilica (no. 58) is plausibly shown as an extension of the Golden House of Nero. A medal inset into the *veduta* adds further support to his conclusion, which is discussed in detail in the index.[23]

The central part of the *Antichità* is devoted to a greatly expanded treatment in Volumes II and III of the original *Camere Sepolcrali*, introduced by secondary frontispieces of a 82, 83 particularly febrile ingenuity. This disproportionate attention

80 *Basilica of Maxentius*, from *Antichità Romane*

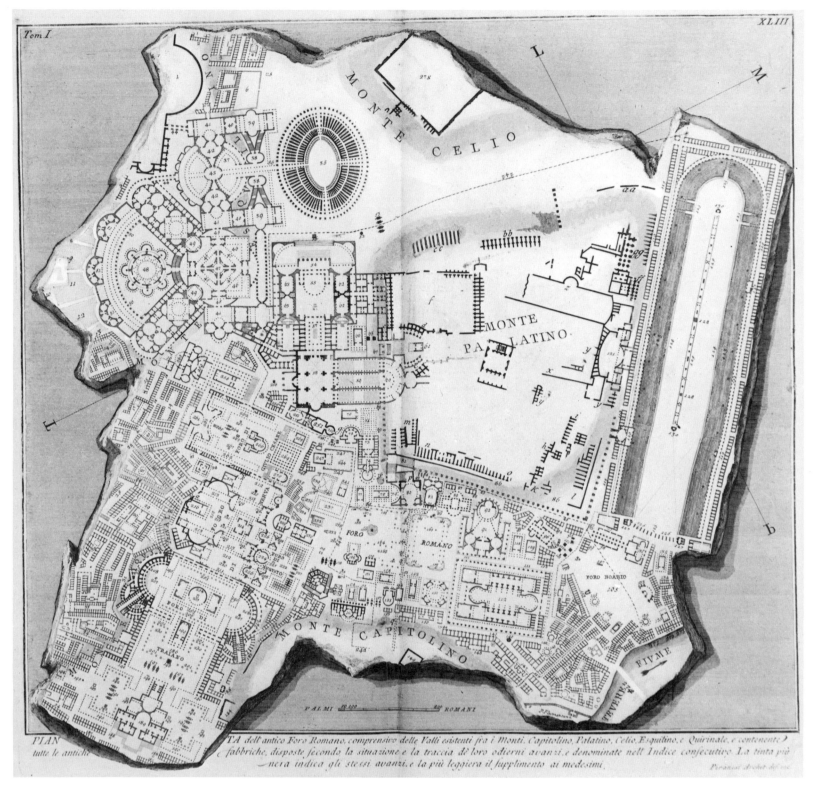

PIAN   TA dell'antico Foro Romano, comprensivo delle Valli esistenti fra i Monti. Capitolino, Palatino, Celio, Esquilino, e Quirinale, e contenente
tutte le antiche   e fabbriche, disposte secondo la situazione e la traccia de' loro odierni avanzi, e denominate nell'Indice consecutivo. La tinta più
nera indica gli stessi avanzi, e la più leggiera il supplimento ai medesimi.

81 Reconstructed plan of the Forum Romanum, from *Antichità Romane*

paid by Piranesi to funerary architecture can be explained in terms of the sheer extent of its survival. Being mainly located outside the city walls according to Roman burial practice, tombs often escaped the more violent despoliation and offered greater scope for a study in depth. Moreover, it was often in these works that Piranesi discovered the complexity which he wished to offer for the inspiration of modern designers.

Much of the material in these two volumes is later in date than the small plates in the opening one, as shown not only by the increased size of plates but also by the far greater sophistication of illustrative techniques, often based on earlier authorities. For example, Ficoroni's crude section of the tumulus of Alexander Severus, published in 1744, is completely transformed by Piranesi.[24] Not only are the monument's structure and individual materials carefully rendered, but the system of internal spaces is methodically corrected by excavation and measurement. In addition, the original level of the entrance tunnel with its steps is indicated, along with various levels of accumulated debris caused by subsequent deterioration and despoliation. In the text below, these findings are supported by reference to an earlier excavation described by Flaminio Vacca at the end of the sixteenth century.

82 Second frontispiece of Volume II, *Antichità Romane*
83 Second frontispiece of Volume III, *Antichità Romane*

84 Francesco de' Ficoroni: *Tumulus of Alexander Severus*, 1744

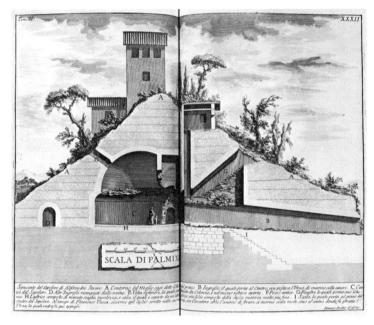

85 *Tumulus of Alexander Severus*, from *Antichità Romane*

86 Gateway to a crematorium, from *Antichità Romane*

87 Details of paving, Via Appia, from *Antichità Romane*

Entirely original, on the other hand, are those diagrams which demonstrate in detail the constructional system of Roman building, as in the instance of the gateway to a crematorium (*ustrino*) on Via Appia. Here, as if with a corpse laid bare for anatomical dissection, Piranesi shows the structural function of the triangular facing tiles in double and quadruple patterns. In a succeeding plate, a heightened degree of reality is achieved in the cyclopean effect of polygonal blocks composing the surface of the neighbouring roadway, with the bedding gravel combining pictorial and didactic functions.

Individual techniques of illustration apart, the combination of images, together on one plate or in a sequence of plates, is one of Piranesi's most remarkable contributions to technical illustration. A particularly vivid instance of this approach is provided by the six plates devoted to the Tomb of Cecilia Metella. A *veduta* places the monument in its setting, as related to Via Appia, and indicates later additions made by the Caetani family when transforming it into a fortress during the Middle Ages. Another plate incorporates within its compass all the basic facts of the surviving tomb, stripped of these additions,

88–92 *Tomb of Cecilia Metella.* Series of plates from *Antichità Romane* showing (top left) the position of the mausoleum on Via Appia, with later additions; (top right) elevation, plan and section of the original structure, together with details of the facing; (centre left) part of the façade, carefully chosen to show both the ornaments of the frieze and the construction of the rubble core; and (bottom left) details of the sarcophagus. The two remaining plates demonstrate the originality of Piranesi's approach to antiquity; they illustrate (centre right) probable building methods, as reconstructed by the artist from blocks of cut stone found on site, and (bottom right) designs for lifting tackle based on a wedge devised by Brunelleschi

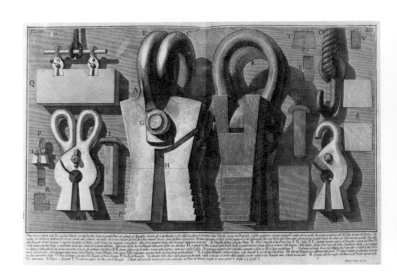

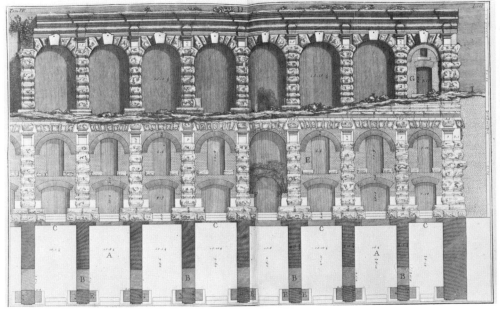

93 Curia Hostilia, showing substructure which was buried in Piranesi's time, from *Antichità Romane*   94 Excavated substructure of the Curia Hostilia

in terms of plan, section, elevation and details of the drum's facing blocks. Then comes a close focus on a portion of the frieze, ingeniously selected to show not only the principal ornaments and the inscription, but also, by means of an existing break (clearly seen in the elevation), the construction of the rubble core behind the facing ashlar. Here the lighting picks out the smallest details of deterioration while investing the frieze of bucrania, swags and trophies with an almost hallucinatory clarity. The original sarcophagus, then in Palazzo Farnese, is described by one of the most original plates yet. In addition to the plan, section and principal elevation of this object are supplied details of all the salient ornaments and their profiles. In all, some eleven separate aspects (accompanied by a detailed commentary in the caption below) are combined in a visually satisfying composition where information is enhanced by the sheer juxtaposition of detail.

The final two plates of the sequence, devoted to reconstructing the method of erecting the tomb and the type of lifting tackle used, introduce an aspect of the *Antichità* strangely at variance with its otherwise sobre accuracy, namely the use of deliberate exaggeration both in scale and in structure. A clue to the situation lies in a phrase in the explanatory text below the plate depicting the superhuman exploits of construction: *fatte più dalla Natura che dall'arte* ('executed more by nature than by art').

Towards the mid-1750s, Piranesi's reasoned commitment to celebrating the Roman achievement had begun to turn into an impassioned defence. As early as 1752, Caylus had exalted Greece over Rome in the *Recueil*, and in Venice the following year the British architects Stuart and Revett, when advocating the value of their proposed expedition to the Aegean, referred in their prospectus to 'Rome, who borrowed her Arts and frequently her Artificers from Greece'.[25] By 1755, the anonymous author of a *Dialogue on Taste*, later identified as the Scottish painter Allan Ramsay, who was a close associate of Piranesi's at the time, had extended the debate still further.[26] Without doubt, however, the work which affected Piranesi most deeply in the years prior to the publication of the *Antichità*

was M. A. Laugier's *Essai sur l'architecture*. Published in Paris in 1753, when it won immediate acclaim, this vigorous defence of Greek originality with pejorative comments on the servility of the Romans would swiftly have become the subject of heated debate among Piranesi's acquaintances at Palazzo Mancini.[27]

The laws of nature as inspiration for the constructional genius of the Romans was to become a deeply held truth for Piranesi, as his later theoretical writings show. The plates of the final volume of the *Antichità*, the latest in terms of stylistic development, demonstrate a far greater attention to structural expression in considering the bridges, theatres and porticoes of Rome. The massive arcades of the so-called Curia Hostilia, 93 actually part of the substructure of the Temple of the Divine Claudius on Monte Celio, offered promising material to support this view. Modern excavations have, in fact, largely 94 confirmed what Piranesi intuited in his majestic sectional elevation, which runs almost as deep again as the portion above the existing ground level, itself scrupulously indicated in the plate.

However, with the largest of all the tombs, the Mausoleum of Hadrian (the medieval Castel S. Angelo), and the related Pons Aelius, Piranesi intensified the drama of Roman technology to an unprecedented pitch. A hint of what was to come was provided by the *veduta* of Castel S. Angelo, issued *Ved 37* shortly after the *Magnificenze di Roma* in 1751, and in marked contrast to the contemporary plate of the Curia Hostilia, still representing a relatively controlled statement of fact. Formidable as the mausoleum appears in this heroic composition, greater 95 drama still is reserved for the sectional plate revealing cyclopean foundations of the utmost complexity. If the portrayal of these excessively conservative substructures was not enough to support Piranesi's case for Roman genius, his subsequent plate 96 in the *Antichità* of the cliff-like abutments of the mausoleum brings his argument to a sonorous finality.

Yet more improbable, considering the relative modesty of its superstructure, are the exposed foundations of the Theatre of 97 Marcellus. Here the revetments and interlocking masonry set upon a forest of piles resemble nothing so much as the *murazze*

95 Section of the foundations of the Pons Aelius and of Castel S. Angelo (detail), from *Antichità Romane*

96 Foundations of the Castel S. Angelo, from *Antichità Romane*

97 Foundations of the Theatre of Marcellus, from *Antichità Romane*

or stone sea defences which Piranesi's masters in the Magistrato delle Acque had erected against the predatory Adriatic.

The roots of this increasing obsession with the virtues of stone construction can be traced to another aspect of Piranesi's early years in Venice – the teachings of Pietro Lodoli. Although they did not appear in print until Francesco Algarotti's partial publication of them in his *Saggio sopra l'Architettura* in 1756, Lodoli's views were certainly discussed extensively in the Lucchesi circle.[28] The technology of stone and its appropriate modes of expression appear to have occupied a major part of the friar's projected thesis.[29] His belief in the operation of natural laws of construction, as embodied in the stone architecture of the Etruscans, was also to have a profound effect as Piranesi evolved his theoretical position later in the Graeco-Roman debate.

Closely related to the polemical exaggeration of Roman structural techniques in the *Antichità* is an equally pronounced concern with richly complex and decorative forms. As the decade of the 1750s advanced, Piranesi's original intention behind the *Antichità* – the application of archaeology to the service of contemporary design – gradually began to merge with his developing defence of Roman originality, giving his inclination for visionary reconstruction an even greater impetus. Just as the Tomb of Cecilia Metalla and the Curia Hostilia provided points of departure for excursions into structural fantasy, so the discovery of relatively complex planning in antiquity bore even stranger fruits in his imagination. Apart 99 from the evidence of several ingenious plans among the Roman 66 tombs, especially those appearing in Montano's putative records, the remains of Hadrian's Villa provided an unprecedented range of planning concepts on a more monumental scale. In 1752 Ligorio's pioneering plan of the Villa had been republished, and over the next two decades Piranesi was working frequently at Tivoli preparing a new plan, ultimately to be published posthumously in 1781 by his son Francesco.[30]

Piranesi's debut in the field of imaginary planning, the 19 *College*, was largely achieved by extending the elaboration of Palladian formulae in a design like Longhena's S. Maria della Salute. Later in the decade, as his training in the experimental medium of Baroque stage design was harnessed to an expanding knowledge of ancient structures and greater familiarity with fantasies by predecessors like Montano and Kircher, Piranesi's abilities reached an entirely new level of ingenuity. Such, indeed, was the success of his plate 81 reconstructing the plan of the Forum Romanum, that the careful distinction between actual and conjectural forms by graded hatching appears almost pedantic. When no longer circumscribed at all by the evidence of any substantial remains, Piranesi's architectural imagination is less sublimated, as in the 98 extravagant *Nymphaeum of Nero*. Here all that was given were the boundaries of the substructure formerly occupied by the Temple of the Divine Claudius (no. 275 on the plan of the Forum Romanum), to which the Curia Hostilia belonged (see no. 17 on the plan of the Nymphaeum). Although Baroque in feeling, this plan nevertheless remains unique in its orchestration of distinct geometrical shapes, and the final production is far more sophisticated than any of the possible sources in Ligorio, Montano or in the literal evidence of antiquity itself.

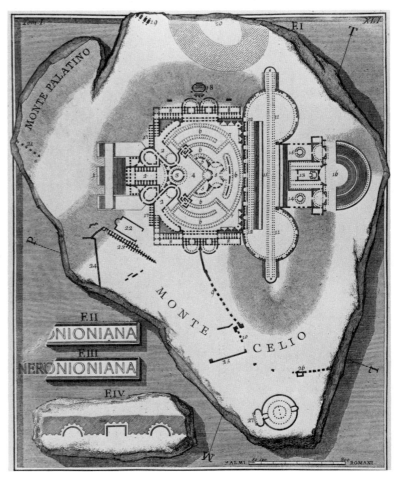

98 Reconstructed plan of the Nymphaeum of Nero, from *Antichità Romane*

99 A sepulchral building near Torre degli Schiavi, from *Antichità Romane*

100 Sir William Chambers: design for a mausoleum for the Prince of Wales, 1752 (Victoria and Albert Museum, London)

The overriding importance to Piranesi of this dialogue between archaeological investigation and the concerns of modern architectural design are revealed in his varying relationships with the visiting British designers referred to previously. William Chambers, who first arrived in Rome in 1750, had already been substantially conditioned by his previous training in the Parisian atelier of J. F. Blondel.[31] He was conservative by temperament, and his ensuing contacts with Piranesi were tempered by considerable reservations, only to find expression many years later in the 1791 edition of his influential *Treatise on Civil Architecture*. The cautionary anecdote then added to his discussion of the architect's exercise of imagination in formulating a design (evidently referring to
19 Piranesi's *College*) is worth quoting in full:

A celebrated Italian Artist whose taste and luxuriance of fancy were unusually great, and the effect of whose compositions on paper has seldom been equalled, knew little of construction or calculation, yet less of the contrivance of habitable structures, or the modes of carrying real works into execution, though styling himself an architect. And when some pensioners of the French academy at Rome, in the author's hearing, charged him with ignorance of plans, he composed a very complicated one, since published in his work; which sufficiently proves, that the charge was not altogether groundless.[32]

In private, however, Chambers was more willing to admit the stimulus of Piranesi's imagination, and in a letter of advice written in 1774 to his pupil Edward Stevens, then about to visit Rome, urged him to visit 'Piranesi, who you may see in my name; he is full of matter, extravagant 'tis true, often absurd, but from his overflowings you may gather much information'.[33]

Significantly, the principal influence of Piranesi upon Chambers, who left Rome in 1755, firmly in favour of Roman virtues, lay in the monumental constructions of the *Antichità*. One
100 of his earliest designs, a projected mausoleum for the Prince of Wales, which was designed in Rome during 1752, renders it in a ruined state using the informative techniques of Piranesi's
88–92 plates of the Tomb of Cecilia Metella.[34] Some two decades later, when at the height of his career, Chambers gave to the massive substructure of the Thames façade of Somerset House (begun in 1776) a rusticated grandeur partly derived from Piranesi's
93 interpretations of the Curia Hostilia.

The Scottish engineer Robert Mylne, studying in Rome between 1755 and 1758, was understandably more affected still by the technical studies of Piranesi. His investigation of the Roman water system was probably undertaken with Piranesi's assistance, and although his prize-winning design of 1758 for a palace at the Concorso Clementino owes more to Peyre and Soufflot, strong debts to Piranesi occur in his executed design for Blackfriars Bridge (begun in 1760) which the latter engraved, as under construction, in 1764 from a drawing 101 supplied at his request.[35]

By far the most sympathetic and productive relationship was that of Piranesi and Robert Adam between 1755 and 1757 – years particularly crucial to the form finally taken by the *Antichità* and for the gestation of Piranesi's theoretical views as revealed in the ensuing Graeco-Roman debate. In Adam Piranesi found a kindred spirit with an understanding of the peculiar nature of his attitude towards antiquity; also a designer who shared something of the same ambitions for the reform of contemporary architecture by a creative application of antiquity.[36]

Within a short time of their meeting in June 1755, Robert Adam was reporting in letters to his brother James in London the various joint expeditions, often including his French colleague Clérisseau and Allan Ramsay, to Hadrian's Villa, the Imperial thermae and Via Appia, with the stimulating discussions and arguments on these occasions.[37] Adam, commenting on his rival Chambers's failure to achieve the same rapport with Piranesi, wrote enthusiastically: 'so amazing and ingenious fancies as he has produced in the different plans of the Temples, Baths and Palaces and other buildings I never saw and are the greatest fund for inspiring and instilling invention in any lover of architecture that can be imagined'.[38]

The archaeological fantasies of the mid-1750s, both perspective reconstructions and plans, which were devised by Piranesi as part of an evolving defence of the Roman genius for invention, have more complex origins than his equally innovatory concern with structural techniques. A tradition of highly imaginative archaeological reconstructions can be traced, as already mentioned, from Ligorio via Montano and Kircher to Fischer von Erlach and Bianchini. Francesco Bianchini, the Veronese antiquary, had reconstructed the Imperial palaces on the Palatine in his *Del Palazzo de' Cesari*, which was published posthumously in 1738. This work, based on excavations carried out between 1720 and 1724, featured a substantial fold-out reconstruction by Nicoletti da 102 Trapani, couched in a contemporary architectural idiom and showing minimal concern with the broader urban or geographical setting of the complex. Where Piranesi's visionary perspectives, such as the secondary frontispieces to the *Antichità*, 82 transcend this less adventurous type of reconstruction is in the accuracy of the ornamental detail and in the totally convincing manner in which each structure has been worked out architecturally in relation to its physical setting. For instance, the actual ground plan of the Circus Maximus in plate XLIII 81 of Piranesi's reconstructed Forum Romanum is an important constituent of the Circus fantasy. Yet it would be pointless, on 83 the other hand, to attempt a specific identification of the whole composition, as certain scholars have done. Piranesi's plate represents neither an idealized Circus Maximus, nor the Circus

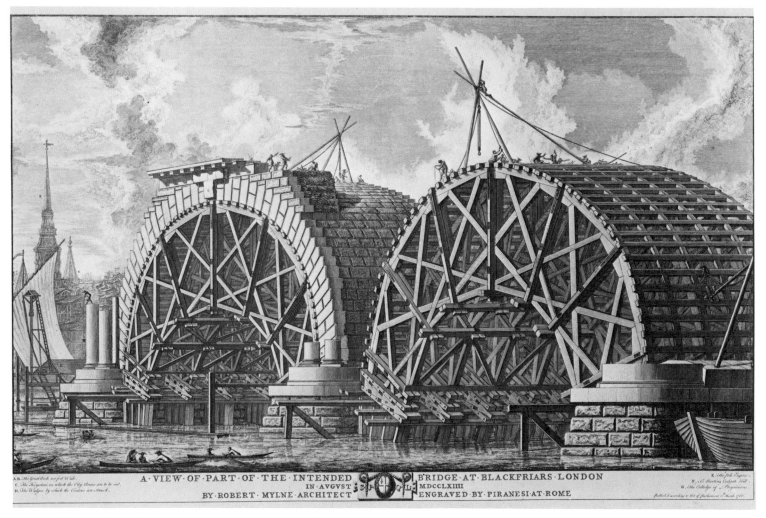

101 Blackfriars Bridge under construction, etching by Piranesi from a drawing by Robert Mylne

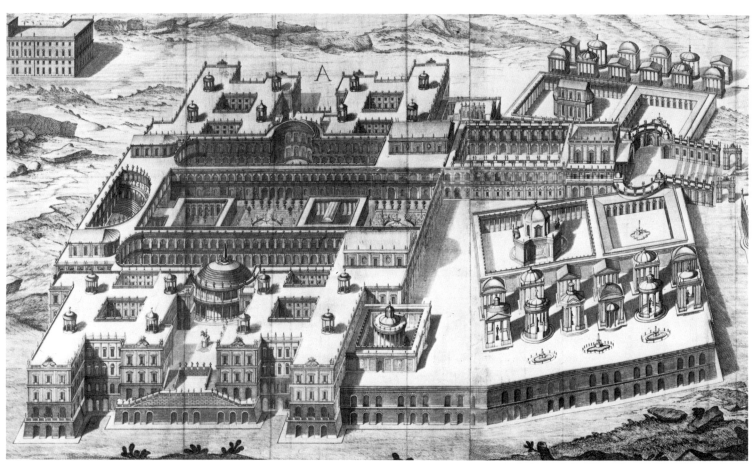

102 Nicoletti da Trapani: reconstruction of the Imperial palaces on the Palatine (detail), from Francesco Bianchini's *Del Palazzo de' Cesari*, 1738

103 *Imaginary Composition*, drawing (Sir John Soane's Museum, London)

of Caracalla near Via Appia, but a conflation of *all* Roman circuses – it is Dryden's 'Nature raised to a higher pitch'.

82   This is equally true of the visionary Via Appia, which represents an apotheosis of Roman tomb design derived from assorted elements in the factual achievement recorded in clinical detail in the succeeding plates. Whereas Chambers and the more prosaic minds of the architectural profession dismissed these compositions as grotesque or, at the worst, mere ravings (Vanvitelli once referred to the 'mad Piranesi'), it took a sympathetic and open mind like Adam's to recognize the wealth of formal inspiration which lay within this approach.[39] Indeed, such fantasies may be considered as much a legitimate medium for uninhibited experiment as the temporary festival
18   architecture of the *Chinea* in the 1740s.

Something of the stimulus of this phenomenon as it affected Adam's development during the mid-1750s can be shown by
103   comparing a fantasy drawing executed for him by Piranesi with
104   one of Adam's own mature essays in the genre.[40] When the time came for Adam to return to Britain in 1758, the conventional Palladian upbringing of his pre-Roman career in Scotland had been replaced by a far broader approach towards design: an approach which, even if subdued by Piranesian

standards, would not have possessed the same imaginative breadth without these Roman experiences.

The advent of Adam in Piranesi's career came at an equally opportune moment for the latter, since by 1755 the relationship with Charlemont was rapidly deteriorating, largely through Parker's hostility rather than Charlemont's indifference. Piranesi clearly began to feel his confidence in this patron misdirected, and it was probably under these circumstances that Adam wrote in June 1755 that Piranesi 'threatens dedicating his next plan of ancient Rome to me'.[41] Evidently this particular work was intended as the climax to the *Antichità*, but by the following September Robert was describing to James how he had succeeded in persuading Piranesi to publish the work separately. Thus when the *Antichità* appeared some nine months later, the plan of Rome was referred to as due for publication.[42] Piranesi's esteem for Adam was nevertheless registered in the *Antichità*, where both he and Ramsay were given symbolic   82
tombs of honour in Via Appia.[43] On his farewell visit to Piranesi in April 1757, Adam had the satisfaction of finding the artist at work on the dedicatory inscription to the plan.[44]

By this time Charlemont's failure to supply his promised backing for the *Antichità*, let alone to reply to Piranesi's

104 Robert Adam: *Imaginary Palace*, detail of drawing (Sir John Soane's Museum, London)

remonstrating letters, provoked the artist to an action which was violent but nevertheless appropriate within the spirit of his publication. After the sale of forty copies of the work, the original dedicatory frontispiece to Volume I was suppressed. The Earl's self-composed citation was solemnly deleted from the marble slab and his heraldic achievements defaced as if hammer and chisel had been taken to the stone. Virtually all other references to the patron in the subsidiary frontispieces were treated likewise, Piranesi finding a suitable Roman precedent in Caracalla's erasure of his murdered brother's inscription from the Arch of Septimius Severus. A fresh inscription was cut on the marble slab in the third state of the original plate – *Utilitati publicae* – and after further silence from the unworthy patron, Piranesi finally published three of his original letters (one of them to Abbé Peter Grant, who had unwisely tried to mediate) in the pamphlet *Lettere di Giustificazione scritte a Milord Charlemont* in 1757.[45]

Apart from rehearsing the tedious details of the affair as Piranesi saw it (amplified by a complete visual record in miniature of the various acts of deletion, together with certain satirical material), the *Lettere* reinforce the artist's conception of the *Antichità* as a work transcending the function of the conventional antiquarian treatise. As he put it, 'This work is not of the kind which remains buried in the crowded shelves of libraries. Its four folio volumes comprise a new system of the monuments of ancient Rome.'[46] The principal theme of his general remarks is the nobility of artistic reputation and the imperishable nature of art: 'As a nobleman must consider his ancestors, an artist who will leave his name to posterity must consider his own reputation and think of his descendants. A nobleman is the latest of his name, an artist the first of his: both must act with equal delicacy.'[47]

Within a short time of the *Antichità*'s appearance, Piranesi's confidence in its appeal was justified. Copies were acquired by leading authorities throughout Europe, such as the Marquis de Marigny, *Directeur des bâtiments royaux*, and by heads of state such as the Empress of Russia. But for him the greatest accolade was his election in April 1757 to an Honorary Fellowship of the Society of Antiquaries of London, as proudly displayed on the title page to the *Lettere di Giustificazione*.[48]

It was not for another five years, however, that the missing climax to the *Antichità*, the plan of Rome, finally appeared as the *Ichnographia* of the Campus Martius in a folio dedicated appropriately to a fellow architect. The *tour de force* of six contiguous plates had almost certainly been completed in 1757, the date of the dedicatory inscription to Adam, whose head appears with Piranesi's, as if forming a duumvirate, in one of the two medallions.[49] This visionary Marble Plan, which must be considered together with those other 'fragments' depicting the Forum Romanum, the Capitoline Hill, the thermae, the Nymphaeum of Nero and the Praetorian Barracks, completes the calculated sequence of the *Antichità*. Thus, starting with the primal sources of evidence, the master-plan of the surviving remains within the city walls, the reader is taken on a journey of discovery in terms of the Roman genius for construction, planning and ornamental design, until presented with the final act of reconstruction – the vision of a new Rome.

The modern archaeologist will look in vain for the correlation with factual evidence, although the remaining portions of the past are skilfully incorporated in their proper place – the Pantheon, Theatre of Marcellus, the Imperial mausolea, the Stadio Domitiani (Piazza Navona) and the buildings of the Tiber Island. Via Flaminia, on the other hand, is strangely diverted from its accepted route direct from Pons Milvius (Ponte Molle) to the Capitoline Hill in accordance with a statement by Strabo. This matter had already been introduced in the *Antichità* with the discussion of the aqueduct system as it related to the Campus Martius, and Piranesi had demonstrated this contrary opinion in his map of the water system. Beyond these matters, however, Piranesi is out to present by an overwhelming demonstration of principles, analogous to his exaggeration of Roman structures, the *potential* fertility of design revealed by the study of archaeology. In so doing, he comes closer to conveying the spirit of Imperial planning than centuries of earnest enquirers since Ligorio's comparable panoramic map, which he clearly sought to emulate.

105 Frontispiece of Volume I, *Antichità Romane*, 3rd state

106 Frontispiece to *Lettere di Giustificazione scritte a Milord Charlemont*

The year before the *Antichità Romane* appeared, a little-known German scholar, Johann Joachim Winckelmann, had published in Dresden an essay on the imitation of Greek works, *Gedanken über die Nachahmung der griechischen Werke in der Malerei und Bildhauerkunst*, which was to have a more catalytic effect for the European conception of Greek antiquity than the works of Caylus and Laugier and all the subsequent folios of Le Roy, Stuart and Revett combined. By applying an outstanding imagination, unfettered by antiquarian prejudices, to the modest evidence of gems, coins and Roman copies of Greek painting and sculpture he opened up a new perspective on the past. In the same year Winckelmann reached Rome, subsequently becoming librarian to the great collector Cardinal Alessandro Albani, and by the end of the decade he had placed the Graeco-Roman debate on a new level.

For all the divergent attitudes and opinions that were to place Piranesi and Winckelmann at the heads of the opposing camps, their respective approaches to Classical antiquity are far closer to one another than to the work of any scholar or antiquarian before or during their own time. By similar acts of intuition, stretching the imagination beyond the immediate scope of the evidence and the methods of conventional scholarship, each in his way formulated a completely new conception of antiquity, which in a certain sense were to prove complementary. Where Winckelmann exploited the literary powers of poetic imagery, Piranesi resorted to the visual potential inherent in the *capriccio* and architectural fantasy to reach new truths and a fresh kind of historical information. What Hegel was later to say about the achievements of Winckelmann may be considered equally true of Piranesi: that 'by the contemplation of the ideal works of the ancients he received a sort of inspiration, through which he opened up a new sense for the study of art'.

IV

Controversy

BY the close of the 1750s archaeology had become a major influence on Piranesi's development as an architect and designer and was to involve him in a decade of vigorous polemical activity. Although his prominent entry into the international arena of the Graeco-Roman controversy during the 1760s has been seen as an abrupt change from the patient recording of antiquity, there are already warning signs in the previous decade. The rhetorical character of certain illustrations in the *Antichità Romane* reveals an earlier and more gradual involvement in the debate, closely bound up with his artistic development.

A fresh interest in Greek antiquity and its architecture had begun to emerge in Europe during the middle years of the century.[1] Since many of its principal theories and seminal publications originated as part of the contemporary architectural scene, they were bound to affect Piranesi, especially through his close connections with the French Academy in Rome.[2]

Beyond the awakening Greek Revival, moreover, there was Piranesi's long established concern with the imaginative uses of antiquity, first introduced in the *Prima Parte*. Such a controversial standpoint in itself was bound to involve him in any debate which hinged upon the nature of artistic originality – a fundamental issue of the developing Graeco-Roman quarrel. In this respect Piranesi's contribution to the ensuing exchanges must be seen as an episode, however critical, in his gradual development towards a theoretical and artistic position of extreme originality by the mid-1760s.

Piranesi's earliest statement as an architect in his dedication to the *Prima Parte* involved an attack on contemporary designers for lack of imagination as well as on patrons for their undiscriminating taste. His arrival in Rome during the early 1740s had coincided, as mentioned earlier, with the close of the unusually productive phase of public works initiated with De Sanctis's Spanish Steps (1723–6) and closing with Galilei's Lateran façade (1733–6) and Fuga's façade of S. Maria Maggiore (1741–3).[3] The practical building world of the early eighteenth century, with its restrained version of the Baroque carried on by Fontana's followers, was unlikely to attract a designer such as Piranesi whose sympathies lay with the imaginative language of theatre design and the *capriccio*. Appropriately, it was Juvarra's opinion about the decline in architectural taste which he was to quote in support of his own artistic credo in the *Prima Parte*.

By fulfilling Piranesi's intention to explain his ideas through drawings, the plates of this work show the swift maturing of his visionary capacity from the Bibienesque *Great gallery* to the striking originality of the *Ancient mausoleum*. There is also sufficient evidence among the surviving sketches made at this time to show that such designs were worked out in a thoroughly architectural manner.[4]

By the 1750s Piranesi's collaboration with the radical group of student *pensionnaires* at Palazzo Mancini had placed him at one of the most significant centres of architectural thought in Europe. After early exchanges with designers like Le Lorrain in the 1740s Piranesi's own independently organized designs, as represented in the *College* plan of 1750, were to influence a new generation of students, notably Peyre and De Wailly. Besides making available in this form the inspiration of Roman thermal planning, Piranesi's dissemination of the decorative vagaries of Roman ornament with the plates of the *Trofei* of 1753 was expressly aimed at practising artists and designers.

While accumulating archaeological material during this decade, as eventually published in the *Antichità*, Piranesi began to move away from the circle of the French Academy, particularly as it had now become the focus for certain theoretical ideas based on the primacy of Greek art. By 1756 his introduction to the *Antichità* repeated even more forcibly his strictures against modern designers for failing to profit from the lessons of Roman antiquity. These were not only directed against the continuing conservatism in Rome but were now, by implication, also levelled at certain restrictive views among the progressive French and British designers. Three distinctive features of the *Antichità* plates reveal his growing isolation from this avant-garde thought in particular. Firstly, there is a marked increase in the sheer complexity of his plans, for example those reconstructing the Nymphaeum of Nero or the vanished portions of the Forum Romanum. Then there is a greater density of archaeological detail and a frenetic elaboration of form in his architectural fantasies, notably in the secondary frontispieces to Volumes II and III. This tendency is also reflected in the contemporary *capricci*, such as those executed for Robert Adam. Finally and most significantly, he places an exaggerated emphasis on the structural and engineering exploits of Imperial Rome.

Such phenomena, while originating from Piranesi's earlier works, clearly represent his initial reactions to the growing attention paid to Greek architecture both in theory and in

107 Le Roy: *The Erechtheum*, from *Les ruines des plus beaux monuments de la Grèce*, 1758

108 One of the *Tempietti Greci* added by Marchionni to Villa Albani

practice throughout the decade. The defence of Greece had been introduced early in the eighteenth century by French theorists such as Frézier and De Cordemoy as an offshoot from the protracted quarrel between the Ancients and Moderns.[5] It was Caylus, however, who gave it fresh significance in Volume I of his *Recueil d'antiquités* of 1752 when asserting that the Greeks had carried the arts 'to the greatest perfection; in Rome where [the arts] could not excel unaided, after having struggled for some time against barbarism, they were buried with the fall of the Empire'.[6]

The following year a more specific application of these ideas to contemporary architectural design appeared in Venice with Stuart and Revett's *Proposal* for their publication *Antiquities of Athens*. Dismissing Rome 'who borrowed her Arts, and frequently her Artificers from Greece', they claimed that

a work so much wanted will meet with the approbation of all those Gentlemen who are lovers of Antiquity, or have a taste for what is Excellent in those Arts, as we are assured that those artists who aim at Perfection must be infinitely more pleased, and better instructed the nearer they can draw their Examples from the Fountain-head'.[7]

But above all, it was the Jesuit Marc-Antoine Laugier, in his *Essai sur l'architecture* of 1753, who was to create the greatest impact by advancing a more specific philosophy of design in support of Greece.[8] He endeavoured to base architecture on the fundamental principle of the imitation of nature, as represented by Vitruvius' description of the rustic hut as a functional paradigm:

Never has a principle been more fertile in its effect. From now on it is easy to distinguish between the parts which are essential to the composition of a work of architecture and those which necessity has introduced and caprice added to them ... let us never lose sight of our little rustic hut.[9]

This introduced a highly potent idea, comparable to Rousseau's conviction that one should return to the beginnings of human history to discover the norm by which the present should be guided and, if necessary, corrected. The consequence of this austere criterion for architecture was the repudiation of those Baroque ideals of artistic licence which lay at the centre of Piranesi's system of invention and composition. In Laugier's view, the abuses of the primitive state of architecture were to be laid at the door of such designers as Borromini and his followers.[10] Caprice was now a crime.

Although having little knowledge of actual examples at this stage, Laugier was drawn to the conclusion that 'architecture owes everything that is perfect to the Greeks', their works serving as models to the Romans 'to whom architecture is under moderate obligations only'.[11] Thus on two fronts was Piranesi to find himself threatened – culturally and artistically.

Actual visual evidence in support of these challenging assertions, however, was slow to appear, still slower to offer any serious challenge in terms of an alternative style to Roman Classicism. As early as 1750 Soufflot's measured drawings, made during his historic expedition to view the Greek temples at Paestum with De Marigny and Cochin, were under discussion in the French Academy. Pancrazi's engravings of the temples at Agrigentum appeared in his *Antichità Siciliane* in 1751–2, and in 1754 Le Roy returned with material from his brief field trip to Greece sponsored by the Academy. But Greek architecture only began to present a more serious threat in the second half of the decade with the publication of Le Roy's *Les ruines des plus beaux monuments de la Grèce* in 1758. His plates, of 107 far greater calibre than previous records if somewhat inaccurate, supported the assertion that architecture was a Greek invention from which all Roman buildings derived, albeit as defective copies.

Meanwhile the aesthetic ideals of Winckelmann's 'noble simplicity and quiet grandeur', first advanced in 1755 as characterizing Greek art, only began to assume a greater effect after the close of the decade. Admittedly he had issued a brief account of the temples at Agrigentum in 1759, based on a survey made two years before by Piranesi's Scottish colleague Robert Mylne, and had referred to Paestum in a further essay in 1760.[12] But Marchionni's pair of *Tempietti Greci* added to Villa 108 Albani at about this time, with their Hellenistic incrustations of ornament comparable to the Rococo character of Mengs's *Parnassus* ceiling there, are probably a far closer reflection of Winckelmann's tastes than the stern austerity of the archaic Doric. By 1760, therefore, Piranesi could have seen few effects upon contemporary design, if Stuart's remote Greek Doric temple at Hagley in Warwickshire of 1758 is discounted. The threat still remained largely on a theoretical basis, backed by engravings rather than by buildings.

Piranesi's appetite for controversy, fought with publications and ingenious methods of visual satire, had already been sharpened by his encounter with Lord Charlemont over the *Antichità Romane*.[13] Moreover, the Irish peer, as an active member of the Society of Dilettanti, had himself taken a modest part in the promotion of Greek art. Apart from his support of James Stuart, he was also patron of Richard Dalton, whose *Musaeum Aegyptiacum et Graecum* of 1752 had resulted from an expedition with Charlemont to Greece and the Levant in 1749. Piranesi, in the *Lettere di Giustificazione scritte a Milord Charlemont* in 1757, had defended the *Antichità* not only as recording the past but as celebrating the creative genius of Rome for posterity. So closely was the defence of Rome identified with his own artistic beliefs that an attack upon the former amounted to a personal affront. Such was the complex mixture of scholarly and artistic motives which led to Piranesi's first major polemical work, *Della Magnificenza ed Architettura de' Romani*, in 1761.[14]

The publication of this handsome folio of two hundred pages of text with thirty-eight plates, completed the previous year, was delayed over the engraved portrait of Clement XIII to whom it was dedicated. It appears, however, to have been already under way by 1758, when the appearance of Le Roy's work led to its amplification.[15] Considerable parts of it, indeed, are likely to have been written still earlier in the form of a refutation of an anonymous pamphlet, *The Investigator. No. 332: A Dialogue on Taste*, published in London in 1755, and later found to be by Allan Ramsay, a friend of Piranesi and Robert Adam.[16]

The opening pages of *Della Magnificenza* set out in considerable detail to refute *The Investigator*'s assertion that the Romans were untutored in the arts of peace before contact with Greek civilization following the sack of Corinth in 146 BC. The learned array of Classical authorities used to counter Ramsay's somewhat superficial pamphlet suggests a heavy reliance on scholarly advice, as Bianconi claimed in his early biography of Piranesi.[17] However, a considerable portion of the visual evidence in the plates is highly personal to the artist, enlarging on pictorial themes first introduced in the *Antichità*.

Piranesi's main argument in *Della Magnificenza* rests on the Etruscans as sole founders of Roman civilization. According to his thesis, not only were the latter an older race than the Greeks, but they had perfected painting and sculpture as well as the technical arts long before the Greeks and were for some time the only teachers of the Romans.

Many of these tendentious ideas were derived from the recent developments in Etruscan scholarship described earlier. Although Piranesi quoted Dempster and Gori extensively, his theories about the cultural originality and inventive capacities of the Etruscans were drawn from the controversial views of Guarnacci, then in currency in the circle of Clement XIII and the Rezzonico family before they were published in 1767.[18]

A far broader contribution to Piranesi's approach, if more elusive to document, was provided by the theories of the Neapolitan historian Giambattista Vico, much admired by Lodoli and the Venetian Enlightenment during Piranesi's youth.[19] In his original methods of historical research, set out in

109 *Cloaca Maxima*, from *Della Magnificenza*

the *Scienza Nuova* of 1725, Vico had combined a philosophical system of enquiry with philological techniques of assessing linguistic and archaeological evidence (*i grandi frantumi dell'antichità*). Piranesi, besides sharing Vico's conclusions on the autonomy of Roman civilization as ultimately derived from Etruscan sources, also echoed his belief in the undying capacity of great nations such as Rome for cultural revival (*il ricorso delle cose umane nel risorgere che fanno le nazioni*). This idea of revival, or *ricorso*, was to become a particularly dominant belief as Piranesi's later theoretical position evolved.

Accompanying this cultural defence of Rome was an architectural one, specifically directed against Le Roy and, by implication, Laugier, who is not in fact mentioned. According to a particularly questionable thesis, Piranesi likens the severity of Etruscan building to that of the Egyptians, attacking the Greeks for affecting an empty prettiness (*una vana leggiadria*) in their architecture. As evidence of the functional austerity of early Roman buildings as inherited from the Etruscans, he cites their impressive engineering achievements in road construction, drainage and the complex aqueduct system. Among the specific examples described and illustrated are technical feats such as the Cloaca Maxima, the revetments of the Capitoline 109 Hill, and the Emissarium, or drainage outlet, of Lake Albano.

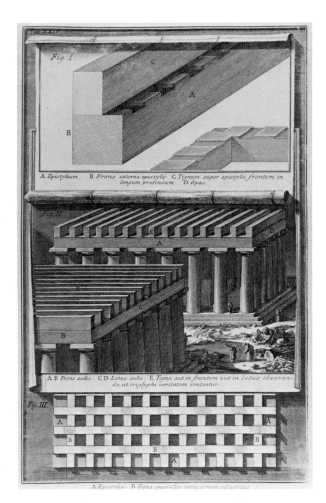

As already found in certain parts of the *Antichità*, Piranesi's imaginative faculties developed and expanded his theories by means of particularly ambitious plates, many of them folding out to accommodate the wealth of evidence assembled through his polemical ardour. In combining cultural and formal evidence in support of Italic originality in temple design, he reconstructed the Etruscan temple described by Vitruvius. Elsewhere a series of complex diagrams, specifically directed 110 against Laugier's primitive hut thesis, is related to the Vitruvian account of the development from wood to stone architecture. In discrediting this theory as manifestly illogical, Piranesi was clearly indebted to the views of Lodoli, who also had admired the unadorned character of Etruscan stone buildings for their uncompromising functionalism.

This having been said, however, it is noticeable that a disproportionate space is given in well over two-thirds of the plates to celebrating the richness and sheer variety of Roman architectural ornament. Here Le Roy's austere line engravings of Attic details are illusionistically pinned on to plates crowded 111 with Roman fragments, rendered with the richest effects of texture and chiaroscuro at Piranesi's command. Quotations from Le Roy and satirical interpolations reinforce Piranesi's undisguised relish in this area of the treatise. In the text, however, he vainly attempts to justify the apparent contradiction on the principle that the Romans, when eventually adopting Greek taste under the Empire, could not fail to correct and to surpass it.

110 Diagram of temple construction, from *Della Magnificenza*   111 Roman Ionic capitals contrasted with Greek, from *Della Magnificenza*

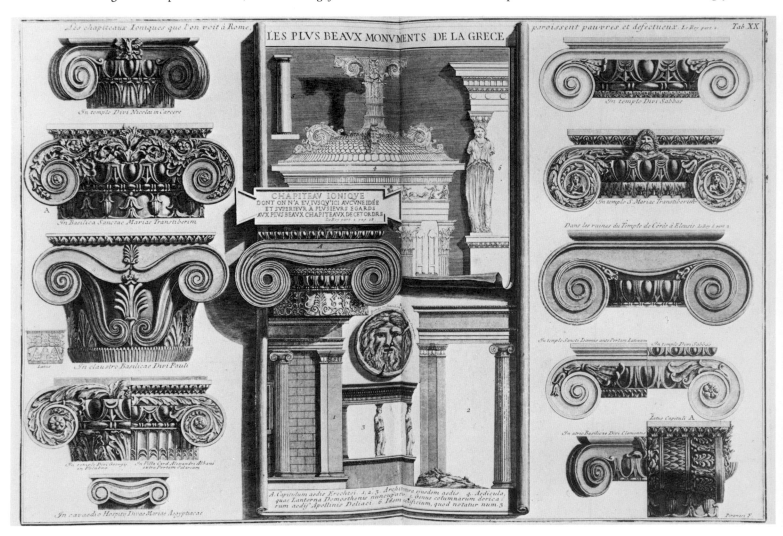

Despite its polemical character and ostentatious erudition, *Della Magnificenza* cannot be said to represent a really significant change of direction for Piranesi. Its genesis over the later 1750s coincided with and, indeed, grew out of the wide range of antiquarian studies initiated by the *Antichità*. The fruits of these researches were to appear in separate treatises during the first half of the following decade, together with others which explored in greater detail leading themes of the polemical debate in terms of Etruscan civilization and early Roman engineering and utilitarian buildings. Seen within this broader context, the striking contradictions in *Della Magnificenza* between the rational defence of austerity in the text and the undisguised enthusiasm for Imperial Roman decorative invention in many plates can best be explained by the contingencies of debate. Clearly Piranesi had got out of his depth intellectually, pursuing certain arguments further than he probably intended at the outset. Contrary to his basic predilection for complexity and idiosyncratic design, he had fought unwisely on limited issues determined by his opponents rather than in accord with the material rapidly accumulating from his comprehensive interests. It is not unduly surprising, therefore, that he was shortly to abandon an intellectual position made increasingly irrelevant by his own artistic development.

Among the first of the works to enlarge on both the *Antichità* and *Della Magnificenza* was the *Rovine del Castello dell'Acqua Giulia* of 1761, which reconstructed the technical character of the *mostra* or head fountain of the water system terminating on the Esquiline Hill. In the *Trofei* Piranesi had already published 70 the decorative fragments transferred from these ruins to the Campidoglio in 1590. His present concern, however, was to pursue his earlier studies of the water-courses in the form of a specific case-history. As shown earlier, he had carefully identified fragments of the various aqueducts in relation to the 73 urban structure of the ancient city, establishing the direction of water flow by measurement and by correlating this practical fieldwork with literary authorities like Frontinus. The treatise opens with a brief disquisition on his general conclusions, together with a commentary on Frontinus' account of methods adopted by the Roman water-magistrates to regulate domestic consumption from the public system through graded bronze cups.

The principal feature in this work, however, is the sequence of plates giving a complete record of the structure of 112 the *mostra* by means of plans, cross-sections, elevations and details. An extensive technical knowledge, harnessed to his acute imaginative powers, transformed this amorphous pile of ruins into a beautifully elaborate system of ducts, channels and sluices together with their plumbing and mechanical apparatus. 113 What sets out ostensibly to be a study of purely utilitarian achievement becomes a celebration of architectural complexity, bearing out Piranesi's claim in *Della Magnificenza* that a combination of the first two Vitruvian criteria of good building – strength and usefulness – could on occasion produce the third, a beauty independent of surface enrichment.

112–113 Diagram from the *Rovine del Castello dell'Acqua Giulia*, showing (left) section of the head fountain and (right) details of the filtering system

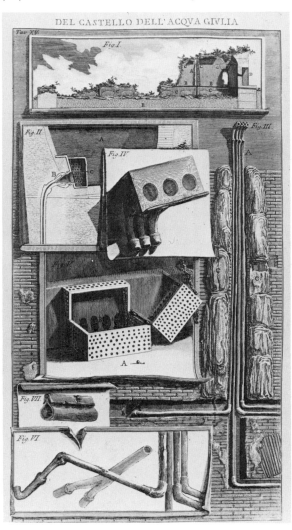

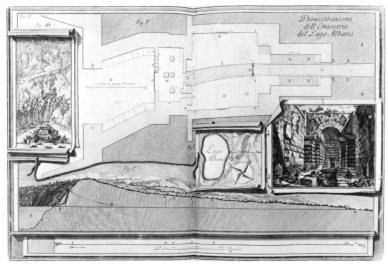

114 Plan of drainage outlet of Lake Albano, from *Descrizione e Disegno dell'Emissario del Lago Albano*

115 View of tunnel entrance, from *Descrizione e Disegno dell'Emissario del Lago Albano*

116 Subterranean grotto, from *Di due Spelonche*

A similar transformation from an exhaustive factual study to polemical evidence of a visually striking character is found in the *Lapides Capitolini* of 1762. As before, the emphasis is placed on visual impact, here provided by a large fold-out plate portraying pieces of a vast inscription from the Forum Romanum listing all the Consuls, the triumphs and the major games. Piranesi reproduces these fragments as they were set into Michelangelo's frame in Palazzo dei Conservatori, and skilfully fills the gaps with sculpture and classical fragments mainly derived from the Capitoline collections as relevant to the Republic, such as the She-Wolf and friezes of sacrificial instruments. The Latin text which follows displays a formidable erudition about the history of the inscription and earlier scholars' opinions on it, together with transcripts of absent pieces and references to literary sources covering the years missing. This and the monumental index listing all the Consuls is clearly directed at those adversaries, such as Ramsay, who had dismissed the early Romans as little more than a pack of naked slaves.

In *Della Magnificenza* Piranesi had attempted to account for the absence of the remains of public buildings from the heroic age of Rome which he had praised so generously by the inevitable destruction caused by the great fire under Nero in A D 64 and the gradual replacement of indigenous buildings through a fashionable taste for things foreign. He had also advanced a more ingenious argument: if the utilitarian works which had survived, particularly those below ground such as the drainage systems, were so impressive, how much more remarkable must the public works have been. Besides the Cloaca Maxima, another of his key examples was the remarkable engineering represented by the drainage outlet of Lake Albano. This work was now to be featured in one of his most impressive acts of technical research, the *Descrizione e Disegno dell'Emissario del Lago Albano*, in 1762.

Livy describes how the Romans, while besieging Veii in 398 B C, had responded to an oracle which required the level of Lake Albano to be lowered in order for victory to be assured them. Accordingly, within a year they had dug an outlet in the form of a tunnel, five feet high by three feet broad and some 1500 yards in length. Given these facts and the remains of the work, still in use, Piranesi extracted the maximum visual drama to accompany his scholarship. He provides a sequence of plates 114 combining plans, cross-sections, reconstructed elevations and modern views of the entrance and outlet structures. These also demonstrate the stages of boring the drain below the original water level, the problems of dispersing the spoil through a series of transverse shafts (certain of which he had discovered to his own satisfaction) and the character of the elaborate masonry facing. The fact that this epic task was achieved some two and a half centuries before the conquest of Greece, and not under Domitian as sometimes claimed, encouraged Piranesi to amplify the *terribilità* of the surviving remains in four *vedute*. 115 Applying here the calculated distortion in scale employed in the contemporary views of Tivoli to stress the almost superhuman dimensions of construction, he came close, both in feeling and in motif, to the refashioned *Carceri*. In the latter, however, man is an actor, albeit helpless, on a colossal stage, while here the introduction of humanity serves more mundane ends. Although rendered almost irrelevant by the conflict between the achievements of a super-race and the combined forces of time and nature, the fishermen and antiquarians serve to locate the drama in the present. And whereas ambiguity is a major constituent in the *Carceri*, the explicit record of the Emissarium's triumphant survival involves a mode of argument in the Graeco-Roman debate which might be termed 'poetic truth'. In this category of visual rhetoric, it is the conceptions rather than the executed facts of the archaeological past that lead Piranesi away from the rationalism of *Della Magnificenza* to a situation where the inspiration of antiquity, especially Roman antiquity, represents a living force, the artist being an agent for its transmission to the modern world.

While exploring the same area, Piranesi also recorded two subterranean grottoes in the cliffs overlooking the lake, which he published as *Di due Spelonche ornate dagli Antichi alla Riva del Lago Albano*. The work opens with an essay on Roman *nymphaea* and the probability that these particular examples were used for the orgies of Clodius denounced by Cicero. With customary thoroughness Piranesi provides plans and sectional views, carefully indicating the levels of debris, together with a few highly emotive *vedute*. In these latter works polemical concern with structural achievement is combined with a taste for the highly ornamental richness of the interiors. The *veduta* of the larger grotto is arranged like a theatre set, lit and equipped with the sublime rhetoric of Salvator Rosa. It is not hard to imagine it as a setting for the following anecdote about Piranesi told by Legrand:

He was drawing a grotto called del Bragantino, and was measuring the sections, perched on a ladder, accompanied by one Petrachi. The weather was stormy and for eight days the thunder had been grumbling almost without a break. A fisherman had been watching him for a long time in his odd dress (our artist was wearing an enormous hat with the brim turned down and a little hunting coat, very short, which gave him rather a fierce appearance) and he imagined that this singular character who was gesticulating, writing and often talking to himself, must be a sorcerer, and that he was moreover responsible for the bad weather which had gone on continuously since his arrival; he spread the idea, the alarm was given and the villagers armed and went off to do away with the sorcerer. . . . It was only by the timely arrival of the Pope's official that he was saved from his fate.[20]

Owing to the proximity of the Pope's summer residence overlooking the lake at Castel Gandolfo, Clement XIII took a keen interest in these enquiries. At his suggestion Piranesi concentrated on other remains in the area which were eventually published two years later in the *Antichità di Albano e di Castel Gandolfo*. Here again close attention was paid to the technical character of surviving structures, notably the House of Pompey, the Amphitheatre of Domitian, two subterranean reservoirs, some monumental tombs and a particularly well preserved length of the Via Appia. If building science was the ostensible reason for these investigations, the end products, especially the *vedute* concerned, reached an unprecedented amplitude and majesty of statement. For instance, in the interior view of the vast underground reservoir in the grounds of the Jesuits at Castel Gandolfo, Piranesi's use of the theatrical device of *scena per angolo* combines the maximum amount of physical information with a grandeur arising from a sense of almost limitless space. Once again, we come close to the world of the later *Carceri*, and a fine preparatory chalk study made on the site shows the degree of calculation behind this formidable statement.

117 Interior of cistern, Castel Gandolfo, from *Antichità di Albano e di Castelgandolfo*

118 Preparatory drawing for the previous plate (Private Collection, Cambridge, Mass.)

Pursuing his enquiries, Piranesi now went further afield in search of material to demonstrate the independent technical achievements of the Italic races in Latium. He selected Cori, one of the most ancient settlements in Italy, which, like the Tuscan city of Cortona, attributed its foundation to Dardanus of Troy.

The opening illustration in the *Antichità di Cora* of 1764 is a particularly ambitious folding plate portraying the cyclopean town walls of the sixth century BC. Here various medieval structures have been stripped away to reveal a system of *opus reticulatum* of such precision in its jointing that, according to Piranesi, it appeared more a work of nature than of man. A comparison with a similar composition published some eight years earlier in the *Antichità Romane* – the foundations of Hadrian's Mausoleum – shows the remarkable progress made by Piranesi in exploiting formal devices for didactic ends. Bolder contrasts in lighting are now produced by the deeply bitten areas of the plate, while a more rapid movement into depth is effected by a series of diagonals plotted by a number of gesticulating figures.

119 Town walls of Cori, from *Antichità di Cora*

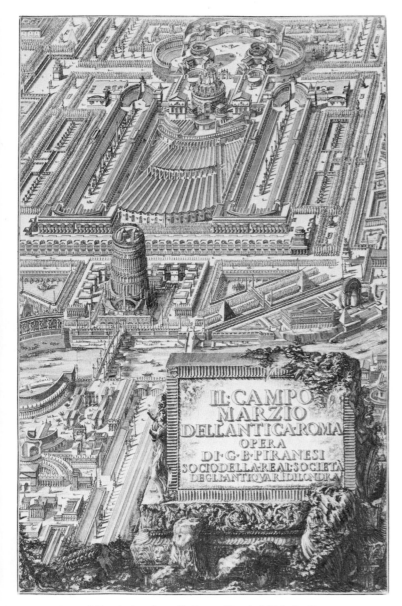

120 Second frontispiece from *Il Campo Marzio dell'Antica Roma*

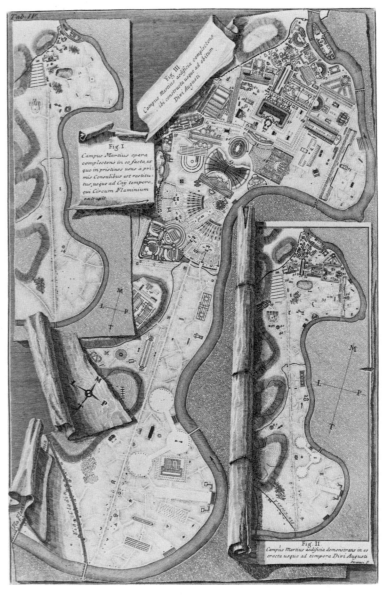

121 Maps showing evolution of the Campus Martius, from *Il Campo Marzio dell'Antica Roma*

Predictably, the so-called Temple of Hercules occupies a substantial portion of the folio, since its surviving portico represented a particularly early example of the Doric, or Tuscan, order. Detailed diagrams indicate the idiosyncrasies in the entablature of this temple as symptomatic of the evolution of the Tuscan order with an obdurate indifference to the possible influence of the neighbouring Greek colonies of Campania.

Among these polemically directed treatises of the 1760s, there is one which stands apart by virtue of its originality as well as by its intimate connection with Piranesi's artistic development – *Il Campo Marzio dell'Antica Roma*. Although published in 1762, like *Della Magnificenza*, its preparation extends well back into the previous decade, originating as a rejected part of the *Antichità Romane*. Certain implications in its general approach, however, anticipate a significant change taking place in Piranesi's intellectual and artistic life by the mid-1760s.

The *Campo Marzio* had grown out of the *Ichnographia*, the large map reconstructing the monumental quarter of Rome between the modern Via del Corso and the Tiber. This itself was envisaged as complementary to the 'fragments' containing

Piranesi's reconstructed plans of the Nymphaeum of Nero, the 98 Forum Romanum and the Capitoline Hill in the *Antichità*. 81 The preparation of the *Ichnographia*, moreover, was closely related to the tense if productive relationship between Robert Adam and Piranesi in 1755–7. Before Adam's final departure from Rome in April 1757, Piranesi had already begun work on the dedicatory plate at the top of the map (actually dated that year), presumably having a basic conception of the portion overlaid by the inscription.[21] By then he had also decided that the map should form a part of a complete treatise devoted to this area of monumental Rome.

As characteristic of the Enlightenment, the *Campo Marzio* set out to record the physical evidence of historical change and the patterns of urban growth determined by the interrelation of physical factors and political forces. The polemical function of the work, therefore, depended on the sheer weight of evidence and the immense span of time covered in reply to those evolutionary theories advanced by Winckelmann in support of Greece.

In his dedication to Adam, Piranesi described the thorough investigations undertaken since the idea first arose from their

122 Maps showing evolution of the Campus Martius, from *Il Campo Marzio*

123 *Scenographia* – aerial panorama – of the Campus Martius, from *Il Campo Marzio*

discussions when exploring the site. He also justified the conjectures and the hypothetical reconstructions necessary in an area where many important structures remained embedded in or below the medieval townscape. The thirty-three pages of text that follow contain a display of erudition based on literary authorities and later scholarship, but, as in the other folios of these years, it is the sequence of plates which constitutes the key element in this celebration of Roman magnificence.

Initially, the geography of the physical setting is provided by 122 a map which also locates the sites of the principal remains. Then, almost to rival views of the ruined Palmyra set in the sterile expanse of the Syrian desert as illustrated by Wood and Dawkins in 1753, this is followed by the *Scenographia* – an 123 awesome aerial panorama of the entire site with the remains starkly isolated on the plain, as if the Middle Ages had not intervened.[22] A sequence of maps follows plotting each phase in 121 the evolutionary story from the virgin site via the contributions of Romulus, the Tarquins and the early Consuls to the dramatic flowering of an urban plan of great complexity under Augustus. The finale, however, is reserved for the *Ichnographia* – endpap a giant plan of six plates reconstructing Rome during the later Empire. Piranesi, adopting the same illusionistic techniques as in the master-plan of the *Antichità*, shows the *Ichnographia* as a 72 vast fragment of an even larger work.

In the thirty-seven plates which follow, Piranesi produces the raw material from which this speculation originated, developing further the various didactic techniques of the *Antichità* with a comparable rhetoric. Medieval accretions are removed from the fragmentary structures like the Theatre of Marcellus. Elsewhere, the aid of the Marble Plan is involved in 124 recovering the remains of the Theatre of Pompey from its urban 125 conglomeration, and its seating system is reconstructed from surviving fragments. Engineering facts are given prominence in such overwhelming plates as that of the Ponte Molle. Even more intractable material, such as the battered remains of the

124, 125 Fragments of the Marble Plan relating to the Theatre of Pompey and (below) air-view of the Theatre of Pompey, both from *Il Campo Marzio*

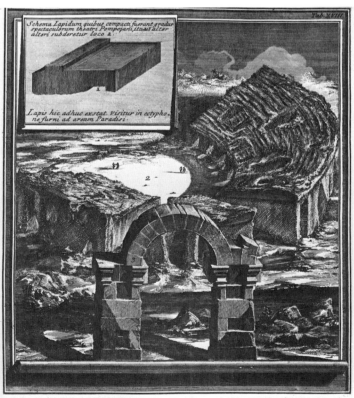

Mausoleum of Augustus, is given significance by the deployment of lighting and texture in order to isolate significant components in its masonry core.

For the first time in his archaeological career, Piranesi provides perspective renderings of his reconstructed plans in the *Campo Marzio*. Selecting certain portions of the *Ichnographia* for this treatment, he depicts the area of Hadrian's Mausoleum in the second frontispiece, together with three other bird's-eye 120 views of important zones: those of the Theatres of Marcellus 126 and Balbus, the Pantheon with the Baths of Agrippa, and the 127 Amphitheatre of Statilus Taurus adjoining the Orologium, or giant sundial, of Augustus. Piranesi's reasons for this new approach can be seen as part of his increasing concern with a mode of architectural design growing out of antiquity rather than with the mere reproduction of the past. While he was influenced to a minor extent by earlier perspective recon- structions by Kircher and Fischer von Erlach, Piranesi's 12 individual buildings in these aerial views show a new conception of design which departs from his 'Baroque' compositions of the 1750s. Despite lingering traces also of Palladian formulae, his buildings are now composed of distinct geometrical forms with frequent emphasis on plain surfaces and abrupt superimpositions of one element of Classical decoration on another.

It is in the *Ichnographia*, above all, that Piranesi's formal originality is brought to a sudden maturity. The idea of a total reconstruction of Rome belongs to a tradition dating back to the large engraved map of 1561 by Pirro Ligorio, the principal 65 forerunner of Piranesi in the field of visionary archaeology. But whereas Ligorio's Rome was an aggregate of individual buildings, symbolizing literary references and largely indifferent to interrelationships and setting, Piranesi's ingenuity is stimulated by the physical limitations of the site. The architect and antiquarian are now joined by the topographer.

Among the sources of inspiration for this enormous network, antiquity itself provides a major element, especially in the ancient Roman procedure of aligning groups of monumental buildings on a common axis, as already shown by Piranesi's plan of the Forum Romanum. Moreover, his 81 contemporary survey of Hadrian's Villa, published posthum- ously in 1781, clearly offered him even more complex planning patterns in terms both of combinations and of individual forms.[23] But in Piranesi's global concern with the Roman architectural inheritance, the character of the Baroque city should not be overlooked with its scenic planning of monumental townscape in relation to structures like the Colosseum and the early Christian basilicas.

In the design of individual components in the *Ichnographia* debts can again be traced to Ligorio as well as to Montano; also 66 to the Baroque predilection for clusters of spatial forms. These influences excepted, the actual mode of composition – as already noted in the aerial perspectives – departs from Baroque style in the arrangement of distinct geometrical components. Here Piranesi is far closer to the emerging ideals of European Neo-Classicism, even if at this date no other designer had pushed this logical process of pattern-making to such extremes.[24]

Throughout the *Ichnographia* antiquity provides a mine of elemental shapes for this novel process of elaboration. For

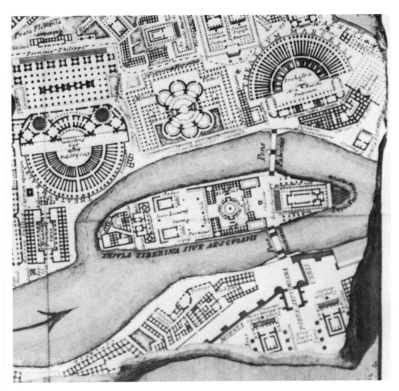

126, 127 Two plates from *Il Campo Marzio* showing (below) three aerial views and (above) a detail from the *Ichnographia* representing the area of the upper view with the Theatres of Balbus and Marcellus

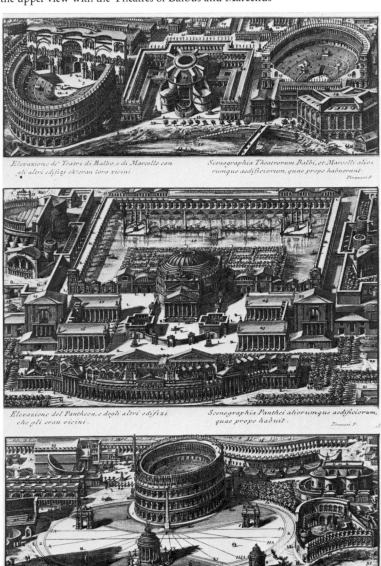

instance, such an unorthodox concept as the group of radial corridors which fan out from Hadrian's Mausoleum clearly derives from the plans of amphitheatre construction. Elsewhere, thermal planning is combined with other systems of design involving complexes of multiple units such as those found in the Imperial palaces on the Palatine. In such a procedure the ramifications are limitless, and Piranesi is at pains to justify this with reference to nature, who never repeats herself. For him variations and multiplications are major symptoms of creative architecture.

This celebration of the virtues of complexity, already evident as a basic preoccupation in Piranesi's early work, is clearly directed at the growing influence of Winckelmann. The German scholar, as the leading exponent of unadorned simplicity, had praised the beauty inherent in the proportions of Greek buildings. While accepting the theoretical justification of ornament in buildings in his *Remarks on the Architecture of the Ancients* in 1762, Winckelmann had traced a progression from Paestum to Athens, followed by a sharp decline under the Romans, especially as exemplified by Palmyra and Baalbek. An increased use of ornament and, by inference, general complexity, were associated with a decline in taste:

Architecture suffered the same fate as the old languages, which became richer when they lost their beauty; this can be proved by the Greek as well as the Roman language, and as architects could neither equal nor surpass their predecessors in beauty, they tried to show that they were richer.[25]

For Piranesi on the other hand, whether in planning or in ornament, complexity and variation meant life, and the unorthodoxy of modern designers was often anticipated by the ancients themselves. As he observes in the dedication to the *Campo Marzio*:

I am rather afraid that parts of the Campus which I describe should seem figments of my imagination and not based on any evidence: certainly if anyone compares them with the architectural theory of the ancients he will see that they differ greatly from it and are actually closer to the usage of our own times. But before any one accuses me of falsehood, he should I beg, examine the ancient [Marble] plan of the city . . . he should examine the villas of Latium and that of Hadrian at Tivoli, the baths, the tombs and other ruins outside the Porta Capena and he will find that the ancients transgressed the strict rules of architecture just as much as the moderns. Perhaps it is inevitable and a general rule that the arts on reaching a peak should decline, or perhaps it is part of man's nature to demand some licence in creative expression as in other things which we sometimes criticise in buildings of our times.[26]

Not without point the *Ichnographia* is shown as a fragment of a new Marble Plan, implying that the fecundity of Roman inspiration is limitless, not only in space but in time. Less than his previous works a document for the antiquary, Piranesi's map is supra-historical, both as a polemical weapon and as a vigorous exhortation to contemporary architects such as Robert Adam.[27]

With this affirmation of belief in the creative stimulus of antiquity and his active concern with modern design, Piranesi's polemical activity had begun to move away from the narrow issues of stylistic debate. He had already shown interest in Egyptian designs before his discussion of such matters in *Della Magnificenza*, and, despite his satire at the expense of Le Roy, had begun to adopt Greek elements just as the Romans

themselves had done. In fact a minor indication of this shift in
position is found in the aerial perspective of the Pantheon in the
Campo Marzio where he introduces a colonnade of caryatids,
features previously dismissed in *Della Magnificenza* as
symptomatic of the Greek trivialization of architecture. Of far
greater significance is the bold combination of Greek and
Egyptian motifs with Roman forms in a set of ten small
imaginary compositions added to the *Opera Varie* sometime in
the early 1760s.[28] In one he uses the part-fluted Doric columns
of Delos and in another the squat archaic colonnades of
Agrigentum. The tendency to break with a Baroque fluency of
transition in favour of abrupt juxtaposition of forms, together
with discordant superimpositions already hinted at in the
Campo Marzio perspectives, is developed here more boldly than
ever.

A new phase in the international Graeco-Roman debate
opened in 1764 with a reply to *Della Magnificenza* published in
the *Gazette littéraire de France* by the critic Mariette. Developing
Caylus's view of Hellenic originality further, he rejected the
Etruscans' claims on the grounds of their being Greek colonists.
Hence all Roman art had derived from Greece, being carried
out in Rome by Greek slaves, where it underwent a decline.
Meanwhile the pure Greek style maintained *une belle et noble
simplicité*. This phrase merely reinforced the growing stress laid
on austerity by Winckelmann, who in the same year published
his most ambitious work of Hellenic justification, *The History of
Ancient Art*.

Piranesi's rejoinder appeared in 1765 in a publication
composed of three elements. In the *Osservazioni . . . sopra la lettre
de M. Mariette* he repeated the leading arguments of *Della
Magnificenza* in a text set out in two parallel columns in which
he endeavoured to refute Mariette sentence by sentence. The title
page, however, reflects the more complex situation at which
Piranesi had arrived intellectually over the past few years.[29]
Ostensibly the dominant feature of the design is the Tuscan
order as an invention of the Etruscans, fully independent of the
Greek Doric and exhibiting all the primal functionalism of
Laugier's rustic hut. For Piranesi, on the other hand, the issue
of artistic originality was more profound, as two contrasting
insets on the left-hand side of the plate make clear. Mariette's left
hand is shown writing his letter under the motto *aut cum hoc*
while below, in the profile of the column, occur the tools of the
artist denoted *aut in hoc*. In short, the discussion of such matters
is beyond the experience of armchair critics like Mariette, and
can only be resolved by active designers like Piranesi, in far
closer touch with the creative spirit of antiquity through modern
practice.

Following the *Osservazioni*, in close connection with this title
page, comes one of Piranesi's most significant works, the *Parere
su l'Architettura*, presenting a viewpoint of the greatest
significance not only for Piranesi's own development but for
European artistic theory in general. Imitating Ramsay's
Investigator, this takes the form of a Socratic dialogue between
two architects, Protopiro and Didascolo. Protopiro represents
the progressive school of designers, nurtured in Laugier's
functionalist theories and committed to Winckelmann's view
of Hellenic austerity. Didascolo, as Piranesi's mouthpiece,
expresses his criticism of the limitations of such an attitude,
favouring the creative licence of the designer.

128 Title page of *Osservazioni sopra la lettre de M. Mariette*

129 Imaginary architectural design, dedicated to the Society of
Antiquaries, from *Parere su l'Architettura*

130 Architectural fantasy, endpiece from *Parere su l'Architettura*

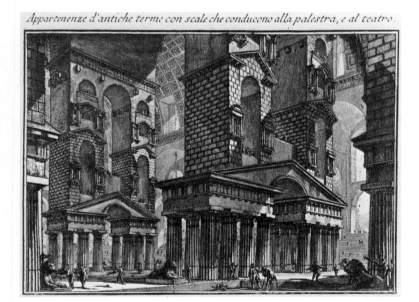

131, 132 Above and below: two architectural fantasies, added to the *Opere Varie* in the 1760s, *An ancient school* and *Remains of ancient baths*

The encounter is brief, since the issues are no longer obscured by inconclusive wranglings over literary authorities and highly tenuous evidence. In certain respects the debate represents a revival of the seventeenth-century quarrel between the Ancients and the Moderns, except that here both parties appeal to antiquity as the ultimate source of wisdom. One side acknowledges a series of truths derived from antique precedent; the other, a belief in the unlimited capacity of the modern designer to create new methods of design from a broad study of the past. Tradition is set against innovation. Piranesi's evidence in support of the latter view is no longer drawn from specific monuments of antiquity, but quotes examples of modern invention such as James Adam's design for a British order.[30] In 208 support of the unfettered imagination, Didascolo points to the dangers of following Mariette's worship of *une belle et noble simplicité*. Furthermore, quoting Le Roy against himself, Didascolo observes that such narrow criteria would reduce architecture to *un vil métier où l'on ne feroit que copier*. Worse still, the logical reduction of a building to its most essential functional elements, according to Laugier's system, would arrive at a bare field!

The original text of the *Parere* was illustrated by a couple of 129 vignettes showing original architectural designs by Piranesi 130 according to a method of composition first appearing in the small plates added to the *Opere Varie* in the early 1760s. In the 131, building dedicated to the Society of Antiquaries of London, all 129 the rules of Vitruvian and Palladian composition are broken with a Mannerist penchant for reversing conventional elements, in terms both of their position and of their relative proportions. Furthermore, Etruscan and Roman motifs are combined with an indefinable hint of Egyptian expression. More significantly, the formal language of the late Baroque, still the current language of contemporary design in Rome, is replaced by a system of disproportionate and sharply defined units, juxtaposing austere surfaces with highly dense areas of enrichment.

This approach to design was greatly developed and exaggerated for polemical effect in a set of six plates added to the *Parere* at some date after 1767, when Piranesi began to inscribe himself *Cavaliere*, or Knight. In these works, several of them only portions of structures, the last traces of conventional forms 133 disappear. Greek as well as Egyptian motifs are now crowded together with Etruscan and Roman ornament. Many of them include inscriptions underlining the basic principles and the challenge of this innovatory system of design. Reaffirming the lessons of the *Campo Marzio*, Piranesi quotes Ovid: 'Nature renews herself constantly – to create the new out of the old is, therefore, also proper to man.' As an answer to the pedantry into which the Graeco-Roman debate had sunk, in another plate he affirms in the words of Terence that 'it is reasonable to know yourself, and not to search into what the ancients have made if the moderns can make it'. Most scathing of all is his rejoinder to critics and members of his profession, quoting Sallust: 'They despise my novelty, I their timidity' (*Novitatem* 135 *meam contemnunt, ego illum ignaviam*).

The final element of his multiple publication was grandly entitled *Della Introduzione e del Progresso delle belle arti in Europa ne' tempi antichi*. Despite a promise to develop his ideas extensively on the originality of the Etruscans, however, he is content to

133 Preparatory drawing for a plate in *Parere su l'Architettura* (Kunstbibliothek, Berlin)

restate his thesis about the priority of Italy over Greece. By way of illustration, he adds several plates depicting the variety of patterns to be found among the Etruscan tombs which he had investigated at Chiusi and Corneto.

With the *Parere* Piranesi had arrived at a point where his intellectual standpoint was fully in harmony with his basic preoccupations as a visionary designer. While this theoretical volte-face in relation to his rationalist position in *Della Magnificenza* can be partly explained as manoeuvring to counter the arguments of his adversaries, especially Winckelmann, its main significance comes from his increasing activities as a practising designer and architect during the decade. Largely through the discerning support of Clement XIII and members of the Rezzonico family, he was given some relatively ambitious commissions to fulfil on his own terms. In 1763 he was invited

176– 180 by the Pope to submit schemes for a new tribune for the west end of the Lateran. This was to complete the programme of modernization begun by Borromini with the nave in the 1640s and continued into the eighteenth century with Galilei's façade. For the Pope's nephew, Cardinal Giambattista Rezzonico, Grand Prior of the Order of Malta, he reconstructed and

159– embellished the priory church on the Aventine, adding a new
175 entrance screen and ceremonial piazza. During these same years Piranesi carried out various schemes of interior decoration for the Pope at Castel Gandolfo, for Cardinal Rezzonico at the

Quirinal and for Senator Abbondio Rezzonico in the Palazzo 181–184 Senatorio, all of them involving furniture. In the mid-1760s he had also provided the Caffè degli Inglesi in Piazza di Spagna 200 with some of the earliest interiors anywhere in the Egyptian style. During this period, moreover, he was developing a series of remarkable chimneypiece designs, some of which were executed for foreign connoisseurs such as the Earl of 192 Exeter and the Dutch merchant John Hope. Before the end of 190 the decade many of these works were published in his final polemical treatise, *Diverse Maniere d'adornare i Cammini*, of 1769. 134

The plates of the *Diverse Maniere* set out to illustrate a lengthy essay, *An Apologetical Essay in Defence of the Egyptian and Tuscan Architecture*, containing Piranesi's most considered discussion of the innovatory views first introduced in the *Parere*. While Piranesi's actual works and activities as a designer must be considered separately, it is necessary to examine his intellectual position at the close of a complex and productive development over three decades.

The *Diverse Maniere* is addressed to Piranesi's most sympathetic patron, Cardinal Rezzonico, to whom he attributes support for the kind of innovations demonstrated here in practice as well as justified in theory. Such a patron, we are told in the dedication, dissatisfied with modern fashions in architectural decoration, requires the designer to emulate the creative eclecticism of the Romans, who had first utilized Etruscan ideas and then proceeded to absorb Greek and Egyptian material into their living system of design.

The *Essay* is addressed in three parallel texts – Italian, French and English – to an international audience of connoisseurs and designers rather than to the scholars of the earlier stage in the debate. It constitutes a fully reasoned justification of the artist's freedom to select material from the past solely on the basis of visual criteria, uncircumscribed by narrow theories and academic prejudices. The *Essay* also represents a final and conclusive attack by Piranesi on contemporary practice in the name of the visionary ideals first introduced three decades previously in the *Prima Parte*. Just as Winckelmann a few years earlier had established style as the interpretative key to antiquity, so Piranesi now discusses the application of visual laws – 'the rules of art' – to an assessment of past achievements. From such a standpoint not only Palladio but even Mannerists like Peruzzi and Ligorio, with whom Piranesi had greater sympathy, had fallen short in their imaginative uses of antiquity.

Piranesi attempts to forestall two major criticisms of his own designs. To supporters of simplicity, like Mariette, who objected to the overcrowding or ornament, he justifies himself on the principle of aesthetic control and formal balance, using analogies of musical counterpoint to refute Montesquieu's dictum that a 'building crowded with ornament is like a poem of enigmatic thoughts'. As for the boldness and stiffness of his use of Egyptian and Tuscan ornaments, he provides a remarkably advanced defence of stylization in architectural design: 'Art, seeking after new inventions, borrowed ... from nature ornaments, changing and adapting them as necessity required.'[31] Antique examples of this abstraction are provided by Piranesi in a comparison between the Greek and Egyptian lions of the Acqua Felice Fountain, and in the sphinx capitals *Ved 54* of Villa Borghese which he had recently exploited on his façade 165 to S. Maria del Priorato.

134 Frontispiece to *Diverse Maniere d'adornare i Cammini*

135 Architectural fantasy, with quotation from Sallust, plate added to *Parere su l'Architettura* after 1767

136 Etruscan bases and shell forms, from *Diverse Maniere d'adornare i Cammini*

Finally, this consideration of how the modern designer should learn from antiquity to borrow from nature leads him to a defence of Etruscan art, first introduced eight years earlier in *Della Magnificenza*. Here, however, he is no longer concerned in justifying the originality of this race by historical and literary evidence alone, but on aesthetic grounds, selecting their vase forms (later established as Greek imports) to illustrate their inspiration from natural patterns, especially those of shells. While Piranesi is now willing to admit certain unique qualities possessed by the Greeks, he insists on detailing the multifarious achievements of Etruscan invention as codified in an accompanying diagram. With such a wealth of inspiration before him, how much more should the modern designer be encouraged to greater originality. As he triumphantly concludes:

Let us at last shake off this shameful yoke, and if the Egyptians and Tuscans present to us, in their monuments, beauty, grace and elegance, let us borrow from their stock, not servilely copying from others, for this would reduce architecture and the noble arts [to] a pitiful mechanism, and would deserve blame instead of praise from the public, who seek for novelty, and who would not form the most advantageous idea of the artist, as was perhaps the opinion some years ago. No, an artist who would do himself honour, and acquire a name, must not content himself with copying faithfully the ancients, but studying their works he ought to show himself of an inventive, and I had almost said, of a Creating Genius; and by prudently combining the Graecan, the Tuscan, and the Egyptian together, he ought to open himself a road to the finding out of new ornaments and new manners. The human understanding is not so short and limited, as to be unable to add new graces and embellishments to the works of architecture, if to an attentive and profound study of nature one would likewise join that of the ancient monuments.[32]

V

The Fever of the Imagination

MANY years ago, when I was looking over Piranesi's *Antiquities of Rome*, Mr Coleridge, who was standing by, described to me a set of plates by that artist, called his *Dreams*, and which record the scenery of his own visions during the delirium of a fever. Some of them (I describe only from memory of Mr Coleridge's account) represented vast Gothic halls: on the floor of which stood all sorts of engines and machinery, wheels, cables, pulleys, levers, catapults, &c. &c. expressive of enormous power put forth and resistance overcome. Creeping along the sides of the walls, you perceived a staircase; and upon it, groping his way upwards, was Piranesi himself: follow the stairs a little further, and you perceive it come to a sudden abrupt termination, without any balustrade, and allowing no step onwards to him who had reached the extremity, except into the depths below. Whatever is to become of poor Piranesi, you suppose, at least, that his labours must in some way terminate here. But raise your eyes, and behold a second flight of stairs still higher: on which again Piranesi is perceived, by this time standing on the very brink of the abyss. Again elevate your eye, and a still more aerial flight of stairs is beheld: and again is poor Piranesi busy on his aspiring labours: and so on, until the unfinished stairs and Piranesi are both lost in the upper gloom of the hall. – With the same power of endless growth and self-reproduction did my architecture proceed in dreams.[1]

In this celebrated passage from *The Confessions of an English Opium Eater* of 1821 Thomas De Quincey provides an insight into the central mystery of Piranesi's *Carceri*, or Prisons, which first appeared around 1745 and were re-issued in the early 1760s – both critical moments of his intellectual and creative development.[2] De Quincey, examining the workings of the imagination stimulated rather than provoked by opium, recognized in Piranesi's plates a phenomenon comparable to the mechanism of his own thought processes.[3]

When they first appeared in the mid-1740s, the fourteen plates of the *Invenzioni capric di Carceri* represented an intensely private work, far ahead of its time in both form and content. Piranesi's considerable diffidence in offering it to the public is suggested not only by the absence of any indication of authorship on the frontispiece and most of the plates, but also by their being priced at one *paolo* apiece as opposed to 2½ *paoli* for the individual *Vedute di Roma* some years later.[4] Hastily etched in a highly idiosyncratic style, these works arose from what was little short of a creative crisis, providing an outlet for Piranesi's frustrated architectural imagination as reflected in the admonitory tone of the dedication to the recently published *Prima Parte di Architetture e Prospettive*.

As their frontispiece indicates, the *Carceri* were essentially a series of *capricci* or *scherzi di fantasia* in the manner of Tiepolo, whose influence upon Piranesi during his recent return to Venice was to be of paramount importance for his maturing etching technique. They consist of hastily sketched forms, traced on the plate with the same fluency and abbreviated notation as is found in Tiepolo's fantasies. They also contain an equally personal language of arcane imagery which, like that of the *Grotteschi*, continues to defy all attempts to impose a coherent iconographic solution. But quite unlike Tiepolo's *Scherzi* and later *Capricci*, the *Carceri* represent an experimental field of composition, as reflected in their barely resolved forms and loosely suggested structures. In this respect they constitute improvizations on a theme somewhat analogous to the ideas fashioned by contemporary musicians from a sequence of brilliant extemporizations, pushing both instrument and technique to the utmost limits of their capacities. Thus, far from being the products of drug-induced hallucinations as claimed by De Quincey, the *Carceri* reveal the processes of a highly controlled discipline, exploiting to an unprecedented degree Baroque illusionistic devices of perspective and lighting.[5] The irrational and elusive concepts thus adumbrated are almost a gesture of defiance to the patrons and architects of Rome who had failed to measure up to the creative possibilities suggested by the 'speaking ruins' surrounding them.

The fact that the *Carceri* are rooted in the creative process of the early 1740s is borne out by their evident origins in Piranesi's formative training in stage design, both in Rome and in Venice. The prison scene was a relatively common subject in surviving designs for early eighteenth-century stage sets, if rarely appearing in engraved works such as Giuseppe Galli Bibiena's influential *Architetture e Prospettive* of 1740. Examples can be found in the drawings of Ferdinando Bibiena, Marco Ricci, Daniel Marot and, notably, Filippo Juvarra, whose designs for Cardinal Ottoboni's theatre in the Cancelleria were a source of particular inspiration for Piranesi, in technique as much as in composition.[6]

The first evidence of Piranesi's thinking in this direction occurs in the *Dark prison* of the *Prima Parte*, with its stage-like composition and exaggerated structural system reflecting the artist's early engineering training in Venice. If the transition

137 Frontispiece to the *Carceri*, 1st state

138 Filippo Juvarra: stage design for a prison scene, drawing, 1712 (Biblioteca Nazionale, Turin)

140 *Dark prison*, from the *Prima Parte*

139 Ferdinando Bibiena: stage design for a prison, watercolour (Albertina, Vienna)

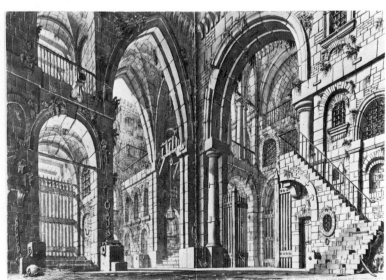

141 *Carceri*, pl. VI, 1st state

142 *Group of columns*, from the *Prima Parte*

141 from this particular conception to plate VI of the *Carceri* is
evident, no less important was the armature provided by a
142 composition such as the *Group of columns* of the *Prima Parte*,
143 which anticipates the arrangement of staircases in plate VIII.
Similarly, the idea of the sweeping spiral staircase around a
177 monumental circular structure in the *Temple of Vesta* finds a
144 counterpart in the layout of plate III, with a similar ambiguity
in the surrounding space, suggested rather than defined by
curvilinear forms. Although the surviving preparatory
drawings for the *Carceri* are rare, this mode of transposition
from aulic to penal subject-matter is strikingly confirmed by a
145 study for a palatial interior, now in the British Museum, which
146 if reversed with appropriate modifications becomes the setting of
plate XI.[7]

In contrast to the extremely ornate decoration of the majority
148 of the *Prima Parte* compositions, Piranesi reduces the *Carceri* to a
drama of stark economy, an almost abstract play of structural
forms rendered in terms of pure masonry where the proportional
system of Vitruvian ornament no longer inhibits the
imagination. Reflected in these expressions of utilitarian
architecture are memories of his father's craft and of the
engineering world of the Magistrato delle Acque. There is also
something of Lodoli's admiration of the functional probity of
stone construction as experienced by Piranesi in the
monumental language of Venetian architecture – the rusticated
façades and entrance halls of Sansovino, Sanmichele and
Longhena, as well as of Lucchese and Scalfarotto.

The compositional devices of perspective developed from the
Bibienesque *scena per angolo* in the plates of the *Prima Parte* exert a
powerful new effect of unease within this near-abstraction of
form. Two patterns in particular inherited from the earlier work
are those of the *Great gallery*, with its subordinate spaces leading 7
by means of staircases to larger areas, and, from the *Monumental* 8
bridge, a distant vista framed by a vast foreground arch. Unlike
the *Prima Parte*, however, the *Carceri* compel the spectator to
undergo an optical journey of frenetic motion by means of a 156
succession of stairs, ramps, bridges, balconies, catwalks and
galleries – a nervous continuum with no point of stability or rest
throughout. If this were not sufficiently disorientating, Piranesi
also contrives a system of conflicting illusions preventing one
from adjusting to the environment at any one moment in that
progression from its beginning in the immediate foreground –
often without the reassuring scenic frame – to the far distance
where the journey continues out of sight.

Closely bound up with these restless spatial experiments is
the originality of the technique itself. The essentially pictorial
nature of Piranesi's etching, much criticized by Vasi, depends
here upon a network of interweaving lines and contradictory
hatching in which conventional orthogonals and transversals
are further confused by inexplicable areas of light and shadow.
Lightly bitten areas are played off against zones of blank paper,
the latter occasionally representing mysterious plumes of smoke 146
which, by masking crucial junctions, remove any reassuring
points of spatial reference. Seen by itself each structural element,

143 *Carceri*, pl. VIII, 1st state

145 Study for a palatial interior, drawing (British Museum)

146 *Carceri*, pl. XI, 1st state

144 *Carceri*, pl. III, 1st state

whether arch, pillar, vault or beam, exists as a credible form until related to its context. Furthermore, pulley ropes, cables, grilles, joists and bars serve to produce a mesh of visual snares as menacing and brittle as a spider's web.

141 Populating this shadow-world of perpetual flux is a race of amorphous figures, grouped together in imponderable rites or set apart in total seclusion, unrelated one to another in these labyrinthine halls. Lacking the confidence of the humanity in the *Prima Parte* or the wiry energy of the populace in the early *vedute*, these figures merely punctuate the meaningless transitions to infinity where architecture is the prime subject-matter.

In the *Carceri* we have reached a situation where each plate no longer simply represents but *is* an architectural experience in itself. Through the most complex system of decoding where conventional perspective sets up expectations only to deny them by introducing fresh patterns, the spectator becomes inescapably involved in the creative process. Each plate embodies a set of endless possibilities. As never before, the Western system of pictorial space is questioned with all its implications concerning the nature of perception. The challenge was not be met again until the revolution of Cubism.

Significantly, few drawings survive to enable us to plot the compositional evolution of the *Carceri*. Indeed, the very techniques of the plates with their hastily sketched forms suggest a considerable degree of spontaneous composition, etched straight on to the copper. Apart from two particularly close
147 preparatory designs (in reverse) for plates VIII and XII, now in Hamburg and Madrid respectively, two other drawings can be associated specifically with the evolution of the most complex of
148 the *Carceri*, plate XIV.[8] In the Edinburgh drawing the concept
150 is first introduced in terms of a single arcade at the centre, heavily
149 blocked out in areas of light and shadow.[9] The London design, also in reverse, brings into the composition the series of ambivalent relationships with additional ruined arches, giving to the executed version its compelling force as a tantalizingly inseparable weave of structures.[10]

The *Carceri*, although clearly achieving little success when first appearing under the name of their publisher, Giovanni Bouchard, were reissued with the views of the *Magnificenze di Roma* in 1751.[11] Already something of their creative stimulus upon Piranesi's formal development is apparent in the compositional breadth and imaginary language of the colossal
22 fantasy, the *Great harbour*, in the *Opere Varie* of 1750, with its unparalleled display of anti-Vitruvian forms. The effect of the *Carceri* in spatial terms may also be sensed in the enormous
19 complexity of the *College* plan belonging to the same work. In fact, this might well pass for an ideal key to their otherwise irreconcilable systems of halls, vestibules, stairs and galleries. Similarly, when Piranesi came to celebrate the massive
96, 95 substructures of Hadrian's Mausoleum and the Pons Aelius in the *Antichità Romane*, the megalomania of the *Carceri* contributed an essential ingredient to their polemical expression. Even the speculative apparatus for reconstructing
90 the Tomb of Cecilia Metella was to inherit the macabre effects of the instruments of torture indicated in certain of the *Carceri*. But literal images apart, it was Piranesi's dissatisfaction with conventional modes of Classical design established by the Renaissance which the *Carceri* first revealed, and which was to introduce a new formal language as the 1750s came to a close.

As Piranesi's imaginative world grew more estranged from the contemporary developments in architectural design found in the hellenizing circle of the French Academy, so a further creative crisis emerged by the 1760s. Significantly, at the very time when he was becoming deeply embroiled in the pedantic exchanges of the Graeco-Roman controversy with the publication of *Della Magnificenza*, he turned once more to the *Carceri* as a source of self-analysis and of creative release.

The re-publication around 1760 of the original fourteen plates, together with two additional ones, as the *Carceri d'Invenzioni*, created a version which not only reflected many new preoccupations, formal as well as thematic, but was to capture the imagination of a new and more receptive generation.[12] Never again were they allowed to become a neglected part of Piranesi's works. On the contrary, in time they were to eclipse many of his other achievements, creating a serious distortion to his reputation which has persisted for over a hundred and fifty years.

Formally, the most striking change to overtake the original plates was the effect of an intensive reworking of the majority of them in terms of heightened tonal contrasts and the introduction of more explicit details. In the conversion of a collection of *scherzi* into a sequence of dramas, the final traces of Rococo linear and atmospheric subtleties were to be replaced by strongly bitten lines and broad areas of tonal contrast. This transformation, apart from reflecting the formal development of Piranesi's graphic style around 1760, is also connected with his personal control over the actual printing process in his new establishment at Palazzo Tomati. As with the large *Vedute di Roma*, the *Carceri* continued to play a major part in his graphic experiments. Current research is revealing that, while he issued no further edition of these plates as a group after the early 1760s, Piranesi continued to explore new possibilities in the printing of individual plates well into the next decade.[13] This was done with regard to the effects of ink, in both extent and colour.

Thematically, the major changes incline towards the expression of melodrama. With few exceptions, the physical horror of prisons was now rendered explicit in terms of their structural immensity and spatial complexity. An extended 157 system of staircases, galleries and roof structures recedes into infinity with that spirit of self-generation that De Quincey considered a property of the highly developed imagination out of control. Also now inserted is a complete repertoire of penal apparatus in the form of chains, cables, gallows and sinisterly indistinct instruments of torture, many of them infused with a sense of decay through endless use. Animating this punitory hell is an increased number of figures, together with certain episodes of punishment being enacted. Although this latter feature already appears once in the original version with plate X, there the group of bound prisoners thrust forward on a 151 cantilevered slab possesses the effect of sculpture in the mode of Michelangelo's *Slaves* rather than that of the pathetic huddles of oppressed humanity in the later version of the plates.

The key to this crucial transformation of the *Carceri* lies in the substitution of explicit imagery for the implicit ideas which had given the earlier state a more potent, if elusive, sense of fear. Through the intervening decade of the 1750s Piranesi had addressed himself to tackling a series of fresh problems related to archaeology and to aesthetic controversy. With the preparation

147 Preparatory drawing for *Carceri*, pl. VIII (Kunsthalle, Hamburg)

149 Right above: preparatory drawing for *Carceri*, pl. XIV (British Museum)

150 Right below: preparatory drawing for *Carceri*, pl. XIV (National Gallery of Scotland, Edinburgh)

148 *Carceri*, pl. XIV, 1st state

151 *Carceri*, pl. X, 1st state

of the *Antichità Romane* and its associated works he was concerned with the study of neglected aspects of the Roman achievement, together with their effective communication through cogent images. In this respect the atmospherics of the 17 *Grotteschi* and the linear arabesques of the *Archi Trionfali* were 32, 33 no longer adequate to register the detailed systems of masonry 97 construction intuited in the *Theatre of Marcellus*, or to distinguish the precise textures of material decay as found in the 88–92 *Tomb of Cecilia Metella*. As the violence of controversy overtook these disinterested studies towards the end of the decade, a fresh need arose for rhetorical images to set against the evidence of Le Roy and to discredit the theories of Laugier and Winckelmann. Joined to this development in polemical expression was Piranesi's wish to develop a new language of architectural composition, by 1760 of overriding importance to him.

Three plates in particular – the two added to the series as plates II and V together with the original closing one reworked 152 as plate XVI – reveal these new concerns in a more overt form. In each case compositional clarity is sacrificed to a didactic superabundance of detail, in marked contrast to the other plates which retain their initial cohesion. In the first two, the architectural system is created by the superimposition of a series of vast arcades reminiscent of the Curia Hostilia and the 94 Tablinium of the Capitol. Incorporated into these epic settings is a variety of reliefs, inscriptions and large ornamental fragments, as if these plates were additional illustrations to the prolix arguments of the contemporary *Della Magnificenza ed Architettura de' Romani*.

The general theme, therefore, concerns *Romanità* and its roots in the time of the Kings and early Republic; also the origins of Italic civilization in the Etruscans. Research into the individual inscriptions and reliefs has revealed that these three plates in particular represent polemical statements exploiting the theme of the *Carceri* within a specific iconographic programme.[13] Among the principal arguments brought against the Greeks by Piranesi in the early pages of *Della Magnificenza* was the superior character of the *Lex Romana*, founded upon civil virtue and equity in primitive times, especially under the Kings. Among the inscriptions in plate XVI that on the Egyptian lotus column 152 – AD TERROREM INCRESCEN AUDACIAE – is taken from

Livy's life of Ancus Martius, which refers to the creation of the Mammertine Prison in the Forum by Servius Tullius.[15] Furthermore, the quotation immediately above the columnar relief to the right – INFAME SCELUSS.. ..RI INFELICI SUSPE.. – is a paraphrase of a passage in the same work describing the just if nominal punishment under Tullius accorded to the Horatius who had killed his sister for favouring an enemy of Rome.[16] Although a third inscription appearing on the prominent stela is more elusive, this may also be indirectly derived from the same source.

More complex if more specific still is the revealed meaning of plate II, featuring prominently a scene of torture with energetic executioners and animated spectators. Set high above this episode in the crown of the main arch is a row of inscribed portrait reliefs. The names supplied can be identified with victims punished unjustly by Nero, as recorded in the *Annals* of Tacitus.[17] The fragmentary names of three others appear on the left-hand pillar supporting a relief with giant heads, all of these emphasizing the decline of Roman law under a philhellene emperor. The same theme also appears to be extended to plate V, where a giant relief in a late Imperial style depicts a prisoner led to punishment.

Given the way in which the revised *Carceri* reflect and incorporate live concerns in Piranesi's intellectual and artistic evolution, it is not surprising to find in plate II evidence of his growing search for a novel system of architectural design. The early indications of a change in Piranesi's architectural thinking run parallel, and at times counter, to the rationalist theories set out in *Della Magnificenza*. This is evident not only in the complex character of much of the material illustrated in this work but, more strikingly, in the group of small architectural fantasies included in an edition of the *Opere Varie* around the same time. In the *Ancient school* and the *Remains of ancient baths* architectural forms are manipulated in an extremely idiosyncratic manner as found in the exterior façade over the torture scene in plate II of the *Carceri*. Here a relief strip, boldly superimposed over a Tuscan colonnade, is bent upwards into the pedimental area of a gable to frame four Corinthian columns. It anticipates by half a decade the strange designs of the additional plates to the *Parere su l'Architettura* – an eloquent confirmation that fantasy provided for Piranesi a testing ground of ideas for subsequent development.

Already in Piranesi's time the influence of the later *Carceri* had begun to foster new themes and fresh modes of expression in artists and writers. The literal imagery of vast cavernous halls and galleries with all the gruesome paraphernalia of torture instruments can be seen in the fantasies of the Frenchman Louis-Jean Desprez.[18] Likewise one of the earliest impressions on a literary imagination is recorded in the travel journal of the English dilettante William Beckford. While in Venice in 1780, only a couple of years after Piranesi's death, he recalled his thoughts while floating under the Bridge of Sighs leading to the Ducal Prisons:

I shuddered whilst passing below; and believe it is not without cause, this structure is named *Ponte dei Sospiri*. Horrors and dismal prospects haunted my fancy on my return. I could not dine in peace, so strongly was my imagination affected; but snatching my pencil, I drew chasms and subterraneous hollows, the domain of fear and torture, with chains, racks, wheels and dreadful engines in the style of Piranesi.[19]

152 *Carceri*, detail of pl. XVI, 2nd state, showing inscriptions

153 Louis-Jean Desprez: prison interior with torture scene (Pierpont Morgan Library, New York)

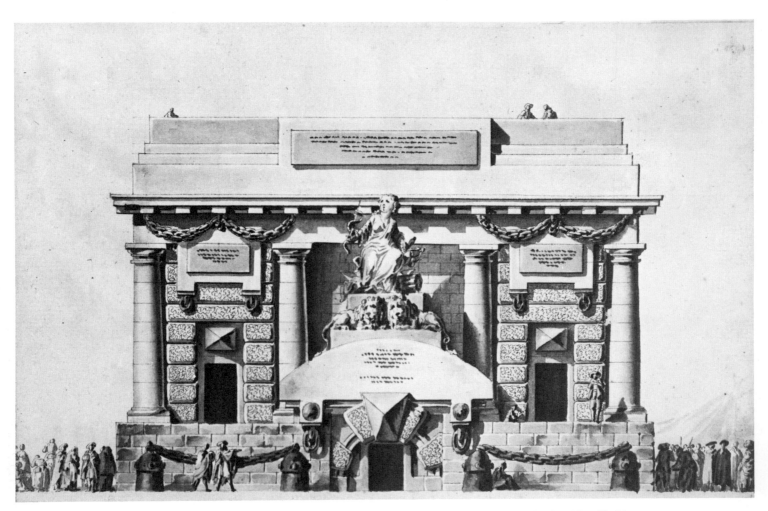

154 Jean-Charles Delafosse: design for a prison façade (Cooper-Hewitt Museum of Design, Smithsonian Institution, New York)

155 George Dance the Younger: doorway, Newgate Gaol, London

The more far-reaching sensations of terror born from the sheer endlessness, magnitude and massiveness of the *Carceri* spoke to the generation educated by Edmund Burke's *Enquiry into the Sublime and Beautiful* of 1757, where the topics of Obscurity, Privation, Vastness, Infinity and Magnitude in Building relate to the emotions of fear induced by infinity and 'greatness of dimension'. Similarly the formal language of retribution in Piranesi's penal architecture, which anticipates by decades the *architecture parlante* of Boullée and Ledoux, already exerted its effect upon the creation of certain prisons in the 1770s. For instance, the French designer Jean-Charles Delafosse, in search of a contemporary system of symbolism, produced an ideal prison façade combining ideas from the *Carceri* with motifs derived from the Neo-Mannerist aesthetic of the *Parere*.[20] In marked contrast, however, to this dense conglomeration of allegorical ornament is the austere statement of George Dance's Newgate Gaol, London, which he began in 1769 within a few years of meeting Piranesi while studying in Rome. Although strong debts to Giulio Romano and Palladio have been identified in this stark building, it was Piranesi's *Carceri* that taught Dance's generation the expressive potential of design based on the highly original handling of Classical forms amplified by exaggeration in scale and texture.[21]

If they can be considered to have a personal meaning for Piranesi himself, the *Carceri* are concerned with this process of

156 *Carceri*, pl. VII, 1st state

157 *Carceri*, pl. VII, 2nd state

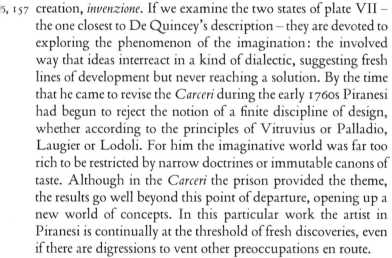

5, 157 creation, *invenzione*. If we examine the two states of plate VII – the one closest to De Quincey's description – they are devoted to exploring the phenomenon of the imagination: the involved way that ideas interreact in a kind of dialectic, suggesting fresh lines of development but never reaching a solution. By the time that he came to revise the *Carceri* during the early 1760s Piranesi had begun to reject the notion of a finite discipline of design, whether according to the principles of Vitruvius or Palladio, Laugier or Lodoli. For him the imaginative world was far too rich to be restricted by narrow doctrines or immutable canons of taste. Although in the *Carceri* the prison provided the theme, the results go well beyond this point of departure, opening up a new world of concepts. In this particular work the artist in Piranesi is continually at the threshold of fresh discoveries, even if there are digressions to vent other preoccupations en route.

In the final analysis, however, the *Carceri*, with their polemical ardour and didactic intensity crossed with speculative ideas of far-reaching consequence, defy a unitary solution. This is hardly surprising considering Piranesi's discursive interests poured into these plates in two critical phases of his development, together with the visual ambivalences and contrived irrationality of space formulated in the early version and extended for new creative ends in the later one. In no other work, except perhaps in certain drawings, are we able to come so close to the workings of Piranesi's febrile imagination with all its complex blend of fact and fantasy, the plausible and the impracticable. Where the sequence of the *Vedute di Roma* constitutes public evidence of his artistic progress, the *Carceri* remains a more intimate and elusive work which barely supports the considerable weight of scholarly exegesis which has been applied to it. Creative frustration engendered the first version when the young Piranesi faced a lack of opportunity as a designer in the contemporary architectural scene. The second version redefined his problems in more specific areas which were to be at least partly resolved in the decade which now lay ahead.

158 D. Cunego and Piranesi: Pope Clement XIII, frontispiece of *Della Magnificenza*

159 Giuseppe Vasi: *View of the Aventine*, 1771, detail showing S. Maria del Priorato on the left, with the Pyramid of Cestius and S. Paolo fuori le Mura in the distance (British Library)

VI

Freedom in Design

BY the early 1760s when the refashioned plates of the *Carceri* appeared, Piranesi had reached a climacteric point in his career. He was acknowledged as the leading *vedutista* of his adopted city, with almost sixty large plates of the *Vedute di Roma* to his credit. These images were rapidly becoming a determining influence on the European vision of antiquity as acquired by visiting tourists as well as by an increasing number of artists studying in Rome. In the world of international scholarship he was recognized as a leading archaeologist through the *Antichità Romane* and various related treatises. His election to the Society of Antiquaries of London was followed by his admittance in 1761 to the Accademia di San Luca, marked by the later execution of a vigorous portrait bust by the young British sculptor Joseph Nollekens.[1] Through the vicissitudes of debate in the Graeco-Roman controversy, moreover, he was beginning to develop a new approach towards contemporary design. In his view antiquity presented a live issue as a rich and varied source of inspiration for the modern artist. Yet despite all these achievements, his creative aspirations as a trained architect were still largely unfulfilled except through the medium of his graphic fantasies and his indirect influence upon other designers. He needed not only suitable opportunities but, in particular, sympathetic and discerning patronage. This was now to be rectified by the enthusiastic support of the Venetian Pope, Carlo della Torre Rezzonico, Clement XIII, together with members of his family. They were to promote Piranesi's manifold activities throughout the decade; by its end a wealth of fresh opportunities was to open up from an increasing number of foreign clients.

Within a short time of his election in 1758, Clement XIII had shown a practical gesture of support by contributing towards the costly undertaking of *Della Magnificenza*.[2] In dedicating this treatise to him, Piranesi placed as its frontispiece a portrait of the Pope, significantly set against a background of Imperial Roman ornament – the prime inspiration of the decade.[3] Other dedications to Clement XIII followed in swift succession with the *Acqua Giulia*, *Lapides Capitolini*, *Emissario del Lago Albano* and the *Antichità di Albano*. The last two works were given particular encouragement since the Pope's residence at Castel Gandolfo was close to these antiquities, and Piranesi became a regular visitor to the palace.

Two important architectural commissions from this new source of support occurred for Piranesi within the first half of the 1760s – the design of a fitting conclusion to Borromini's nave at the Lateran, and the reconstruction of the priory church and headquarters of the Order of Malta on the Aventine.[4] Although, sadly, the former scheme had to be abandoned, many of the brilliant ideas in the various projects recorded were to influence the executed design of the Aventine church, and it is this commission that we must first consider.[5]

Cardinal Giambattista Rezzonico, a nephew of the Pope, had been created Grand Prior of the Knights of Malta in 1761 and was anxious that the modest sixteenth-century buildings of his priory should be given a more impressive appearance. As with the Lateran, large sums of money were not available, so that the existing structure had to be adapted to modern tastes with the greatest resourcefulness. In accomplishing this, Piranesi's work on the Aventine was fully documented throughout in a detailed account book, now in the Avery Architectural Library of Columbia University. These accounts, compiled by the contractor Giuseppe Pelosini, cover the period between 2 November 1764 and 31 October 1766 when considerable structural renovations were carried out along with an elaborate decorative scheme.[6]

The priory had been first established on the Aventine towards the end of the fourteenth century, and after various vicissitudes its setting, the former Benedictine church of S. Maria de Aventina, had been rebuilt in 1556.[7] At the same time an adjoining building was reconstructed as the Villa di Malta, and during the next century a fine garden containing a coffee house was laid out by Cardinal Pamphili, featuring the avenue of laurel with its celebrated vista of St Peter's. At this time, apart from a steep road to the church from the banks of the Tiber, entrance to the priory was obtained from the unprepossessing extension of an ancient road, the Vicus Armilustri, the modern Via di S. Sabina, which ran north-east along the crest of the Aventine. As can be partially seen in Giuseppe Vasi's *veduta* of 1771, a profusion of vineyards, orchards and gardens lay to the south of the property, extending as far as the Baths of Caracalla and Porta S. Sebastiano with the Pyramid of Cestius beside it. Such was the arcadian setting of the noble piazza which Piranesi produced by widening the *vicus* into a ceremonial space.

202

158

159

160, 161 Two views of the Piazza de' Cavalieri di Malta: (top) the entrance screen to the convent and (above) the walls opposite

162 Below: fragment of a Roman frieze now in the Capitoline Museum, Rome

163 Central stela of south wall, Piazza de' Cavalieri di Malta

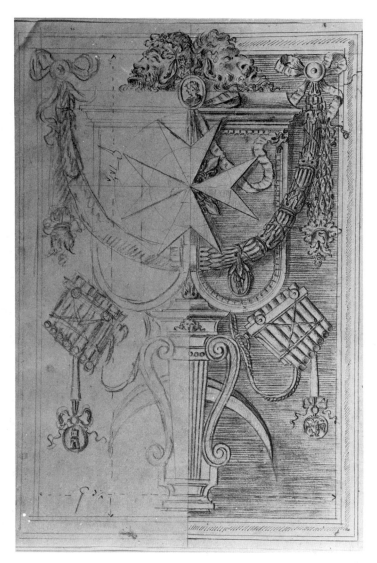

164 Drawing for one of the side stelae, Piazza de' Cavalieri di Malta (Pierpont Morgan Library, New York)

160 To the north of what is now the Piazza de' Cavalieri di Malta, Piranesi placed an entrance screen against the priory garden wall and sited on the axis of the laurel avenue. Here a Palladian formula, probably derived from a modest woodcut by Serlio, provided the departure for a compositional *scherzo*.[8] The conventional rhythms implied by the pilasters and blind niches are rearranged with an ambiguity which, accentuated by rich passages of ornamental relief, is comparable in quality to Piranesi's favourite Mannerist works such as Ligorio's Casino di Pio V at the Vatican.[9]

163 Along the wall opposite to this screen Piranesi set a group of highly original stelae, or commemorative pillars, bearing decorative reliefs. The outer ones were flanked by obelisks and the whole group embellished further by urns and ball finials. On the shorter end wall of the piazza was placed another stela between obelisks, bearing an inscribed tablet recording the circumstances of the construction.[10] Today, the subsequent growth of the cypresses placed behind the walls of the piazza and the later buildings of S. Anselmo have dwarfed the composition and obscured distant views over the Campagna. Only at night does the setting regain a certain atmosphere of awesome solemnity.

164 The strange mode of composition of the decorative reliefs on the stelae, for which some meticulous working drawings survive, not only reflects Piranesi's developing concern with the innovatory system of design advanced in the *Parere* of 1765, but demonstrates his belief in the continuing function of ancient symbolism.[11] The iconography of the Order, both naval and military in character, is ingeniously blended with the embattled tower and twin-headed eagle of Rezzonico heraldry, all of them in terms of motifs taken from Roman sources such as various friezes in the Capitoline Museum, the Trophies of Marius, Trajan's Column and the aquiline relief at SS. Apostoli.[12] In addition, however, are included many images with Etruscan associations for Piranesi, significantly arising from his continuing obsession with the Italic roots of Rome. Many of these motifs, such as the lyre, the cornucopia, the serpent, the bird's wings and the shepherd's pipes, are to be found in Piranesi's tendentious anthology of Etruscan inventions later published in the *Diverse Maniere*. They also possess a considerable local relevance here on the Aventine through its associations with the early history of Rome and various ancient cults introduced from Etruria.[13] It is even possible that the military character of this ceremonial space may tacitly refer to the *Armilustrium*. In this ancient ceremony, which had taken place annually on the Aventine, the weapons and equipment of the Roman army were ritually purified at the close of the summer campaign – a Roman parallel to the Order of Malta's peaceful retirement to its sacred precincts after the heroic phases in its history.[14]

165, 166 S. Maria del Priorato: (above) façade and (below) the nave looking towards the high altar

167 Sphinx capital, detail from *Della Magnificenza*

The church of S. Maria del Priorato, rebuilt in the sixteenth century at the south-west angle of the hill, was originally a simple rectangular structure comprising a nave of four bays with rudimentary transepts and a shallow apse. Its only external embellishment was a pedimented west front, articulated by pairs of pilasters to either side of a doorway with a circular window above. Piranesi, in order to give this unassuming façade a greater degree of pomp, added an attic storey (subsequently destroyed in 1849) and continued on its façade both the formal complexity and the thematic programme from the piazza reliefs.

As with the entrance screen, the Neo-Mannerist aesthetic, first tentatively explored in the small architectural fantasies of the *Opere Varie* around 1760 and developed in the imaginary compositions of the *Parere*, led Piranesi to enliven but not to disrupt the existing Palladian conception of the applied temple front. Besides the application of Maltese symbols in the pediment together with the standards and parade swords flanking the door below, decorative emphasis is concentrated at the centre of the façade. This takes the form of a reeded sarcophagus with serpentine brackets, set within a series of abruptly interrupted mouldings. Placed at a salient point on the Aventine, Piranesi's façade attracts any available light on its richly worked surface, and perhaps only a Venetian could have exploited the movement of the sun to such effect. Indeed, when seen under strongly oblique light, the overall effect is of a crisply etched plate with its intense concentration of detail offset by unrelieved areas of brilliant highlights and deep shadow.

Among the façade ornaments, Piranesi's current polemical concern is represented by the Ionic capitals with sphinxes confronting the Rezzonico tower, closely following antique versions at Villa Borghese and in Robert Adam's collection as featured in a plate of *Della Magnificenza* a few years before.[15] Meanwhile, the boldly fretted frieze above relates to Etruscan tomb decoration at Chiusi, as illustrated with the *Parere* in 1765.

Inside the church, the brittle flatness of the façade reliefs is exchanged for an impressive sense of space in the cool white nave, culminating in the intensified drama of the high altar. Ideas then being developed for the Lateran tribune probably suggested to Piranesi the use of certain scenographic devices of Venetian church design, as first evolved by Palladio at Il Redentore and elaborated in the next century by Longhena at S. Maria della Salute.[16] Accordingly, the particularly sculptural altar is set against an apsidal screen of columns and amplified by the sensuous effects of concentrated lighting introduced from the east window behind it.

168, 169 S. Maria del Priorato: (above) drawing for the central panel of the nave vault (Pierpont Morgan Library, New York) and (below) detail of vault, as built

170 S. Maria del Priorato: vault over the high altar

Of almost equal importance in Piranesi's transformation of this modest interior is the influence of Borromini's vaulting designs, especially that of the Propaganda Fide with its elaborate weave of intersecting ribbing. Placed at the centre of Piranesi's design is an elaborate relief panel celebrating the 169 Order and its maritime history, its exquisite detailing of an archaeological precision faithfully carried out by the *stuccatore*, Tommaso Righi, from the preparatory drawing.[17] 168 Further towards the altar is a lantern, originally giving indirect lighting to the altar below, its oculus surrounded by a four- 170 lobed moulding of eight delicately rendered scenes illustrating the *Life of the Baptist*, patron of the Order and of its Grand Prior.

Piranesi also enhanced the nave of four bays with a series of ingenious trophies or decorative cartouches, incorporating 221 medieval tombs and monuments of the Order within a scheme of modernization clearly inspired by Borromini's comparable work at the Lateran. As before, a personal manipulation of Classical forms is fused with antique symbolism to glorify the naval prowess of the Knights of Malta.

The high altar exercised Piranesi's greatest imaginative skill, 174 in terms of both theme and visual impact, as revealed by three preparatory drawings. As in many other of his surviving designs, a vigorous initial sketch now in New York introduces 171 the basic concept from which the final solution evolved. This consists of a sarcophagus serving as *mensa*, with a superstructure behind it bearing a relief of the Madonna and Child. The superstructure, in turn, supports a highly expressive tableau featuring the *Apotheosis of St Basil*, protector of the first priory church in the Forum Romanum.[18]

The definitive form of the altar emerges in a drawing now in 172 Berlin where the candelabra are abandoned in favour of a greater complexity in the central structure.[19] This now consists of two sarcophagi, the rear one supporting a third, with the tableau of St Basil hastily sketched above it. A similarity between this mode of composition and Piranesi's earlier exploration of new forms in the etched fantasies of the 1750s will be clear when the altar is compared with the strange monument to the right of the *Circus* fantasy introducing Volume III of the 83 *Antichità Romane*.[20]

In a highly finished design in New York for the lower part of 173 the altar, virtually as executed by Righi, Piranesi combines a considerable variety of decorative sources with the same personal selection and mode of sharp fragmentation of elements as found on the entrance façade.[21] In this latter respect a specific 165 gesture of continuity is made by repeating the oculus motif on the front of the *mensa* and the scrolled brackets on the rear sarcophagus. A strong contrast is provided by the figure group 174 surmounting the sphere in the executed work, which is absent

171, 172 Two preparatory studies for the high altar of S. Maria del Priorato (above, Pierpont Morgan Library, New York; below, Kunstbibliothek, Berlin)

173 Design for the lower part of the high altar of S. Maria del Priorato (Pierpont Morgan Library, New York)

in the drawing. The precise form taken by the *Apotheosis* may have been left to Righi, whose later monument to the writer Balestra in SS. Martino e Luca – subject of an acrimonious debate involving Piranesi – shows a marked similarity, particularly in the treatment of the *putti*.[22] In contrast to this Baroque fluency of form is the sharp definition of Piranesi's elemental shapes, as rendered all the more effective when viewed, however unintentionally, from the rear of the altar. Here we see a composition of geometric astringency anticipating by decades the formal purism of Ledoux and Boullée in their most revolutionary designs.

Concern with the setting of a highly complex altar was central to Piranesi's contemporary designs for the projected tribune of the church of St John Lateran.[23] Borromini's brilliant reconstruction of the nave interior during the previous century had stopped short of the transepts at the west end, although it is likely that the Seicento master had formulated an equally original sanctuary.[24] Early in the eighteenth century the eastern exterior of the basilica had been given an impressive façade by Galilei, but it was not until Clement XIII that a fresh attempt was made to complete the process of modernization.

The earliest reference to the scheme occurs in September 1763 when Natoire, Director of the French Academy in Rome, informed the Marquis de Marigny that the Pope had commissioned a new high altar from Piranesi.[25] Within a brief span of time, however, the idea had developed into a major remodelling of the entire western portion of the basilica. At least five distinct solutions can be discerned amongst the surviving twenty-three drawings, now at Columbia University, which were presented by Piranesi to Cardinal Rezzonico shortly after the whole scheme had been abandoned in 1767.[26]

Although the sequence of ideas does not necessarily follow the order imposed by Piranesi in his subsequent numbering of the set, it is interesting to find that the initial two projects for the tribune take a relatively modest form which is succeeded by a dramatically ambitious solution, totally impracticable in terms of available money as well as of the weak nature of the existing foundations. These three versions are then followed by a further two in which features of the initial conceptions are combined with those of the third scheme to produce a design close in character to the form taken by the east end of S. Maria del Priorato. This process of design, stimulated by flights of near-fantasy, is eminently characteristic of Piranesi's approach to a variety of creative solutions throughout the decade, as will be seen in his ideas for furniture and decorative schemes.

The third project, involving a powerful blend of Venetian scenic effects and north Italian decorative forms, as related to Juvarra in particular, represented Piranesi's ideal solution. While certain elements recall the conceptions of the *Prima Parte* – notably the *Temple of Vesta* – the prime inspiration was unquestionably Borromini's nave, which acted both as a challenge and as a yardstick for Piranesi. Among the drawings (two of them now missing), at least seven are concerned with recording this particular solution in all its aspects from plans and sections to enlarged passages of the decorative treatment. None of these superb works of draughtsmanship comes closer to registering Piranesi's ideals of Roman magnificence than the longitudinal section of plate VIII. Here we are shown how light is directed upon the altarpiece and giant columnar screen

Margin references: 175, Ved 88, Ved 6, 178, 179, 178, 177, Ved 88, 178

174, 175 High altar of S. Mario del Priorato, with (below) the back view

176 Design for the high altar of St John Lateran, pl. XX (Avery Library, Columbia University, New York)

177, 178 *Temple of Vesta*, from the *Prima Parte*, and (below) longitudinal section of St John Lateran, pl. VIII (Avery Library)

from a clerestory hidden in the arch between exedra and sanctuary; further light filters laterally through side windows in the altar walls of the ambulatory. A dense concentration of exquisite ornament in the apse is organized within the structural pattern of ribbing which relates to the Borrominesque pilaster bays with aedicules continued from the nave right round the ambulatory. As at the Aventine church, the profusion of individual decorative motifs shows a Neo-Classical fidelity to antique sources, but the total cohesion is that of the Baroque, and Piranesi can be seen as the conscious heir to Borromini's aspirations.

In this ambitious scheme the papal altar with its *baldacchino* and crypt containing the reliquary of St Peter and St Paul is set in the transept, as it had been in Borromini's time. An alternative design for this project, plate XII, shows the altar 180 with the exedra taking a form extremely close to Borromini's style. It embodies winged seraphs, flowing palms and sinuous festoons, with considerable groups of statuary composed of saints, allegories and angels to either side of the *mensa*.

The fourth project returns to the simple plan of the first two 179 solutions but elaborates still further a highly sculptural altar composition and flanking candelabra, close to the preliminary sketch for the Aventine. The altarpiece is set against the rear 171 wall and supported to either side by screens of columns, with the ambulatory now raised above sanctuary level. Finally, the fifth project evolves from this solution, with an extension of the exedra by an additional unit to repeat a complete bay of Borromini's nave.

Following the individual projects are three further designs for a papal altar and *baldacchino*, executed in a somewhat prosaic fashion by an assistant, together with several enlarged details of

179, 180 Transverse sections of St John Lateran: (above) pl. XV showing the choir, (below) pl. XII showing choir and transept (Avery Library, Columbia University, New York)

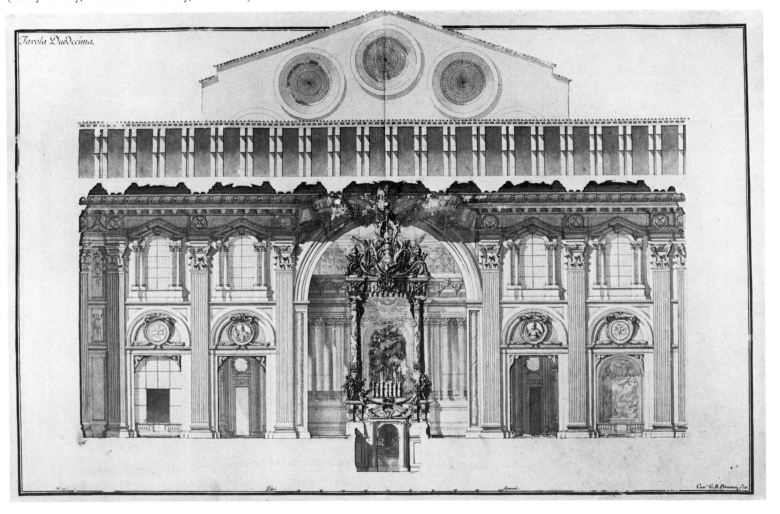

181 One of the side-tables designed for Cardinal Rezzonico (Minneapolis Institute of Arts)

182 Detail of another of the Rezzonico tables (Rijksmuseum, Amsterdam)

the elaborate third scheme. However, another study for the altar by Piranesi himself (plate XX) shows striking evidence of a 176 fresh stylistic development in the later 1760s.[27] The prime characteristics resemble the violent distortions and bolder handling of architectural forms in the plates added to the *Parere* after 1767. As in these latter, the altar design of plate XX is composed of abruptly juxtaposed elements, lacking the effortless transitions of the earlier Lateran designs or even of the executed work on the Aventine. Hazardous as it is to impose a consistent stylistic development on Piranesi's later works, this particular design seems to confirm a broader and more monumental tendency in his expression towards the late 1760s, becoming more pronounced in the following decade.

Probably in part compensation for the abandonment of the Lateran commission, Clement XIII conferred the knighthood of the *Sperone d'Oro*, or Golden Spur, upon Piranesi. The investiture was held, appropriately, in the completed S. Maria del Priorato during the Pope's visit in October 1766, although the artist was not able to use his new title, *Cavaliere*, until the issue of the relevant papal brief on 16 January the following year.[28] It was during 1767 that Piranesi, who was naturally anxious to capitalize upon his recent labours, brought together the surviving designs for the Lateran and presented them to Cardinal Giambattista Rezzonico. When the *Diverse Maniere* was dedicated to this patron in 1769, the artist was inscribed on the title page as *suo architetto*. In the preceding years he had 134 been actively involved in various schemes of decoration and furnishing for the Cardinal and other members of his family. These, unlike the Lateran scheme, are still subject to considerable conjecture, but while nothing so far has come to light of the interiors produced for the Pope at Castel Gandolfo, certain evidence survives in the plates of the *Diverse Maniere* for some pieces of furniture executed for the apartments of the Cardinal at the Quirinal and those of Senator Rezzonico in the Palazzo Senatorio.

Most notable is a plate appearing towards the end of the book 183 with the design for an elaborate side-table, stated in the inscription to be in the Cardinal's apartments along with other unspecified items shown elsewhere among the plates. This has been impressively confirmed in recent years by the discovery of both executed versions of the work, now at Minneapolis and 181 Amsterdam respectively.[29] The fact that these tables follow the 182 etching so closely, apart from the omission of the pendant husks, suggests that many others of the hundred pieces of furniture of the *Diverse Maniere* may not be simply flights of Piranesi's unfettered imagination. Admittedly their appearance in the plates is frequently ambiguous, whether because they are insecurely placed, as the giant clock on the Rezzonico table, or because their function is indistinct, as in the case of certain commodes.[30]

While Piranesi's architectural imagination worked within a tradition derived from Mannerist and Baroque sources, here the link with the Rococo idiom of his early years in Venice is particularly striking. Something of the curvilinear basis of his design, already growing obsolete in contemporary France, is seen in a sheet of preparatory studies for sconces, one of which 185 appears to the top left of the same plate as the table.[31] In the latter work, however, for all the Rococo character of the structure, a more specific Neo-Classical reference is found in the ornament,

Queste tavolino ed alcuni altri ornamenti che sono sparsi in quest'opera, si
vedono nell'appartamento di Sua Eccza Monsig.r D. Gio. Batta Rezzonico
Nipote e Maggiorduomo di N.S.PP. Clemente XIII.

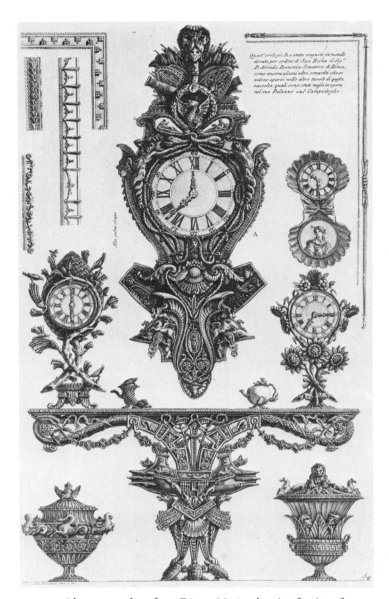

183, 184 Above: two plates from *Diverse Maniere* showing furniture for
the Rezzonico family, including the table shown opposite

185 Left: preparatory study for sconces (Pierpont Morgan Library, New
York)

especially in the chimeras and goat legs, as derived from bronze
furniture then being uncovered at Herculaneum and Pompeii.[32]
Predictably, the main influence of Piranesi upon the course of
European design in the applied arts lay in the extremely original
manner in which he applied antique motifs to traditional
furniture types.

Further evidence of an executed commission is found in the
Diverse Maniere with a wall-clock in ormolu made for Senator 184
Abbondio Rezzonico's rooms in the Palazzo Senatorio. Here a
change in style is also evident, since the freely curvilinear forms
of Rococo clock design are replaced by a symmetrical
arrangement, while the plethora of constituent motifs such as
trophies, helmets, shells and tritons are sharply defined. This
procedure is even more apparent in the bizarre pier-table placed
under the clock, which may also have been designed for the
same commission, since it is built up of elements taken
exclusively from an antique marble relief in the Capitoline 162
Museum, used by Piranesi as a source for various symbols in the
Aventine scheme.[33]

The actual setting of these pieces of furniture, which is of
major importance to their individual effect, remains uncertain.
Various hints, however, can be gleaned from the plates

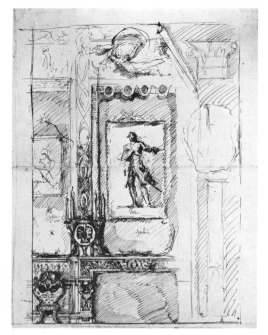

186 Sketch for a decorative scheme (Kunstbibliothek, Berlin)

187 Chimneypiece from *Diverse Maniere* related to the design shown left

188, 189 Chimneypiece from *Diverse Maniere* with the preparatory drawing above (Pierpont Morgan Library, New York)

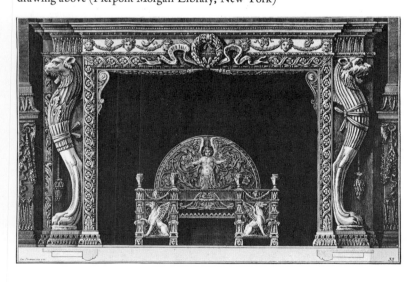

featuring chimneypiece designs, which constitute the major part 187 of the *Diverse Maniere*. Some of these show adjacent portions of the wall scheme with occasional items of furniture such as chairs, mirrors and sconces. Otherwise, one of the most extensive pieces of evidence is provided by an incomplete sketch 186 in Berlin for an unidentified commission incorporating a version of one of the most elaborate of the etched chimneypiece 187 designs.[34] Here the vivacity of the Rococo is replaced by a more monumental weight and rectangularity that goes beyond the contemporary Louis XVI expression towards the Napoleonic Empire style.

The chimneypiece attracted Piranesi as the architectural member of a decorative interior offering the maximum scope for applying his innovatory aesthetic to a strictly modern need. The sixty-one etched chimneypiece designs of the *Diverse Maniere* can be broadly divided into two main groups: those of the utmost complexity devised with a propagandist intention similar to that of the *Parere* plates, and those which balance innovation with the practicable and acceptable. With fantasy, therefore, as the point of departure, Piranesi, like Adam after him, selected from his more ornate confections certain ideas to develop. A preparatory drawing in New York for one of the 188 etched designs allows us to see this selective process at work.[35] 189 Here a monopod, or elaborate claw-footed bracket with animal head, of a type appearing in the overwrought chimneypiece 187 design related to the Berlin sketch, becomes the dominant motif of the design. This feature in turn was to be extracted for use by 231 later designers, particularly in the Empire era.

The compositions for chimneypieces in the *Diverse Maniere* also suggest an artistic development from mid- to later 1760s, comparable to that discerned in the designs for the Lateran commission. According to Piranesi's captions at least three of the chimneypieces in the book had been carried out before 1769. While that for Senator Rezzonico cannot be traced in the Palazzo Senatorio, the other two can be seen at Burghley House 193

190, 191 Chimneypiece for John Hope: (above) design from *Diverse Maniere* and (below) detail of the executed version (Rijksmuseum, Amsterdam)

192, 193 Chimneypiece from *Diverse Maniere* with (below) the executed version in Burghley House

194 Chimneypiece at Wedderburn Castle

195, 196 Chimneypieces at Gorhambury House: (above) drawing room and (below) library

and at the Rijksmuseum respectively. We also know that most [191] of the chimneypiece plates were already in circulation by 1767, as surviving letters from Sir William Hamilton and from Piranesi to Thomas Hollis indicate. By then the artist was already thinking in terms of a British market for these objects, since Hamilton observes that the proposed collection of designs 'will be very useful in my country where we make much use of fireplaces. The ornaments will be found without end there.'[36] It is possible that the etched design relating to the interior scheme [187] of the Berlin drawing was being developed as early as the mid-1760s, since one element for it appears on another Berlin sheet containing a preparatory design for the Aventine screen.[37]

The chimneypiece installed by the Earl of Exeter in the [193] state bedroom at Burghley House was probably commissioned during his second visit to Rome in 1767.[38] Although the executed work follows the plate closely, except for the painted [192] overmantel decoration added to complete this opening plate to the *Diverse Maniere*, Piranesi was anxious to point out the necessary limitations of the etching. In a special note, he emphasizes the importance of the relief to the composition, as well as the polychromatic effects of the antique fragments incorporated. The plaque, cameos and herms are of porphyry set against Cararra marble, their borders being picked out in ormolu. This warning should also be kept in mind with more complex works where, actually or potentially, the appearance of more involved compositions would have been considerably modified by the use of colour, by projection, and occasionally, as we are told elsewhere in the *Diverse Maniere*, by the flatness of painted ornament on the walls.

Equally restrained in form is the chimneypiece for the [191] merchant John Hope, in which antique fragments, herms and other ornaments are skilfully incorporated into a harmonious composition by the restorer's art. As with the Exeter example, the etched setting for the work was added later although it [190] was certainly Piranesi's intention that his chimneypieces should determine the character of a complete wall scheme.

A far more elaborate pair of chimneypieces was acquired, [195, 1] probably between 1769 and 1770, by Piranesi's enthusiastic patrons Edward Walter and his wife. These works, transferred to their present location in the drawing room and library at Gorhambury House sometime after 1774, when Harriet Walter married Lord Grimston, also incorporate various antique and modern reliefs with a polychromatic effect comparable to that of the Exeter work.[39] Clearly Piranesi improvised his com-positions as suggested by available material, but the general effect of the design is bolder than the earlier compositions, reflecting a more monumental style which emerges in certain aspects of Piranesi's work towards the close of the 1760s.

With the opening up of a new field of foreign patronage at this time Piranesi extended his decorative ingenuity to other contemporary forms such as sedan chairs and coaches. In his early years he had already applied his sense of fantasy to a ceremonial gondola as well as to an exotic coach in the [14] foreground of the first large *veduta* of Piazza di S. Pietro. A [37] preliminary study in New York for one of the coaches in the [197] *Diverse Maniere* appears proudly realized in the foreground of a [198] later *veduta* of the piazza, etched around 1771–3.[40] That not all [199] the eighteen designs for vehicles in the *Diverse Maniere* were *capricci* is borne out by a letter of January 1768 in which the Earl of

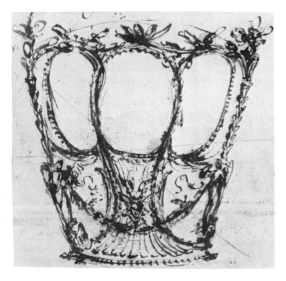

197, 198 Design for a coach: (left) preparatory drawing (Pierpont Morgan Library, New York) and (right) as published in the *Diverse Maniere*

199 Detail from *Piazza di S. Pietro* (see *Vedute di Roma*, pl. 101) showing coach with similar design

Carlisle describes his intention of having a coach made to a design recently purchased from Piranesi.[41]

Also closely connected with British patrons were Piranesi's designs in the Egyptian style, among the most controversial of all the plates in the *Diverse Maniere* both for their uncompromising ingenuity and for their importance to Piranesi's artistic theories.[42] During the mid-1760s he had painted an entire 200 interior in this mode for the Caffè degli Inglesi in Piazza di Spagna, no record of which survives except for two plates showing what were presumably adjacent walls in the scheme.[43] 201 All eleven of the etched designs for Egyptian chimneypieces were in existence by 18 November 1767 when Piranesi sent a proof copy of the *Diverse Maniere* with fifty-seven plates to Thomas Hollis, who subsequently presented them to the Society of Antiquaries. In his covering letter to Hollis, Piranesi was highly conscious of pioneering this taste as part of his programme of contemporary design.[44]

The first indication of Piranesi's concern with the Egyptian style, as opposed to the use of random motifs such as obelisks and pyramids in his imaginary compositions, occurs in one of 132 the small architectural fantasies added to the *Opere Varie* shortly after 1760. Although this composition – *Ancient school in the Egyptian and Greek styles* – reflects the belief stated in *Della*

Magnificenza that the monumental austerity of Egyptian buildings, as opposed to the superficial graces of Greek architecture, was inherited by the Etruscans, he was already experimenting in these plates with the fusion of styles that led to 129 the *Parere*. By the later 1760s Piranesi's concern with Egypt had broadened to embrace a wide range of motifs derived from the discoveries at Tivoli as well as from various books.[45] While the spirit of fantasy which produced the Caffè decoration and certain of the more exotic chimneypieces may be seen as Rococo in approach, the actual expression is distinctly moving towards a heavier and more romantic mood. Because of its advanced character, this aspect of his achievements was much slower to find acceptance, indeed provoking adverse criticism. For instance, the Welsh artist Thomas Jones in 1776 was to dismiss the Caffè as 'a filthy vaulted room the walls of which were painted with Sphinxes, Obelisks and Pyramids from capricious designs of Piranesi, and fitter to adorn the inside of an Egyptian Sepulchre, than a room of social conversation'.[46] It was to be another decade, in fact, before the first signs of Piranesi's Egyptian influence could be found in such designers as Bélanger in France and Playfair in Scotland, and only after 215 the turn of the century did Regency and Empire taste fully 230 accept the potential range of its forms. 229

Altro spaccato per longo della stessa bottega, ove si vedono frà le aperture del vestibolo le immense piramidi, ed altri edifizj sepolcrali ne' deserti dell' Egitto.

Disegno ed invenzione del Cavalier Piranesi

Cav. Piranesi F.

200 Wall decoration for the Caffè degli Inglesi, Rome, from the *Diverse Maniere*

The Egyptian style was to prove a major issue when Piranesi published the *Diverse Maniere* in 1769 at the end of an exceptionally productive decade. Although it seems likely that he had already considered publishing a collection of his designs much earlier, by the close of the decade he had accumulated a far greater quantity of material, and several works had been executed for important clients.[47] Frequently with his enterprises it is hard to separate a sense of business opportunism from the altruistic dedication to a cause. Here in the *Diverse Maniere*, however, it is clear from the extent and nature of his *Apologetical Essay in Defence of the Egyptian and Tuscan Architecture* that his polemical and theoretical concerns were foremost in his mind. The last word in the debate remained to be said in the light of practical results.

The closely related text and plates of the *Diverse Maniere* are addressed to clients as much as to designers, and in the dedication to Cardinal Rezzonico Piranesi upholds him as an exemplar of the enlightened patronage whose absence he had lamented in the *Prima Parte* when starting his career some twenty-five years earlier. He goes on to review his various works for this patron and his family on the Aventine and, potentially, at the Lateran, as well as at Castel Gandolfo and in the Quirinal and Capitoline Palaces.

The substance of the *Essay* that follows concerns the nature of style and those rules of art applying it to the broadest range of contemporary needs. At the outset, Piranesi is quick to anticipate criticism of his innovatory mode of expression, demonstrated in the plates which follow the text, on two counts – complexity and stylization.

In meeting the very real objection to his tendency to overload certain designs with ornament, as seen for example in the chimneypiece with flanking chairs, he defends complexity on the grounds that its success depends on a formal balance and consistency maintained throughout an entire scheme. This is why we are encouraged to judge the work in a broader context by hints of decorated walls to either side of certain chimneypieces. Equally important in his consideration is the need to modify the effects of relief, and he cites the advantages of fictive painted ornament as found on the walls of his Caffè degli Inglesi.

The other principal objection, namely that his Egyptian and Tuscan forms are excessively bold and stiff, is dealt with at greater length since it is central to his conception of style as depending on a fine balance between art and nature. He begins with a lengthy digression on the sheer variety and subtlety of Egyptian ornament, most of which had by this time vanished

187

190

200

except for minor art forms such as gems and wall-paintings. By pointing out that considerable realism was frequently practised by the Egyptians, he not only broadens the conventional view of their art as exclusively monumental, but also justifies the richness of motifs in his own exercises in this particular style.

The most original part of the *Essay*, a discussion of the process of abstraction from nature in art, leads him finally to reiterate his defence of the Etruscans. Two diagrams demonstrate his theories that the volutes of capitals and the profiles of architectural mouldings, along with the basic repertoire of classical vase forms, may be traced to shell patterns. Yet despite these polemical undertones he can no longer at this stage of his argument afford to be exclusive, and he recognizes the unique contribution of 'certain elegances and graces' of the Greeks to the development of art.[48] Consequently certain of the fireplace designs involve a fusion of Greek with Roman and Etruscan forms, though this is more didactically than artistically successful.

As the *Essay* and plates of the *Diverse Maniere* indicate, Piranesi's approach to antiquity represents a conscious search for a viable contemporary style possessing the widest possible range of expression. Throughout the Graeco-Roman controversy theory was of secondary importance to him, often being imperfectly engaged to justify his own artistic inclinations. Essentially a Baroque designer to the last, Piranesi was out of sympathy with the emerging aesthetic of Neo-Classicism as fostered by Winckelmann and Laugier. The art of composition by *capriccio* enabled him to avoid the sterility of an art based on axioms of primitive austerity or unrelieved functionalism, even if it did not preserve him from exaggeration or confusion in the end product.

Throughout his active life Piranesi retained the directness of approach and impatience with niceties that characterize a mind largely self-taught. While through his mother's connections he trained in the professional circle of Lucchesi, he retained an artisan cast of mind from his earliest paternal influence in the stonemason's yard. To some extent these complex roots of his early training and the discursiveness of his subsequent interests fostered an originality denied to more narrowly based professionals. For example, as an artist he intuited certain uses of antiquity hidden from the more traditional minds like Vanvitelli's.[49] As an unorthodox archaeologist he introduced into his designs a far wider repertoire of motifs than previously exploited even by the Mannerists. As an architect and engineer he invested his fantasies with a certain structural identity and coherence unknown to other fantasists. As a theorist he evolved from academic controversy new issues which were to provide essential grounds of justification for those designers such as Adam who sought to establish an acceptable philosophy of modern design. As a graphic innovator of genius he was able to disseminate his ideas more swiftly, more extensively and more effectively than perhaps any other artist since Dürer. Finally, lacking the prudence and caution of more conventional minds, Piranesi, in his willingness to experiment freely, generated a far greater range of ideas than even he was capable of handling, which were to be selected and developed by many others during the following decades.

The contemporary world was divided in its opinions of the new aesthetic of the *Diverse Maniere* and the first fruits of its

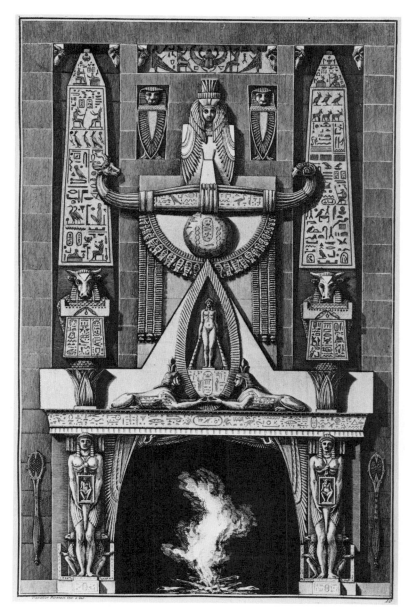

201 Chimneypiece in the Egyptian taste from the *Diverse Maniere*

innovatory system. The British painter James Barry, writing to Edmund Burke in 1769, considered that 'Piranesi will go down to posterity with deserved reputation, in spite of his Egyptian and other whimsies and of his gusto of architecture flowing out of the same cloacus as Borromini's and other hairbrained moderns.'[50] But two years later Horace Walpole recognized the immense stimulus of these bizarre ideas upon a contemporary world which he considered effete and banal. In the 'Advertisement' to the fourth edition of his *Anecdotes of Painting*, he affirmed that

this delicate redundance of ornament growing into our architecture might perhaps be checked, if our artists would study the sublime dreams of Piranesi, who seems to have conceived visions of Rome beyond what it boasted even in the meridian of its splendour. Savage as Salvator Rosa, fierce as Michelangelo, and exuberant as Rubens, he has imagined scenes that would startle geometry, and exhaust the Indies to realize. He piles palaces on bridges, and temples on palaces, and scales heaven with mountains of edifices. Yet what taste in his boldness! What grandeur in his wildness! What labour and thought both in his rashness and details![51]

202 Bust of Piranesi by Joseph Nollekens (Accademia di S. Luca, Rome)

VII

The Closing Years

THE *Apologetical Essay* of the *Diverse Maniere* sets the scene for Piranesi's final achievements and for the practical influence upon contemporary designers exercised through the supporting plates. The text concludes with a reference to the artist's growing collection of antiquities in his *Museo*, or showrooms, at Palazzo Tomati as an immediate source of inspiration for his highly original system of composition. This interreaction between his Baroque imagination and random fragments of Classical ornament was to find a widening scope during the 1770s. Following the inevitable waning of Rezzonico patronage after the death of Clement XIII in February 1769, Piranesi began to exploit the new areas of contact with foreign clients, especially with the British Grand Tourists, which had been established during the previous decade. In addition to a prosperous printmaking business, his main activities as a dealer were to be concentrated in two interrelated fields – the design of quasi-architectural features such as chimneypieces, and the imaginative restoration of antiquities.

By now Piranesi had assembled a team of specialized assistants at Palazzo Tomati, shortly to be joined by his son Francesco who was now in his teens.[1] Particularly fruitful business relationships had been established with other entrepreneurs such as the Britons Thomas Jenkins and Gavin Hamilton, as well as with sculptor-restorers such as Bartolommeo Cavaceppi, Giuseppe Angelini and the young English artist Nollekens.[2]

These business activities may account for the fact that it was Giovanni Battista Visconti and not Piranesi who in 1768 succeeded Winckelmann, sordidly murdered at Trieste that year, as Superintendent of Papal Antiquities. Piranesi appears with the above-mentioned associates in a list of antiquarian dealers drawn up around this time by Monsignor Braschi – the future Pius IV – in connection with the formation of the Museo Pio-Clementino at the Vatican.[3] While Piranesi tended to avoid handling figure sculpture as such, he profited greatly by the growing quantity of ornamental fragments excavated by Hamilton in the Pantanello area of Hadrian's Villa from 1769 onwards.[4]

The production of ornamental chimneypieces incorporating an ingenious mixture of Classical fragments and modern replicas had originally been devised for patrons such as the Earl of Exeter, John Hope and Senator Rezzonico. This had developed into a minor industry by the 1770s, and was increasingly emulated by other Roman designers and dealers.[5] Several new productions were evidently available for sale at Palazzo Tomati by the middle of the decade. This is clear from the surviving correspondence between the Jesuit John Thorpe and Lord Arundell, who was then seeking material to embellish his mansion and private chapel at Wardour Castle in Hampshire.[6] A particularly fine chimneypiece, recommended by Thorpe in February 1774, was swiftly acquired by the Scottish landowner Patrick Home for Wedderburn Castle, Berwickshire, the same spring at the cost of 371 *scudi*.[7] More delicately fashioned than the Exeter and Hope examples, this work relies for its appeal upon the exquisite cutting of classical ornament, together with the inclusion of reliefs and cameos in porphyry. Although Piranesi was described by Thorpe as being reluctant to produce further such works – a familiar business ploy – he nevertheless appears to have made one featuring caryatids that July for an unspecified client in Scotland, and to have sold another to a Russian visitor to Rome.

The Wedderburn work comes extremely close to one of the two chimneypieces referred to earlier as having been originally acquired by Piranesi's patrons Edward and Harriet Walter around 1769–70 for their house at Berry Hill, Surrey.[8] While this particular example, now in the library at Gorhambury House, shows the same restraint and wealth of refined detail as that at Wedderburn, its pair in the drawing room is a far bolder confection with a monumental use of fragments and polychrome reliefs. Apart from implying a certain stylistic development in Piranesi's expression around the 1770s, this marked difference also suggests that he often produced designs to order, adapting the work to the specific dimension and character of the setting. After all, a major principle of the *Diverse Maniere* was that modern convenience should govern the application of antique forms.

The Walters were also Piranesi's clients for restored antiquities, and it is likely that many such collectors purchased chimneypieces together with ornamental objects such as urns and pedestals. By now Piranesi and his thriving workshop had begun to issue individual plates of antiquities as a form of advertisement. Eventually some 110 of these were collected into two volumes published as the *Vasi, Candelabri, Cippi, Sarcofagi...* in 1778, with an international influence almost as extensive as that of the *Diverse Maniere*. Apart from Piranesi's own products, the *Vasi* depicted works in other Roman collections

203 Funerary monument with a rhyton, from the *Vasi*

204, 205 Newdigate Candelabrum: (above) from the *Vasi* and (right) as executed in marble (Ashmolean Museum, Oxford)

or associated with business colleagues such as James Byres, Colen Morrison and Matthew Nulty as well as Hamilton and Jenkins.[9] A large proportion of these plates, moreover, were enterprisingly dedicated to foreign clients, including at least fifty Britons. The Walters alone were connected with seven plates, two of them recording vases acquired from Piranesi and now at Gorhambury, where they formerly adorned the drawing-room chimneypiece.[10]

As characteristic of the blend of business acumen and erudition in Piranesi, the inscriptions to many of the *Vasi* plates provide extensive information about the original discovery and the present location of the works concerned. They indicate, for example, that thirty-five antiquities were then to be seen in twenty-five separate British collections including those of Henry Blundell, Charles Townley, William Weddell and Sir Charles Worsley. These works range from modest lamps found in tombs to the spectacular vase discovered by Gavin Hamilton at Tivoli in 1771 and later acquired by the Earl of Warwick.[11]

The images of the *Vasi*, although largely etched with studio assistance, also indicate something of the aesthetic principles behind Piranesi's unorthodox approach to restoration. At the time, admittedly, a certain degree of repair and completeness was expected by collectors. Where a vase lacked a pedestal, Piranesi would add a suitable one in the plate, taken from another source. Initially, this artistic licence was scrupulously indicated by letters related to the explanatory captions in the supporting text. This practice of decorative synthesis, however, led to increasing liberties both in the actual restoration and in the illustrations involved. In the more ambitious works his imagination was to carry Piranesi to unparalleled degrees of ingenuity where explanations became superfluous. Several of these advanced fabrications were to be acquired by contemporary designers like Sir William Chambers as a private means of stimulus for the faculties of invention. Among the most elaborate was the alleged funerary monument discovered in the tomb of Augustus Urbanus on the Via Appia. This striking piece, featuring an elaborate rhyton ending in a boar's head on a particularly complex pedestal with supporting chimeras, was restored according to Piranesi's directions by Pietro Malatesta. It was eventually sold to Gustav III of Sweden by Francesco Piranesi in 1785 along with the remaining pieces in his father's *Museo*, and subsequently entered the National Museum, Stockholm.[12]

A particular category of reconstruction which held a special interest for Piranesi and which ultimately had a considerable influence on other designers was that of ornamental candelabra. The fragments of several antique examples which had been uncovered by Gavin Hamilton at Tivoli underwent extensive treatment at Palazzo Tomati.[13] In February 1775 Father Thorpe referred to a pair of them as being suitable to flank the main altar at Wardour, and in the following May the connoisseur Sir Roger Newdigate acquired two particularly fine specimens for the University of Oxford.[14] These examples, originally placed in the Radcliffe Camera, had already appeared in the early plates of the *Vasi* as part of Piranesi's collection. Shortly after the transaction a new etching of the more complex work, featuring cranes, was issued to record the sale.

Monumental candelabra as church furnishings had been a major concern for Renaissance and Baroque designers, and

Piranesi had followed this tradition in both his architectural commissions of the 1760s. The earliest evidence can be found in the hastily sketched forms to either side of the Aventine altar in the preparatory study from the Pierpont Morgan Library. More finished candelabra are to be seen flanking the opulent version of the altar projected for the Lateran tribune. This essentially post-Classical formula often served as an armature for the fabricated candelabra of the 1770s, incorporating original material, and something of this procedure of improvization can be glimpsed in a vigorous pen study from the British Museum. As in the restoration of antiquities in general, the absence of substantial fragments often led Piranesi to apply his fantasy to this theme, with arresting results. While several of these candelabra were to find their way into British collections, Piranesi's most extravagant version was reserved as his own funerary monument – an elaborate *capriccio* in the spirit of the bizarre tombs in the secondary frontispiece to the *Antichità Romane*, Volume II. This work, having briefly served its sepulchral function in S. Maria del Priorato, was taken by the artist's family to Paris, where it can now be seen in the Louvre.[15]

Even before the dissemination of Piranesi's ideas through the plates of the *Diverse Maniere* and the *Vasi*, his influence was already beginning to affect certain European designers, pre-eminently the Adam brothers. The initial impression of Piranesi's creative fantasies had begun to take effect within the few years Robert spent in Rome during the later 1750s.[16] This catalytic process was to continue after the Scot's return to Britain, as can be seen in the design of an artificial ruin for Kedleston around 1759.[17] This essay in the imaginative synthesis of antique motifs anticipates by several years Clérisseau's celebrated Ruin Room, painted in the cell of Fathers Leseur and Jacquier at the Trinità dei Monti.[18] It was at Syon House, Middlesex, however, that the first mature effects of Adam's imaginative eclecticism were carried out; they were, in fact, recorded by Piranesi himself in four plates made from the architect's designs in 1761. While these were not published until 1779, in Volume II of *The Works in Architecture of Robert and James Adam*, they had undoubtedly encouraged Piranesi in turn to publish his revolutionary thesis in the *Parere su l'Architettura* of 1765.[19] In the text Piranesi was to draw particular attention to James Adam's design of a capital for a British order, which exemplified the originality fostered by the imaginative adaptation of antiquity.[20] In return, the Adams in their preface to the first instalment of the *Works* in 1773 were virtually to paraphrase the artistic credo of the *Diverse Maniere* in asserting that

if we have any claim to approbation, we found it on this alone; that we flatter ourselves, we have been able to seize with some degree of success, the beautiful spirit of antiquity, and to transfuse it, with novelty and variety, through all our numerous works.[21]

By the 1770s the effects of Piranesi's later works were to be of crucial importance for major developments in the Adam style. In the evolution of chimneypiece design between 1772 and 1777, as recorded in preliminary studies among the drawings in the Soane Museum, Robert Adam's conventional Palladian forms were replaced by a series of far more original conceptions.[22] In these a number of compositional ideas were selected from the *Diverse Maniere*, although purged of much of the Baroque exuberance of the original source. Similarly,

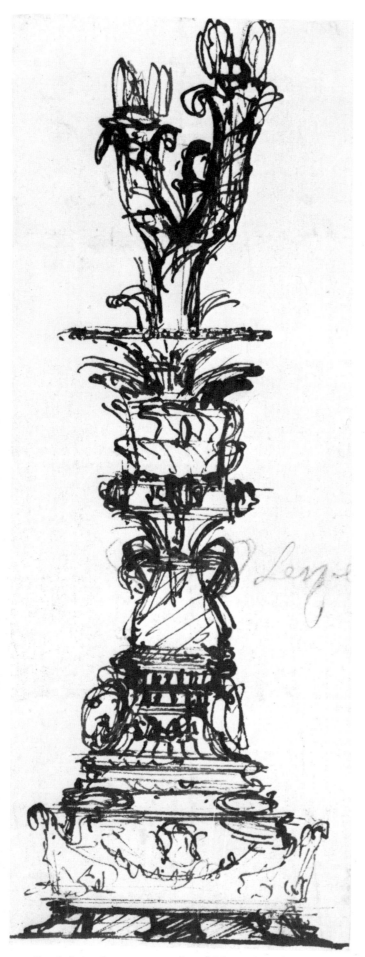

206 Sketch design for an ornamental candelabrum (British Museum)

207 Ornamental candelabrum designed by Piranesi as his own funerary monument (Louvre, Paris)

209 Robert Adam: design for an artificial ruin at Kedleston, *c*. 1759 (Victoria and Albert Museum, London)

208 Below: James Adam: design for a capital of the British order, 1762 (Metropolitan Museum of Art, New York)

210 Centre right: Charles-Louis Clérisseau: design for the Ruin Room at the Trinità dei Monte, before 1766 (Fitzwilliam Museum, Cambridge)

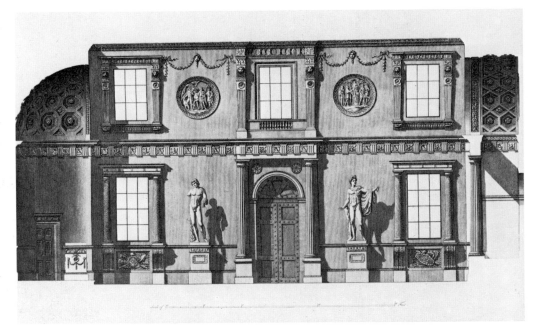

211 Robert Adam: Entrance Hall, Syon House, etched by Piranesi for *The Works in Architecture of Robert and James Adam*, Vol. II, 1779

212 Robert Adam: tripod pedestals for the house of Sir Watkin Williams-Wynn, 20 St James's Square, London (Victoria and Albert Museum, London)

Piranesi's ingenious candelabra conditioned Adam's development of the ornamental candle-stand and tripod pedestal, again with a comparable process of judicious refinement. A particularly impressive exercise in Piranesian synthesis is 212 demonstrated by the stands executed in 1774 for the London house of Sir Watkin Williams-Wynn, a dedicatee of one of the *Vasi* plates.[23]

Perhaps the most comprehensive instance of Piranesi's stimulus, however, is to be found in Robert Adam's approach towards a total decorative scheme, as represented by his series of Etruscan Rooms. In the most complete one surviving, executed 213 at Osterley Park, Middlesex, between 1772 and 1778, certain themes derived from the *Diverse Maniere* are reinterpreted with a comparable degree of ingenuity.[24] Stimulated by such wall 190 decorations as found in the plate of the Hope chimneypiece composed of motifs derived from Pompeian decoration and from vase paintings, Adam achieves the coherence of the modern style advocated only a few years earlier in the *Apologetical Essay*.

In France over the same period of time the impact of Piranesi was more restricted as well as more literal. After the early importance of his visionary compositions for the Roman *pensionnaires* of the 1740s and for the initial phases of French Neo-Classical architecture, the growing austerity in taste associated with Laugier and the Greek Revival provided a less favourable climate. Within the Louis XVI style, however, more unorthodox designers such as Delafosse and, to an extent, Neufforge showed a marked sympathy with Piranesi in their reaction against the current formal restraint. Several designs of

the 1770s in Delafosse's *Nouvelle iconologie historique* and Neufforge's *Recueil élémentaire* show specific borrowings from Piranesi.[25] Apart from Delafosse's design for a prison façade, 154 specifically reflecting one of the plates added to the *Parere*, a number of his chimneypiece designs in the Musée des Arts 214 Décoratifs are based on the more 'Baroque' compositions of the *Diverse Maniere*.[26]

An indirect influence on French interior design can also be traced through the draughtsman Lhuillier, who accompanied Clérisseau on his return to Paris from Italy in 1768 and proceeded to work for the architect François Bélanger on the *pavillon* of Bagatelle. In this building, designed for the Comte d'Artois in 1777, literal borrowings from Piranesi can be found in such surviving evidence from the furnishings as the andirons and a commode in the main bedroom.[27] More substantial debts, however, are represented by certain unpublished designs by Bélanger in his *Livre de cheminées*, now in the Bibliothèque Nationale, produced during the same decade. In the versions produced in the Egyptian style, as in the decorative scheme of 215 1789 for Mme Dervieux's *hôtel*, the architect inserts a repertoire of motifs culled from the *Diverse Maniere* within the geometric 201 forms of the Louis XVI style.[28] This classicizing system, though already moving towards Directoire and Empire expression, lacks that necessary flexibility which made the contemporary Adam style far more responsive to Piranesi's mode of composition.

213 Robert Adam: the Etruscan Room, Osterley Park

214 Jean-Charles Delafosse: design for a chimneypiece (Musée des Arts Décoratifs, Paris)

215 François Bélanger: design for a chimneypiece in the Egyptian taste (Bibliothèque Nationale, Paris)

Running parallel with these early impressions upon European design in the 1770s was a fresh phase in Piranesi's own archaeological studies, chiefly related to sites south of Rome. Recent progress in the excavations of Pompeii as well as Herculaneum had encouraged the artist to make a series of expeditions there from 1770 onwards. The surviving sketches present such a contrast to Piranesi's earlier studies that they have often been attributed entirely to Francesco, who was to etch many of them in the posthumous work *Les antiquités de la Grande Grèce*, published between 1804 and 1807.[29] Executed with a reed pen in a dull brownish ink, their lines are broad and rather coarse, with only the most summary indications of light and texture by means of crude hatching. The figures are equally abruptly rendered in stiff, awkward poses, with an uncharacteristic indifference to their dynamic function amid the ruins. As Hylton Thomas suggests, this perplexing aridity may reflect the lack of inspiration for Piranesi in the utter deadness of the site, with its lack of vegetation and human activity. Even so, when these drawings are compared with the resulting etchings by Francesco, they reveal a greater vitality than might at first appear. As Thomas puts it, 'the moody intensity of the elder Piranesi has become superficial theatricality in Francesco's print'.[30]

This contrast in approach between father and son is even more significant in the last major work of Piranesi, the suite of etchings recording the temples at Paestum, issued posthumously as the *Différentes vues de quelques restes de trois grandes édifices qui subsistent encore dans le milieu de l'ancienne ville de Pesto....* Although the evidence is meagre it would appear that Piranesi,

accompanied by Francesco and their architectural assistant, Benedetto Mori, made an expedition in 1777-8 to examine these Greek temples situated a few miles south of Naples. The father was already suffering from a severe bladder complaint which ultimately caused his death in Rome during the November of 1778. He was to leave behind twenty plates which Francesco completed and published the same year together with a French text.

Although the frontispiece and three of the plates (XVI, XIX and XX) are actually signed by Francesco and others indicate his intervention, the seventeen surviving drawings in London, Paris and Amsterdam are unmistakably in the hand of his father throughout.[31] Although, like the Pompeian studies, many of these contain figures which are strangely insensitive for Piranesi, as a whole the drawings possess a far more finished character than any other sketches surviving from his hand. The considerable distance of Paestum from Rome, and Piranesi's deteriorating health, clearly required a more literal record, particularly as Francesco was forced to take an increasing initiative in the etching process, as many of the later plates of the *Vasi* indicate. Whether in the drawings or the plates, however, nothing is lost of Piranesi's vibrancy of outline where the highly atmospheric light appears to bite into the crumbling surface of the tufa masonry. Nor do his perspective skills, combined with subtleties in tonal recession, fail to describe and evoke an architectural experience of the greatest intensity.

The three great temples at Paestum had first been 'rediscovered' by a succession of visitors to their remote site

216, 217 Preparatory drawing for *The Tavern, Pompeii* (British Museum), and (below) the version etched by Francesco Piranesi, from *Antiquités de la Grande Grèce*

218, 219 *The Basilica, Paestum*: (left) preparatory drawing (Sir John Soane's Museum, London) and (below left) as published in *Différentes vues . . . de Pesto*, 1778

220 Above: G. P. M. Dumont: *Temple of Neptune*, from *Les Ruines de Paestum*, 1769

during the middle years of the century. Their extremely gradual acceptance in the face of a Roman-based Classicism provides a revealing chapter in the evolution of Neo-Classical theory, plotted by a succession of publications with a gradually shifting emphasis.[32] The first serious attempt to record the temples was made by a Neapolitan scholar, Count Gazzola, who introduced the site to Sufflot and Dumont during the former's visit to Italy in 1750. Other measured drawings were added to Gazzola's when they were virtually plagiarized and published by Dumont in 1764. This work was followed by an improved edition with additional illustrations in 1769, the year when the Englishman Thomas Major issued the most detailed account to date. However, it was Piranesi's amplification of the monumental grandeur of these Doric works that played a decisive role in transforming the attitude to Paestum from an archaeological interest into an emotional understanding of these primitive structures. Although he opened the eyes of Europe to the potent expression of Paestum Doric, his publication did not represent a final acceptance of the Greek cause in the protracted controversy. On the contrary, the text and captions play down the Hellenic origins of the site in asserting the monumental values possessed by an architecture born on Italian soil. Creative genius, for Piranesi, was the prerogative of the Italic races, and to be defended to his last breath.

220

Piranesi died on 9 November 1778 after heroic resistance to a particularly painful illness aggravated by his dedicated activities. His body was first interred in his local church, S. Andrea delle Fratte, but shortly afterwards was transferred to a place of honour in S. Maria del Priorato at the direction of his staunch patron, Cardinal Giambattista Rezzonico. In 1779 a full-length statue by Giuseppe Angelini, commissioned by the artist's wife Angela and his family, replaced the monumental candelabrum.[33] This piece of sculpture, although a somewhat frozen image as compared to Nollekens's animated bust of the late 1760s, at least characterizes the artist as he wished to appear – al antica, holding the instruments of the practising artist with evidence of work in progress, a plan of the Temple of Neptune at Paestum.

At about the same time a commemorative portrait in oils was painted by Pietro Labruzzi, closely related to the Nollekens bust and completing the polemical gesture implied in it.[34] Here, shown in contemporary dress, the artist wears the Order of the *Sperone d'Oro* and holds his instruments together with the preparatory drawing of the title page to the *Différentes vues . . . de Pesto*. In the background can be discerned a vase at the Quirinal and the Louvre candelabrum, which had both appeared in the plates of the *Vasi*. Thus characterizing the ultimate concerns in Piranesi's career, this picture also represents the founder of a prosperous business, now to be carried on by his twenty-year-old son and other members of the family.

Very little is known of Laura Piranesi, apart from the fact that she published a series of reduced versions of plates by her father, or of the later publishing activities of Pietro in Rome during the 1800s, but Francesco's highly active life is well documented.[35] Having been trained in architecture by Paris, in landscape by the Hackerts and in etching by Cunego and Volpato, Francesco was clearly groomed to continue his father's work. Apart from his involvement in the later stages of the Paestum plates, he also took a major part in the *Vasi*, along with other members of the workshop at Palazzo Tomati, and brought to completion a number of his father's other projects. For instance, he helped to produce the two volumes on the Trajan and Antonine Columns begun in 1775. In 1781 he published the six-plate plan of Hadrian's Villa, Tivoli, and four years later another of the excavations at Pompeii (a later edition followed, incorporating fresh discoveries up to 1795). A plate of diagrams relating to the Emissarium of Lake Fucino, based on his father's work, was issued in 1791. He also added further plates to the existing series of the *Archi Trionfali, Trofei, Vedute di Roma* and *Antichità Romane*. By way of a supplement to the latter he issued two further volumes in 1780 and 1790 respectively, the *Tempi Antichi*; the second volume was devoted to a fully measured survey of the Pantheon. To consolidate these achievements in 1792 he produced a complete catalogue of the firm's products, dividing the works into thirty-two sections with Roman numerals which he added to the plates at this time.

Francesco's individuality becomes more distinct after 1784 when, following his introduction to the visiting King of Sweden, Gustav III, he was appointed the Royal Agent for the Fine Arts in Italy. The same year he issued a new edition of the *Antichità Romane*, dedicated to Gustav, with a portrait medallion of his father derived from the Nollekens bust. Francesco seems to have seen little future for his antique dealing

221 Giuseppe Angelini: monument to Piranesi in S. Maria del Priorato, Rome

222 Francesco Piranesi: *Egyptian Temple and Temple of Isis, Pompeii*, from a drawing by Louis-Jean Desprez, from *Plan of Pompeii with Three Views*, 1788–89

since in 1785, shortly after acquiring the outstanding sculpture of *Endymion* for the Swedish Royal Collection, he sold the bulk of the *Museo* at Palazzo Tomati to Stockholm, where it remains.[36] By now he was becoming increasingly involved in revolutionary politics, and in 1794 was appointed Swedish Consul at Naples, where he carried on counter-espionage. Returning to Rome four years later he became, with his brother Pietro, a fervent Jacobin, serving office in the short-lived French Republic. However, with the arrival of the British and Neapolitan forces there, the two of them fled with the rest of the family to Paris, taking with them the printmaking business founded on the success of their father's plates.

Established in Paris, the Calcographie des Piranesi frères developed into a prosperous business, reissuing the bulk of the graphic works in a finely printed edition of twenty-seven volumes in 1800–1807. It was for this work that the architect J. G. Legrand, son-in-law of Clérisseau, prepared his life of Piranesi, based on family recollections and an autobiographical manuscript.[37] Apart from setting up a less successful manufactory for terracotta replicas of antiquities formerly in the *Museo* at Palazzo Tomati, Francesco now issued three volumes 217 of the *Antiquités de la Grande Grèce*, largely derived from his 216 father's Pompeian sketches. As has been seen, these plates lack the inspiration of the original drawings, and it is particularly revealing to see how much more successful were those etchings produced by Francesco from the seven detailed drawings by the French architect Desprez and published in 1788–9 along with the plan of Pompeii.

Shortly after the turn of the century Pietro Piranesi returned to Rome, where he published Piroli's *Bassorilievi antichi di Roma*, and in 1810 at Francesco's death the family business came to an end. The total collection of Piranesi's plates was acquired by the Parisian firm Firmin-Didot, which continued to issue impressions until 1839. At that date they were purchased on the orders of Gregory XVI for the Calcografia Camerale (now the Calcografia Nazionale), and returned to Italy.

The later work of Francesco Piranesi, particularly represented by the *Antiquités de la Grande Grèce*, registers a shift of emphasis in the portrayal of antiquity. The delicate working and subtle effects of light in his father's plates, even as late as those of Paestum, are replaced by a greater simplification of form and cruder tonal contrasts. The very last traces of the Rococo are replaced by the bolder and more direct expression of Romanticism, in which an appeal to the emotions is conveyed through the charged language of the Sublime.

Meanwhile the plates of the *Différentes vues ... de Pesto* were to 219 play a considerable role in the emergence of the Romantic consciousness, particularly in the succession of visitors to the site during the last two decades of the eighteenth century. James Adam in 1761 had dismissed the temples as 'of an early, an inelegant and unenriched Doric that afford no detail and scarcely produce two good views. So much for Paestum.' However, in 1787 Goethe was to consider the place as 'the last vision I shall take with me on my way north, and perhaps the greatest'.[38] These stern ruins were now found by artists and designers to be capable of an expressive force denied to the more sophisticated works of antiquity, and their effect on contemporary design became increasingly manifest by the close of the century. One of the earliest instances of this consciously primitive expression is to be found in the interior of Great Packington church, Warwickshire, with its bold columnar 223 supports. This was designed in 1789 by Joseph Bonomi in collaboration with his patron, the 4th Earl of Aylesford, a keen admirer and amateur follower of Piranesi.[39]

By the turn of the century Paestum Doric had become a keynote of progressive design. This heavyweight aesthetic, as largely disseminated through the potent expression of Piranesi's late style, was absorbed into the works of German architects like Gilly, Weinbrenner, Schinkel and Klenze.

223 Joseph Bonomi: Great Packington church, Warwickshire

224 Etienne-Louis Boullée: project for a museum (Bibliothèque Nationale, Paris)

225 Claude-Nicolas Ledoux: entrance arch to the Hotel Thélusson, Paris, from *L'Architecture . . . considérée sous le rapport de l'art*, 1846

226 Sir John Soane: interior of the Bank Stock Office, Bank of England (Royal Institute of British Architects, London)

The cult of massive simplicity, although ironically running counter to Piranesi's earlier predilection for the rich, the varied and the complex, was also to prove of far-reaching importance in visionary design. Particularly revealing in this respect are the works of two French designers who never studied in Italy but were to view Roman antiquity mainly through the eyes of Piranesi – Claude-Nicolas Ledoux and Etienne-Louis Boullée. Both of them, like Piranesi, brought to architectural design a strongly pictorial approach, regarding fantasy as a necessary element in experiment and innovation.

In the domestic works of Ledoux the force of Piranesi's influence is already sensed in the heroic arch framing the entrance vista of Hôtel Thélusson, constructed in 1778–81. 225 Even more impressive are the executed and projected buildings for the salt-works and ideal city of Chaux, with a Utopian master-plan strongly indebted to the sweeping vision of the *Ichnographia* of the Campo Marzio.[40] Moreover, the fertility of *endpaper* concepts stimulated by Piranesi's planning fantasies was to be taken to greater extremes of originality in Ledoux's various solutions for the *barrières*, or toll-houses, of pre-Revolutionary Paris, developed around 1783.[41]

Boullée also shared Piranesi's belief in the prerogative of the designer's imagination to create new forms through pictorial means. He was to come even closer to Piranesi in employing the architectural fantasy exclusively as a means of developing and communicating his most original ideas. For instance, his *Museum* project of 1783 shows close debts to the *Temple of Vesta* 224 composition of the *Prima Parte* some forty years earlier, using a 177 Baroque system of dramatic lighting to amplify the sense of awesome monumentality.[42] The involved plan of this vast complex, like the works of Ledoux, derives from Piranesian concepts entering French architecture through Peyre in the 20 1760s and given fresh stimulus by the *Ichnographia*.

Neither Ledoux nor Boullée, however, was sufficiently removed from the current admiration of antique simplicity to be fully in sympathy with Piranesi's rich eclecticism, any more than Delafosse and Bélanger had been able to escape the Louis XVI style sufficiently to benefit like Adam from the radical system of the *Diverse Maniere*. Once again we have to turn to

England to find a contemporary designer in the Revolutionary era with the same highly personal style based on a broadly imaginative use of the past – John Soane.

Piranesi's influence on Soane's formative years in the 1770s was considerable, both directly through his work and indirectly through Soane's master George Dance and the works of Adam. Although as Professor of Architecture at the Royal Academy from 1806 onwards Soane felt obliged, like Chambers before him, to censure Piranesi's excesses and licence, his actual works belie these academic strictures.[43] After a student exercise in the manner of the *Monumental bridge* with his Gold Medal design for a *Triumphal bridge* in 1776, he studied in Italy. There he met Piranesi briefly during the year of his death and received from him four plates of the *Vedute di Roma*. The impact of Paestum, visited shortly after, may have led to Soane's acquisition of the fifteen preparatory drawings for the *Différentes vues ... de Pesto*, joined subsequently by the two Piranesi *capricci* from the Adam collection.[44] On his return from Italy the full impact of Piranesi's conceptions found its expression in Soane's remarkable reconstruction of the Bank of England from 1791 onwards. As with Adam earlier, it was no longer a question of borrowing specific motifs: it was an original cast of mind, unconstrained by Classical loyalties and adventurous in structure and lighting, which made the Bank the most original work of its time in Europe. So haunted was Soane's mode of vision that he even envisaged the Bank rotunda as a noble ruin. Moreover, at the rear of his house in Lincoln's Inn Fields he built a series of chambers and galleries where he arranged his heterogeneous collections in a Piranesian sequence of eclectic fantasies.

While highly original minds like Adam and Soane were attuned to the spirit of Piranesi's imagination, his posthumous influence on contemporary design in both the English Regency and French Empire styles was tempered by the restraint of later Neo-Classical theory. Yet even here Piranesi's designs exercised a considerable effect in the restricted areas of the decorative arts determined by the plates of the *Diverse Maniere* and the *Vasi*. For instance, when the young Charles Heathcote Tatham visited

227 J. M. Gandy: crypt of Sir John Soane's house in Lincoln's Inn Fields, 1813 (Sir John Soane's Museum, London)

228 J. M. Gandy: Soane's rotunda of the Bank of England as a ruin, 1832 (Sir John Soane's Museum, London)

229 Thomas Hope: Egyptian clock (Royal Pavilion, Brighton)

230 Thomas Hope: Egyptian Room, Duchess Street, London, from *Household Furniture*, 1807

231 Percier and Fontaine: design for a table, from *Recueil de décorations intérieures*, 1801

Rome in 1794–5 to search for ornamental material on behalf of the architect Henry Holland, the resulting *Etchings of Ancient Ornamental Architecture* of 1800 acknowledged debts to Piranesi's compilations.[45] Tatham was also to acquire a number of the remaining fragments from the dispersed *Museo* at Palazzo Tomati, which eventually found their way into Soane's collection by 1821.[46]

While this kind of material enriched Holland's repertoire, it was the connoisseur and designer Thomas Hope who possessed the imagination to extend Piranesi's eclectic methods with considerable ingenuity in his London house at Duchess Street and his Surrey residence, the Deepdene. As well as the incorporation of several fabricated candelabra originating from the Piranesi studio into his schemes, Hope's use of the *Diverse Maniere* contributed to the remarkable sequence of rooms at Duchess Street exemplified by the Egyptian Room.[47] However, 230 its illustration in Hope's *Household Furniture and Decoration* of 1807, by adopting the astringent linear style pioneered by Tischbein and Flaxman in archaeological illustration, excluded the emotive uses of light and diversity in texture and colour inherited from Piranesi. The closest one can come to the romantic imagery of these vanished settings is in the surviving

pieces of furniture, such as the Egyptian clock, based on several 229 motifs taken from the *Diverse Maniere*. 201

In France, meanwhile, the Classic reticence which characterized the designs of Bélanger had developed through the Directoire into the expression of the Empire style. The archaeological exactitude found in the works of Tatham and Hope is paralleled in Percier and Fontaine's *mise en scène* for Napoleon as recorded in the *Recueil de décorations intérieures* of 1801. Here individual motifs are selected from the *Diverse Maniere*, such as the lion monopod translated from a 187 chimneypiece to a writing-desk, though as before the synthesis 231 lacks that elusive spirit of fantasy which enlivened Piranesi's furniture for all its awkwardness and distortion.[48]

The inhibiting restraint and resistance to vibrancy of line reflected in these publications are paralleled in topographical illustration and *vedute* by the mechanical character of Piranesi's most notable successor, Luigi Rossini. While something of the Sublime remains in Rossini's plates to his *Antichità Romane* of 232 1829, the broader effects are achieved at the cost of Piranesi's 233 imaginative detail and sensitivity to light. Such plates have become faithful but lifeless records, a tendency apparent even in the more pedestrian works of Francesco Piranesi. In these

232 Luigi Rossini: *Temple of Minerva Medica*, from *Le Antichità Romane*, 1829

233 *Temple of Minerva Medica*, from *Vedute di Roma* (see *Vedute di Roma*, pl. 74)

234 Pietro Basoli: stage design for an ancient prison (La Scala Museum, Milan)

opening decades of the nineteenth century the greatest influence of Piranesi's visual inheritance was to be felt, appropriately, in the area from which it had originated – the world of the theatre and the pictorial fantasy.

By the early nineteenth century Italian stage designers were beginning to exploit a wealth of technical advances made in presentation, especially lighting. There were also the demands of a public requiring more sophisticated effects in which the architecture was an extension of the drama, not simply a virtuoso performance in itself.[49] Predictably, the various emotive devices of Piranesi's treatment of architecture furnished the designer with an extensive repertoire of compositional effects to satisfy these conditions. Prison scenes in particular were invariably couched in the language of the later *Carceri*, as shown for example by the macabre set for La Scala, Milan, 234 devised by the Bolognese Pietro Basoli and closely based on plate XVI of the series. The appropriate marriage between 152 Beethoven's *Fidelio* and Piranesi's penal imagery was achieved with a greater economy by Simeone Quaglio in 1820. 235

The pictorial fantasy, similarly, became one of the prime themes of the popular exhibition picture of the late eighteenth- and early nineteenth-century salon, exploiting the histrionic values of the contemporary theatre. The link between Piranesi and this indulgent phenomenon can be traced through the works of the French painter Hubert Robert, who had been closely associated with the artist during his stay in Rome between 1754 and 1765. After returning to Paris, Robert was admitted to the Academy in 1766 as a 'painter of ruins', and proceeded to work on a wide range of themes first devised in Italy, such as the *Discovery of the Laocoön* of 1773.[50] As with 236 Piranesi, the power of Robert's spectacular *capricci* depended on the complex relationship between architect and painter. In this particular work, Robert's project for redesigning the Grande Galerie of the Louvre provided a point of departure for this monumental vista, governed by the perspective effects, dramatic lighting and animated figures of the *Vedute di Roma*.

This amplification of architecture by pictorial means was introduced into English art through the inspired topographical work of painters such as John Robert Cozens and Turner.[51]

235 Simeone Quaglio: stage design for *Fidelio* (Theatre Museum, Munich)

236 Hubert Robert: *The Discovery of the Laocoön*, 1773 (Virginia Museum of Fine Arts)

237 John Martin: *Belshazzar's Feast*, mezzotint, 1826

The increasing use of the artist's impression for the effective presentation of a design to the client or to the public at large led to the appearance of specialized architectural draughtsmen such as Joseph Gandy, who rendered Soane's designs with the full repertoire of mood-enhancing effects.[52] The transition from these productions to exhibition works in which architecture reached the ultimate level of visual extravagance was achieved in the products of John Martin, whose spectacular biblical scenes, such as *Belshazzar's Feast* of 1821, leave absolutely nothing to the imagination.[53] Here Piranesi's powers of suggestion and subtle language of composition are reduced to the level of melodrama, an art which Ruskin perceptively dismissed as 'modern bombast as opposed to old simplicity'.[54]

Since the creative forces of the nineteenth century were essentially literary rather than visual, the most lasting and productive influence of Piranesi's work was upon the imaginative world of the Romantic writers. What had begun in England with Walpole, Beckford and De Quincey was to be continued through the nineteenth century in France with a succession of works by Balzac, Hugo, Musset, Gautier, Baudelaire and Mallarmé, extending into the present century with Proust.[55] For all these minds the *Carceri* in particular provided a series of visual analogies for the phenomena of disturbing imaginative experiences. These images of the endless growth and immeasurable depths in the recesses of the imagination are evoked, for instance, in the poetry of Victor Hugo:

> Puits de l'Inde! tombeaux! monuments constellés!
> Vous dont l'intérieur n'offre aux regards troublés
> Qu'un amas tournoyant de marches et de rampes,
> Froids cachots, corridors où rayonnent des lampes,
> Poutres où l'araignée a tendu ses longs fils,
> Blocs ébauchant partout de sinistres profils,
> Toits de granit, troués comme une frêle toile,
> Par où l'oeil voit briller quelque profonde étoile,
> Et des chaos de murs, de chambres, de paliers,
> Où s'écroule au hasard un gouffre d'escaliers!
> Cryptes qui remplissez d'horreur religieuse
> Votre voûte sans fin, morne et prodigieuse!
> Cavernes où l'esprit n'ose aller trop avant!

> Devant vos profondeurs j'ai pâli bien souvent
> Comme sur un abîme ou sur une fournaise,
> Effrayantes Babels que rêvait Piranèse!

> Entrez si vous l'osez!...

> Aux heures où l'esprit, dont l'oeil partout se pose,
> Cherche à voir dans la nuit le fond de toute chose,
> Dans ces lieux effrayants mon regard se perdit.
> Bien souvent je les ai contemplés, et j'ai dit:

> 'O rêves de granit! grottes visionnaires!
> Cryptes! palais! tombeaux, pleins de vagues tonnerres!
> Vous êtes moins brumeux, moins noirs, moins ignorés,
> Vous êtes moins profonds et moins désespérés
> Que le destin, cet antre habité par nos craintes,
> Où l'âme entend, perdue en d'affreux labyrinthes,
> Au fond, à travers l'ombre, avec mille bruits sourds,
> Dans un gouffre inconnue tomber le flot des jours!'[56]*

The struggle of ceaseless experiment which is also found in the *Carceri* struck a chord in those writers who attempted to discover pictorial equivalents in their search for the definition of the obscure truths and the psychological springs of the imagination. Although as a result this particular work received an exaggerated attention at the expense of Piranesi's other achievements, the *Carceri* do perhaps reveal, more than any other work, the intimate processes of a restless search after new modes of expression.

Significantly, those among Piranesi's contemporaries who came nearest to understanding this central aspect of his work were figures like Walpole and Adam, Beckford and Soane who also valued the role of fantasy as a means of transcending conventional modes of thought. To narrower minds, on the other hand, like his biographer Bianconi or the Neo-Classical theorist Milizia who sharply attacked the idiosyncracies of the Aventine buildings, Piranesi remained an enigma, a case of disconcerting genius misapplied.[57] In the final analysis, if there is a key to understanding the motivating forces of this strange and original mind, it is surely in his own words: 'I need to produce great ideas and I believe that were I given the planning of a new universe, I would be mad enough to undertake it.'[58]

---

*O wells of the Indies, tombs, and clustered monuments, where the troubled eye is met by a wheeling mass of steps and ramps, chill cells, lamplit passages, beams hung with the spider's long threads, sinister profiles of jutting blocks; where granite roofs, worn into holes like a thin cloth, afford a view of the distant stars; where crumbling staircases plunge without reason through a chaos of walls, chambers, landings; o vast and gloomy crypts, your awesome vaults filled with religious terror; o caverns where the spirit dare not penetrate: before your depths, as before the furnace or the abyss, I pale – terrifying Babels from the dreams of Piranesi! Enter if you dare....

At those hours when the spirit, wide-ranging, seeks in the darkness to reach the foundation of all things, I have lost myself in these haunts of fear. Often I have contemplated them, saying:

'O visions of granite, grottoes of nightmare, crypts, palaces, sounding sepulchres: you are less misted and obscure, less strange, less deep and desperate than destiny – that cavern peopled by our fears, where the soul, wandering in fearful labyrinths, hears afar, through the shadows, the muffled roar of the flood of Time pouring into the chasm of the unknown.'

Notes on the Text

Preface

1 K. Clark, *The Romantic Rebellion*, London, 1973, p. 46.

2 For Focillon's study of Piranesi, as well as for all other works on the artist referred to in this preface, see the Select Bibliography. This also includes catalogues to the exhibitions mentioned above, as well as key articles containing recent Piranesi research.

I Apprenticeship: Venice and Rome

1 An introduction to the artistic nature of Piranesi's Venice is given in M. Levey, *Painting in XVIII century Venice*, London, 1959, and a detailed discussion of the contemporary social and political background to patronage in the Republic is provided in F. Haskell, *Patrons and painters: A study in the relations between Italian art and society in the age of the Baroque*, London and New York, 1963.

2 For an examination of leading figures in the Enlightenment world of Venice and the Veneto (including Piranesi and his associates) see the exhibition catalogue *Illuminismo e architettura del '700 Veneto* (ed. M. Brusatin), Castelfranco Veneto, 1969.

3 Reference to Piranesi's early ambition to become an architect and his training in Venice is made by his earliest biographer, G. L. Bianconi, in 'Elogio storico del Cavaliere Giambattista Piranesi ...', *Antologia Romana*, nos. 34–6, February–March 1779 (reprinted in Bianconi, *Opere* II, Milan, 1802, pp. 127–40). In addition to this somewhat prejudiced account further support is given by J. G. Legrand in his MS. biography, *Notice sur la vie et les ouvrages de J. B. Piranesi ... Redigée sur les notes et les pièces communiquées par ses fils ...*, Paris, Bib. Nat. MSS. nouv. acq. fr. 5968. A transcription of this text, which was based on information given by the artist's family after they moved their business to Paris in the late eighteenth century, appears in *Nouvelles de l'estampe*, no. 5, 1969, pp. 191ff.
For a discussion of the architectural context of Piranesi's early years in Venice and the works of Lucchesi and Scalfarotto see E. Bassi, *Architettura del Sei e Settecento a Venezia*, Naples, 1962; Brusatin, *op. cit.*; R. Wittkower, *Art and Architecture in Italy, 1600–1750*, London, 1973 (rev. ed.), pp. 252ff.

4 The importance of Palladio for early eighteenth-century Venetian architects is discussed in R. Wittkower, *op. cit.*, and C. L. V. Meeks, *Italian Architecture, 1750–1914*, New Haven, Conn., and London, 1966.

5 For a recent study of Temanza and his varied activities see Brusatin, *op. cit.*, pp. 61–4.

6 Lucchesi's polemic against Maffei occurs in his published letter 'Sopra la serraglia dell'Arco di Tito', *Nouvelle Letterarie*, 1730, pp. 169ff. See also G. Silvestri, *Un Europeo del Settecento: Scipione Maffei*, Treviso, 1954.

7 The controversial architectural ideas of Lodoli are examined in W. Herrmann, *Laugier and eighteenth-century French theory*, London, 1962, pp. 160ff; C. Semenzato, *Arte Veneta*, XI, 1957; and E. Kaufmann Jr, 'Memmo's Lodoli', *Art Bulletin*, XLVI, 1964, pp. 159ff.

8 According to Legrand (*Nouvelles de l'estampe, op. cit.*, p. 195), Piranesi studied not only under the Valeriani brothers in Venice and Bologna but under Ferdinando Bibiena himself. Piranesi's connections with stage design are examined in P. Murray, *Piranesi and the grandeur of ancient Rome*, London, 1971, pp. 7, 8 and 21ff.

9 Marco Foscarini's didactic programmes, especially in connection with Batoni's *Triumph of Venice*, are considered in Haskell, *op. cit.*, p. 258ff.

10 The artistic and social character of eighteenth-century Rome is covered by the exhibition catalogues *Il Settecento a Roma*, Museo di Roma, 1959, and *The Academy of Europe: Rome in the eighteenth century*, The William Benton Museum of Art, University of Connecticut, 1973, as well as the invaluable survey in P. Giuntella, *Roma nel Settecento*, Rome, 1971.

11 The extensive architectural activity in early eighteenth-century Rome is dealt with by Wittkower, *op. cit.*, pp. 246ff.

12 An inventory of Giobbe's library and collection of drawings, made at his death and recently discovered by M. Georges Brunel, is published in *Les actes du colloque 'Piranèse et les Français: 1740–1790'* (1976), Académie de France à Rome (in press).

13 A comparison between Piranesi and Vanvitelli is provided in J. Wilton-Ely, 'The relationship between Giambattista Piranesi and Luigi Vanvitelli in eighteenth-century architectural theory and practice', *Atti del Congresso Vanvitelliano (1973)*, Naples (in press).

14 For Bottari's attitude to art see Haskell, *op. cit.*, pp. 348ff, and for his attitude to contemporary restorations of works by Michelangelo see P. Portoghesi, *Roma Barocca*, Rome, 1966, p. 46.

15 Excavations and the export of antiquities were increasingly controlled by the Papal State through a series of regulations instituted in the seventeenth century and taking their final form with the Edict of Pacca in 1820. Greatest control was exercised by those Popes, such as Benedict XIV (1740–58), Clement XIV (1769–74) and Pius VI (1775–99), who did most to create the major collections of the Capitoline and Vatican Museums.

16 Marliani, *Ritratto di Roma antica*, was first published in 1534, reprinted in 1544 and reissued in 1732. Palladio's influential (un-illustrated) guidebook, *Antichità di Roma*, of 1554 was followed in 1570 by the *Quattro Libri dell'Architettura*, which included a quantity of measured drawings of antique monuments. For a full catalogue of antiquarian guides to Rome see L. Schudt, *Le guide di Roma*, Vienna and Augsburg, 1930.

17 The standard *catalogue raisonné* of Pannini's considerable oeuvre is F. Arisi, *Giovanni Paolo Pannini*, Piacenza, 1961. His place in European topographical painting is evaluated in G. Briganti, *The view painters of Europe*, London, 1973.

18 The various miscellaneous publications containing Piranesi's plates of the *Varie Vedute* and their dating are listed and discussed in the important exhibition catalogue of Messrs P. & D. Colnaghi, *Etchings by Giovanni Battista Piranesi*, London, 1973–4. See also S. Zamboni, 'Il percorso di Giovanni Battista Piranesi', *Arte Antica e Moderna*, V, 1964, pp. 68–9, 81–2.

19 As quoted in the transcript of Legrand's MS. biography in *Nouvelles de l'estampe, op. cit.*, p. 194.

20 The complex history of the plates to the original edition of the *Prima Parte* is investigated in A. Robison, 'Giovanni Battista Piranesi: prolegomena to the Princeton Collections', *Princeton University Library Chronicle*, XXXI, no. 3, Spring 1970, pp. 169ff.

21 English translation by compilers of the exhibition catalogue *Giovanni Battista Piranesi: Drawings and Etchings at Columbia University*, New York, 1972, p. 117.

22 Particular sources for motifs in the *Ancient Campidoglio* can be found in Giuseppe Bibiena, *Architetture e Prospettive*, Vienna, 1740, pt I, pl. 6; pt II, pl. 7; pt IV, pls 7 and 10.

23 The rare copies of the *Prima Parte* containing the *Ancient mausoleum* are examined in Robison, *op. cit.*, pp. 169ff., and the catalogue *Drawings and Etchings at Columbia University*, pp. 69ff.

24 Transcript of Legrand MS. biography in *Nouvelles de l'estampe*, *op cit.*, p. 195.

25 Piranesi's letter to Bottari is printed in F. Cerotti, *Lettere e memorie autografe ed inedite di artisti tratti dai manuscritti della Corsiniana*, Rome, 1860, p. 51.

26 The complete group of Piranesi drawings in the Pierpont Morgan Library is catalogued in F. Stampfle, 'An unknown group of drawings by G. B. Piranesi', *Art Bulletin*, XXX, no. 2, June 1948, pp. 122–41.

27 Transcript of Legrand MS. biography in *Nouvelles de l'estampe*, *op. cit.*, p. 196.

28 For the history of Tiepolo's etchings and various interpretations of their imagery see G. Knox, 'The etchings of the Tiepolos', *Burlington Magazine*, November 1966, pp. 585ff.; H. D. Russell, *Rare etchings by Giovanni Battista and Giovanni Domenico Tiepolo*, New York, n.d.; A. Rizzi, *The etchings of the Tiepolos*, London and New York, 1971.

29 Maurizio Calvesi's interpretation of the *Grotteschi* appears in his introduction to the exhibition catalogue *Giovanni Battista e Francesco Piranesi*, Calcografia Nazionale, Rome, 1967–8. It also appears in an expanded form in his introduction to the Italian translation of H. Focillon, *Giovanni Battista Piranesi*, Bologna, 1967.

30 Recent studies of the early states of the *Carceri* are to be found in Robison, *op. cit.*, p. 172; and the exhibition catalogues *Drawings and Etchings at Columbia University*, pp. 74ff, and Messrs Colnaghi, *op. cit.*
Analyses of the complex design and imagery of these plates are made in U. Vogt-Göknil, *Giovanni Battista Piranesi: Carceri*, Zürich, 1958; P. M. Sekler, 'Giovanni Battista Piranesi's "Carceri" etchings and related drawings', *Art Quarterly*, XXV, 1962, pp. 331–65.

31 Three Piranesi drawings in the British Museum have been identified by E. Croft-Murray as free adaptations of two engravings showing Juvarra's scenery for Amadei's *Teodosio il Giovane*, produced at the Cancelleria in 1711. (One of them is reproduced in H. Thomas, *The Drawings of Piranesi*, London and New York, 1954, pl. 25.) See exhibition catalogue *Giovanni Battista Piranesi: his predecessors and his heritage* (ed. E. Croft-Murray), British Museum, London, 1968, pp. 22–4.

32 The first association between the imagery of the *Carceri* and hallucinations arising from opium was made by Coleridge in describing one of the *Carceri* plates to De Quincey (*Confessions of an English Opium Eater*, London, 1821). This has been subsequently revived in A. Hayter, *Opium and the Romantic Imagination*, London, 1968.

33 The plates of the *Archi Trionfali* are discussed in S. Chamberlain, 'The Triumphal Arches of Piranesi', *Print Collectors' Quarterly*, XXIV, no. 1, 1937, pp. 62–79; also in Messrs Colnaghi catalogue, *op. cit.*, items 5–8.

34 In addition to Arthur Hind's catalogue of the *Vedute di Roma* (see bibliography), more recent and extensive research on the problems of dating the early plates and their stylistic development is contained in A. Robison, 'The "Vedute di Roma" of Giovanni Battista Piranesi: Notes towards a revision of Hind's catalogue', *Nouvelles de l'estampe*, no. 4, 1970, p. 180ff. See also Messrs Colnaghi catalogue, *op. cit., passim*.

35 An important study of the role played by the *pensionnaires* of the French Academy in Rome in developing new architectural ideas is found in J. Harris, 'Le Geay, Piranesi and International Neo-Classicism in Rome, 1740–1750', *Essays presented to Rudolf Wittkower* (ed. D. Fraser), London and New York, 1967, pp. 189ff. The first attempt to emphasize the influence of Le Geay upon Piranesi was in E. Kaufmann, *Architecture in the Age of Reason*, London and New York, 1955, pp. 106ff. This has been challenged in a review by Dr R. Middleton, *Architectural Design*, April 1971, p. 249.

36 A reference to Piranesi's decorations for the Saly celebrations occurs in A. and G. de Montaiglon, *Correspondence des Directeurs de l'Académie de France à Rome*, 1909, X, p. 105. A drawing for this commission, since disappeared, was bought at the Saly sale in Paris, 1776.

37 Recent research has thrown fresh light on the influence of temporary architecture for festivals and official functions upon the development of Neo-Classical architecture in Europe. For Rome in particular, see R. P. Wunder, 'A forgotten French festival in Rome', *Apollo*, LXXXV, May 1967, pp. 354ff.

38 An actual ruin composition, specially devised by Natoire in a small garden near the Forum Romanum for his students, is described in A. and G. de Montaiglon, *op. cit.*, XI, p. 93. Part of it appears in a sketch by Natoire himself at the Musée Atger, Montpellier, reproduced in *Apollo*, CI, February 1975, p. 142 fig. 1.

39 Le Lorrain's various *Chinea* designs are discussed in Harris, *op. cit.*

40 Challe's activities in Rome are examined in R. P. Wunder, 'Charles Michel-Ange Challe: a study of his life and work', *Apollo*, LXXXVII, 1968, pp. 22ff.

41 W. Chambers, *Treatise on the Decorative Part of Civil Architecture*, London, 1791 (3rd ed.), introduction, p. 10 (as quoted on p. 60 of this book).

42 For the influence of Piranesi's *College* upon Peyre's student projects see the present author's entries in the catalogue of the 14th Council of Europe Exhibition, *The Age of Neo-Classicism*, Burlington House, London, 1972, pp. 600–601 (1259–60).

II The Vedutista

1 Giambattista Nolli's *Nuova Pianta di Roma data in luce ... l'anno MDCCXLVIII* is a reduction of a larger version in separate plates and was often inserted after the index to the latter. In this reduced format, drawn by Giambattista Nolli and etched by Carlo Nolli, Piranesi was responsible for the vignettes of townscape to the bottom left (Piazza di S. Pietro) and right (S. Croce in Gerusalemme, Fontana di Trevi and S. Maria Maggiore). Nolli's map represents the first attempt in Roman cartography to produce a scientifically accurate map of the city. Its significance is discussed in A. P. Frutaz, *Le Piante di Roma*, Rome, 1962.

2 The architectural expansion of eighteenth-century Rome is discussed in R. Wittkower, *Art and Architecture in Italy, 1600–1750*, London, 1973 (rev. ed.); its social and political development in V. E. Giuntella, *Roma nel Settecento*, Rome, 1971.

3 Particularly important for Piranesi among the Roman topographical engravers of the seventeenth century was G. B. Falda: *Nuove Teatro delle Fabbriche di Roma*, 1665 (average plate size 18 × 28 cm and 25 × 38 cm); also his series of larger plates (average size 45.5 × 68.5 cm) published by Gian Giacomo de' Rossi and his successor Domenico de' Rossi between 1687 and 1694.

4 The only substantial study on Vasi and his graphic works remains A. Petrucci, *Le Magnificenze di Roma*, Rome, 1946. See also C. Olschki 'Le Magnificenze di Roma', *Emporium*, LXIV, 1926, pp. 312ff. An important discussion of the complex relationship between Piranesi and Vasi in their respective *vedute* of the 1740s appears in H. Millon, 'Vasi, Piranesi, Juvarra', *Les actes du colloque 'Piranèse et les Français: 1740–1790'* (1976), Académie de France à Rome (in press).

5 Among recent surveys on the history and technical development of etching are A. Gross, *Etching, Engraving and Intaglio Printing*, London and New York, 1970; W. Chamberlain, *Manual of Etching and Engraving*, London and New York, 1972. A modern reprint of a classic study is A. M. Hind, *History of Engraving and Etching* (first published London, 1923), New York, 1963.

6 G. L. Barbielli, *Roma moderna distinta per Rioni*, Rome, 1741; F. Amidei, *Varie Vedute di Roma*, Rome, 1745; R. Venuti, *Accurata e succinta descrizione topografica delle Antichità di Roma*, Rome, 1763.

7 A modern German reprint of F. Amidei, *Varie Vedute di Roma* (1748), and Piranesi's later collection, *Alcune Vedute di Archi Trionfali* (1765), is to be found in *Giambattista Piranesi: Die frühen Ansichtenwerke*, Uhl Verlag, Unterschneidheim, 1974.

8 See preceding note. For an early appreciation of these particular plates, see S. Chamberlain, 'The Triumphal Arches of Piranesi', *Print Collectors' Quarterly*, XXIV, no. 1, 1937, pp. 62–79.

9 For a discussion of Piranesi's early *vedute* in relation to Duflos, Bellicard, Barbault and Le

Geay see P. Murray, *Piranesi and the grandeur of ancient Rome*, London, 1971, pp. 31ff.

10 The standard *catalogue raisonné* of the *Vedute di Roma* is A. M. Hind, *Giovanni Battista Piranesi: A Critical Study*, London, 1922, reprinted 1968. An extensive revision of Hind's catalogue is being made by Dr A. Robison, whose preliminary corrections are published in 'The "Vedute di Roma" of Giovanni Battista Piranesi: Notes towards a revision of Hind's catalogue', *Nouvelles de l'estampe*, no. 4, 1970, p. 180ff.

11 The rare set of thirty-four of the *Vedute*, preceding the publication of the *Magnificenze di Roma*, is discussed in A. Robison, 'Giovanni Battista Piranesi: prolegomena to the Princeton Collections', *Princeton University Library Chronicle*, XXXI, no. 3, Spring 1970, pp. 165ff.

12 Mrs K. Mayer-Haunton in the exhibition catalogue of Messrs P. & D. Colnaghi, *Etchings by Giovanni Battista Piranesi*, London, 1973–4, points out that fourteen of the first nineteen *Vedute* are etched on plates measuring 400/410 × 540/545 mm, close in size to those of the *Invenzioni capric di Carceri*, and two others among the nineteen are similar in size (390 × 543/6 mm) to the four *Grotteschi*.

13 Piranesi may have used this drawing (in reverse) for the oblique view of Piazza di S. Pietro seen in the lower half of Nolli's *Pianta di Roma* – see note 1 and front endpaper.

14 For a censure on Piranesi's rejection of Classical ideals in figure drawing see G. L. Bianconi, *Opere*, II, Milan, 1802, pp. 129–30.

15 Canaletto's *Campidoglio* may possibly have been painted from a sketch made during his supposed visit to Rome around 1740. Michael Levey, in discussing the artist's views of Rome at Windsor (*Paintings in the Royal Collection: The Later Italian Pictures*, London and New York, 1964, p. 54), considers the evidence for this visit weak and suggests that Canaletto could have been influenced by his nephew Bellotto, who incidentally exhibited a *View of the Campidoglio* in Venice in 1743. Vasi's etched *veduta* of the subject is very similar to Canaletto's compositional treatment.

16 *Nouvelles de l'estampe*, no. 5, 1969, p. 203.

17 '... vedendo io, che gli avanzi delle antiche fabbriche di Roma, sparsi in gran parte per gli orti ed altri luoghi coltivati, vengono a diminuirsi di giorno in giorno o per l'ingiuria de' tempi, o per l'avarizia de' possessori, che con barbara licenza gli vanno clandestinamente atterrando, per venderne i frantumi all'uso degli edifizi moderni; mi sono avvisato di conservarli col mezzo delle stampe. ...' *Le Antichità Romane*, 1756, I, 'Prefazione agli studiosi delle antichità Romane'.

18 'Dico, Milord, che ne appellerò all'avvenire, perchè ardisco credere ... d'aver finita un'Opera, che passerà alla posterità, e che durerà fin tanto che vi saranno de' curiosi di conoscere ciò, chè rimaneva nel nostro secolo delle rovine della più famosa Città dell'universo.' *Lettere di Giustificazione scritte a Milord Charlemont*, 1757, p. xi.

19 Apart from the formal similarities of this plate to those of the *Antichità Romane*, the style of the prominent lettering is far more intrusive than in the normal *Vedute* and the corresponding captions are far more learned.

20 'Piranesi ne faisait point de dessins finis, un gros trait à la sanguine, sur lequel il revenait ensuite avec la plume ou le pinceau et par parties seulement lui suffisait pour arrêter ses idées, mais il est presque impossible de distinguer ce qu'il croyait fixer ainsi que le papier, ce n'est qu'un chaos dont il démêlait seul les éléments sur le cuivre avec un art admirable.' *Nouvelles de l'estampe*, op. cit., p. 202.

21 'Ne voyez-vous pas que si mon dessin était fini ma planche ne deviendrait plus qu'une copie: lorsqu'au contraire je crée l'effet sur le cuivre, j'en fais un original?' *Ibid.*, p. 220.

22 When Francesco Piranesi issued his own *Catalogo* in 1792, he individually dated the first sixty *Vedute* according to the order set out by his father. This has since misled many scholars, in particular Hind, who based his study on this evidence in 1922 (see note 10). Recent research, however, has shown the unreliability of this order. The sequence, as originally classified by the artist according to subject-matter, juxtaposed works of an extremely disparate style: for instance the two views of S. Paolo fuori le Mura (Hind 6 and 7). From 1761, however, the addition of plates, either singly or in groups, in over twenty-five known states of the *Catalogo*, enables one to plot the artist's development of the series, which he completed with plate 135 in 1778, the year of his death.

23 According to J. Scott, *Piranesi*, London and New York, 1975, p. 303, *n.* 19, the Roman money system during the eighteenth century was as follows:

10 *baiocchi*	= 1 *paolo*		= $2\frac{1}{2}$p
10 *paoli*	= 1 *scudo*		= 25p
2 *scudi*	= 1 *zecchino*		= 50p

(No attempt has been made to give modern equivalent values adjusted for changes in the purchasing power of sterling.)

24 For detailed photographs of the present state of the Pantheon and for a full bibliography on its history, see E. Nash, *Pictorial Dictionary of Ancient Rome*, London, 1962, II, pp. 170ff.

25 'Il gravait au vernis dur et ne croisait jamais les tailles: une seule lui suffisait, mais il en variait le sens pour chaque détail. ... Il couvrait de ces tailles ainsi arrangées avec intelligence la totalité de sa planche, les grossissait ou les serrait pour forcer ses teintes, sans réserver alors les touches des plus vives lumières. Ce n'était qu'après ce travail qu'il les plaçait avec du vernis uni au pinceau, comme on touche un dessin avec du blanc, de cette manière elles acquéraient une franchise et un esprit infinis: la liberté de l'exécution remplaçait alors la précision quelques fois servile de la gravure ordinaire. ... Il mettait ensuite l'eau-forte avec un soin et une patience dont on ne l'eût pas cru, couvrant à mesure les parties à dégrader et revenant ainsi jusqu'à dix à douze fois pour certaines planches.' *Nouvelles de l'estampe*, op. cit., pp. 202–3.

26 References to paintings by Salvator Rosa occur in a complete inventory of Piranesi's collection and effects at his death, published in the Italian reprint of *Il Campo Marzio dell'Antica Roma* (ed. F. Borsi), Florence, 1972, pp. 15ff.

27 For Francesco Piranesi's map, together with details of his father's activities at Hadrian's Villa, see P. Gusman, *La Villa Impériale de Tibur*, Paris, 1904.

28 See J. Fleming, *Robert Adam and his Circle in Edinburgh and Rome*, London and New York, 1962, *passim*.

29 'La vérité et la vigeur de ses effets, la juste projection de ses ombres et leur transparence, ou d'heureuses licences à cet égard, l'indication même des tons de couleur, sont dûs à l'observation exacte qu'il allait faire chaque jour soit nature soit au soleil brûlant, soit au clair de la lune où les masses de l'architecture acquièrent tant de force, et ont une solidité, une douceur, et une harmonie souvent bien supérieures au papillotage de la lumière pendant le jour, il apprenait ainsi les effets par coeur en les étudiant de près, de loin, et à toutes les heures.' *Nouvelles de l'estampe*, op. cit., p. 203.

30 The drawing is unfinished, lacking such architectural elements as the Villas Corsini and Ferroni, which appear in the etched plate. See H. Thomas, *The Drawings of Piranesi*, London and New York, 1954, no. 54, p. 54.

31 Another preparatory drawing for the Colosseum (at 90° to the viewpoint of the one illustrated) in the Kunstbibliothek, Berlin, is illustrated in the exhibition catalogue *G. B. Piranesi: Acqueforti e Disegni*, Galleria Civica d'Arte Moderna, Turin, 1961–2, no. 204, pl. 128.

32 Lord Byron, *Childe Harold's Pilgrimage*, 1812–18, canto cxlv.

III The Artist as Archaeologist

1 Rose Macaulay, *The Pleasure of Ruins*, London, 1950, p. 165.

2 For a survey and bibliography of early Roman archaeology see the introduction to *Pirro Ligorio's Roman Antiquities* (ed. E. Mandowsky and C. Mitchell), London, 1963.

3 Quoted in C. Mitchell, 'Archaeology and Romance', *Italian Renaissance Studies* (ed. E. F. Jacob), London, 1960, p. 470.

4 F. Hartt, *Giulio Romano*, New Haven, Conn., 1958; *Pirro Ligorio's Roman Antiquities*, op. cit.

5 G. P. Bellori, *Fragmenta Vestigii Veteris Romae Farnesianis*, Rome, 1673; P. Santi Bartoli, *Sepolcro Nasonio*, Rome, 1680; idem, *Le Antichi Lucerne Sepolcrali figurati raccolte dalle cave sotterrane e grotte di Roma*, 1691; idem, *Gli Antichi Sepolcri overo Mausolei Romani ed Etruschi trovati in Roma ed in altri luoghi celebri*, 1697; Bernard de Montfauçon, *L'antiquité expliquée et représentée en figures*, Paris, 1719–24; Antoine Desgodetz, *Les édifices antiques de Rome mesurés et dessinés très exactement*, Paris, 1682.

6 For a detailed bibliography of itineraries and guide books to Rome see L. Schudt, *Le Guide di Roma*, Vienna and Augsburg, 1930. For maps and reconstructions of the ancient city see A. P. Frutaz, *Le Piante di Roma*, Rome, 1962.

7 G. B. Montano, *Raccolta de' Tempii et Sepolcri*, Rome, 1638. Montano's drawings were acquired by Cassiano del Pozzo and many of them were published by G. B. Soria between 1624 and 1684, but many in the Soane Museum collection remain unpublished. Among later publications is G. B. Montano, *Li Cinque Libri di Architettura*, Rome, 1691; Athanasius Kircher, *Turris Babel*, Amsterdam, 1679; Johann B. Fischer von Erlach, *Entwurf einer historischen Architektur*, Vienna, 1721; Francesco Bianchini, *Del Palazzo dei Cesari*, Verona, 1738.

8 For the influence of Fischer von Erlach on Piranesi see F. Stampfle, 'An unknown group of drawings by G. B. Piranesi', *Art Bulletin*, XXX, no. 2, June 1948, pp. 124–31, and W. Oechslin, 'Pyramide et sphère', *Gazette des Beaux-Arts*, April 1971.

9 A discussion of Etruscanology in eighteenth-century Italy is given in R. Bloch, *The Etruscans*, London and New York, 1958, pp. 20–28.

10 A. F. Gori, *Museum Etruscum*, Florence, 1737–43; G. B. Passeri, *Dell'Etruria Omèrica*, 1755; idem, *Della Pittura degli Etruschi*, 1755, etc.; M. Guarnacci, *Delle origini Italiche o siano memorie istorice-Etrusche sopra l'antichissimo regno d'Italia, e sopra i di lei primi abitatori*, Lucca, 1767–72.

11 For a selection of the principal archaeological publications relating to Greece and Asia Minor see catalogue *The Age of Neo-Classicism*, Burlington House, London, 1972, pp. 439ff.

12 For the early stages of the Graeco-Roman controversy (discussed in the following chapter) see R. Wittkower, 'Piranesi's "Parere su l'architettura"', *Journal of the Warburg Institute*, II, 1938–9, pp. 147ff.

13 Criticizing the contemporary situation in the *Prima Parte*, Piranesi had observed: '. . . whether for fault of architecture itself, fallen from the highest perfection to which it had risen in the period of the greatest splendour of the Roman Republic and in the times of the all-powerful Emperors who succeeded it; or whether the fault of those who should have been patrons of this most noble art. The fact is that in our own time we have not seen buildings equalling the cost of a Forum of Nerva, of an Amphitheatre of Vespasian, or of a Palace of Nero; therefore, there seems to be no recourse than for me or some other modern architect to explain his ideas through his drawings. . . .' Translation from exhibition catalogue *Giovanni Battista Piranesi: Drawings and Etchings at Columbia University*, New York, 1972, p. 117.

14 C. Pietrangeli, 'Archaeological excavations in Italy, 1750–1850' in catalogue *The Age of Neo-classicism, op. cit.*, pp. xlvi ff.

15 Anne-Claude-Philippe de Toubières, Comte de Caylus, *Recueil d'antiquités égyptiennes, étrusques, grecques, romaines et gauloises: Eloge historique*, Paris, 1752–67, 7 vols.

16 The trophies were involved in several other works by Piranesi. Their original location, the *mostra* of the Acqua Giulia, was the subject of a *veduta*, first used in the *Trofei* and reappearing in the treatise *Acqua Giulia* of 1761. The trophies feature prominently in the later *veduta* of the Campidoglio (*Vedute di Roma*) of the early 1760s.

17 For Charlemont's career and his relationship with Piranesi and other artists and architects see M. Craig, *The Volunteer Earl*, London, 1948, and J. Scott, *Piranesi*, London and New York, 1975, pp. 105ff.

18 The Accademia Ercolanese was founded by Charles de Bourbon in 1752, and eight volumes of paintings and bronzes were published between 1757 and 1792.

19 The history and detailed illustration of the Severan Marble Plan are provided by G. Carretoni, A. M. Colini, *et al., La Pianta Marmorea di Roma antica, Forma Urbis Romae*, Rome, 1960.

20 For a history of the Roman water system and Piranesi's contribution to its study see E. B. van Deman, *The building of the Roman aqueducts*, London and Washington D.C., 1934; T. Ashby, *Aqueducts of Ancient Rome*, London, 1935.

21 Sextus Julius Frontinus, *De Aquis*; translated as *The Stratagems and the Aqueducts of Rome* (ed. M. B. McElwain), Loeb Classics, London and New York, 1925. This basic source had been published in 1722 together with a commentary and illustrations by Giovanni Poleni, whose conclusions Piranesi challenges in the *Antichità*.

22 *Le Rovine del Castello dell'Acqua Giulia*, 1761.

23 The use of coins and medals to aid research in reconstruction appears first to have been employed in illustration by J. B. Marliani, *Antiquae Romae Topographia Romae*, Rome, 1534.

24 Ficoroni's illustration (*Le Vestigie e Rarità di Roma Antica*, Rome, 1744, bk I, pl. 169) is itself derived from a section of the *tumulus* in Santi Bartoli's *Gli Antichi Sepolcri overo Mausolei Romani ed Etruschi* (1727 ed., pl. 80) which, with its greater degree of information, may have been Piranesi's source.

25 Quoted in L. Lewis [Lawrence], 'Stuart and Revett: their Literary and Architectural Careers', *Journal of the Warburg Institute*, II, 1938–9, p. 128

26 (A. Ramsay), *The Investigator. No. 332: A Dialogue on Taste*, London, 1755; subsequently published under Ramsay's name in a collection of essays, *The Investigator*, London, 1762. See A. Smart, *The Life and Work of Allan Ramsay*, London, 1952, pp. 86, 90–93.

27 W. Herrmann, *Laugier and eighteenth-century French theory*, London, 1962.

28 Algarotti was a regular correspondent of Piranesi's first intellectual mentor and patron in Rome, Bottari, whose radical attitudes would have encouraged the ideas the young architect had acquired in the Venice of Lodoli. See E.

Kaufmann, 'Piranesi, Algarotti and Lodoli', *Gazette des Beaux-Arts*, XLVI, 1955, pp. 21ff.; F. Haskell, *Patrons and painters*, London and New York, 1963, pp. 320–22, 364–8; and the exhibition catalogue *Illuminismo e architettura del '700 veneto* (ed. M. Brusatin), Castelfranco Veneto, 1969, pp. 71ff.

29 Lodoli's projected treatise is examined in Kaufmann, *op. cit.*

30 Ligorio's plan of Hadrian's Villa (*Ichnographia Villae Tiburtinae Adriani Cesaris a Pyrro Ligorio e Francesco Continio*) was published during the eighteenth century in *Pianta della Villa Tiburtina di Adriano Cesare*, Rome, 1751.

31 J. Harris, *Sir William Chambers*, London, 1970, *passim*. Chambers stayed in Palazzo Tomati, where Piranesi was to move his studio by 1761.

32 W. Chambers, *Treatise on the Decorative Part of Civil Architecture*, London, 1796 (3rd ed.), introduction, p. 10.

33 Quoted in Harris, *op. cit.*, p. 22.

34 Chambers's design for the mausoleum and its relationship to the work of Piranesi and the *pensionnaires* of the French Academy are discussed in J. Harris, 'Le Geay, Piranesi and International Neo-Classicism in Rome, 1740–1750', *Essays in the History of Architecture presented to Rudolf Wittkower* (ed. D. Fraser), London and New York, 1967, pp. 193ff.

35 For Mylne's studies in Rome see C. Gotch, 'The Missing Years of Robert Mylne', *Architectural Review*, CXXX, September 1951, pp. 179ff., quoting in full Piranesi's letter to Mylne (11 November 1760) in which he requests 'an exact copy' of the design for Blackfriars Bridge. In the Charlemont correspondence (Hist. MSS. Comm., 12th Report, Appendix pt X, Charlemont MSS, Vol. 1, p. 252) Mylne is referred to as 'a scholar of Piranesi' by John Parker in a letter, 20 February 1759.

36 Frequent references to Piranesi in Adam's correspondence from Rome are given in J. Fleming, *Robert Adam and his Circle in Edinburgh and Rome*, London and New York, 1962, *passim*. See also D. Stillman, 'Robert Adam and Piranesi', *Essays in the History of Architecture presented to Rudolf Wittkower, op. cit.*, pp. 197ff.

37 J. Fleming, 'Allan Ramsay and Robert Adam in Italy', *Connoisseur*, March 1956, pp. 78ff.; idem, 'An Italian Sketch-book by Robert Adam, Clérisseau and Others', *Connoisseur*, November 1960, pp. 186ff.

38 Fleming, *Robert Adam and his Circle*, p. 167.

39 According to Vanvitelli in a letter to his brother Urbano in the 1760s, '. . . it is a strange thing that the mad Piranesi [*il Pazzo Piranesi*] dares to be an Architect; I shall only say that it is not a profession for madmen'. As quoted in R. Pane, 'Luigi Vanvitelli – l'uomo e l'artista', *Napoli Nobilissima*, XII, fasc. 1, Jan.–Feb. 1973, p. 42, n. 15.

40 Adam, writing to his brother James in the same letter referred to in note 37 (4 July 1755) concerning Chambers's warning to him of the

impossibility of getting anything from Piranesi, goes on to say 'so much is he out of his calculation that he [Piranesi] has told me that whatsoever I want of him he will do it for me with pleasure, and is just now doing two drawings for me which will be both singular and clever'. The drawing here illustrated probably came to the Soane Collection among the papers from the Adam office.

41 Fleming, *Robert Adam and his Circle*, p. 354, 18 June 1755.

42 At the close of the topographical index in the *Antichità*, Vol. I, p. 40, Piranesi adds: 'Mi reservo pertanto di dimostrare la primiera loro costituzione nella grande Iconografia di Roma antica che sto in procinto di dare alla luce' (I therefore reserve my demonstration of their original composition for the great *Ichnographia* of ancient Rome which I am about to publish).

43 Adam's excitement at finding himself thus honoured is described in a letter to James in April 1756 (Fleming, *Robert Adam and his Circle*, p. 207). The monument concerned appears at the left-hand side of the Via Appia surmounted by a statue of the she-wolf suckling the brothers Romulus and Remus (a witty reference to Robert and James Adam?), with the following inscription: DIS MANIB.. ROBERTI ADAMS SCOT.. ARCHITECTI.. PRAESTANTISS.. I.B.P... FAC COERAVIT.

44 Fleming, *Robert Adam and his Circle*, pp. 230–31.

45 The opposite side to the quarrel with Charlemont appears in the Charlemont correspondence, pp. 227, 231–48. A probable list of intended recipients of the *Lettere* is inscribed in a copy published in the exhibition catalogue *Piranesi*, Smith College, Northampton, Mass., 1961, pp. 65–7, repr. pl. 15. The highly complex circumstances of Piranesi's alterations to various plates in the *Antichità*, together with a discussion of the letters concerned (including two unpublished ones in the Vatican Library), are to be found in L. Donati, 'Giovan Battista Piranesi e Lord Charlemont', *English Miscellany*, Rome, I, 1950, pp. 231ff.; *idem*, 'Piranesiana', *Maso Finiguerra*, Milan, III, 1938, pp. 206–7.

46 *Lettere di Giustificazione scritte a Milord Charlemont . . .*, Rome, 1757, pp. xi–xii.

47 *Ibid.*, p. xiii.

48 P. Murray, *Piranesi and the grandeur of ancient Rome*, London, 1971, p. 46. The reference in the Minute Book of the Society of Antiquaries for 24 February 1757 refers to Piranesi as 'a most ingenious architect and Author of the Antiquities in Rome and its Neighbourhood in V Vols. Folio; and desirous of being admitted an honorary member of this Society. ...' Apart from the four books of the *Antichità*, the fifth referred to is probably the *Trofei*.

49 The date 1757 appears in the left-hand medallion of the dedication.

IV Controversy

1 N. Pevsner and S. Lang, 'The Doric Revival' in N. Pevsner, *Studies in Art, Architecture and Design*, I, London and New York, 1968, pp. 197ff.

2 D. Wiebenson, *Sources of Greek Revival Architecture*, London, 1969.

3 R. Wittkower, *Art and Architecture in Italy, 1600–1750*, London, 1973 (rev. ed.), pp. 246ff.

4 A number of sketch plans in the British Museum show the preliminary organization of several early fantasy compositions such as appear in the *Prima Parte*.

5 The importance of Frézier and De Cordemoy for the development of Greek Revival theory in the later eighteenth century is discussed in R. Middleton, 'The Abbé de Cordemoy and the Graeco-Gothic Ideal', *Journal of the Warburg and Courtauld Institutes*, XXV, 1962, pp. 278ff., and XXVI, 1963, pp. 90ff.

6 Anne-Claude-Philippe de Toubières, Comte de Caylus, *Recueil d'antiquités égyptiennes, étrusques, grecques, romaines et gauloises: Eloge historique*, Paris, 1752–67, I, pp. ix, 119ff.

7 *Proposal* for The Antiquities of Athens, as quoted in L. Lewis [Lawrence], 'Stuart and Revett: their Literary and Architectural Careers', *Journal of the Warburg Institute*, II, 1938–9, p. 128.

8 See W. Herrmann, *Laugier and eighteenth-century French theory*, London, 1962.

9 M.-A. Laugier, *Essai sur l'architecture*, Paris, 1755 (2nd ed.), p. 3.

10 For other contemporary reactions to Borromini in France see Herrmann, *op. cit.*, Appendix VII, pp. 226ff, 229 and 232. For example, C. N. Cochin satirically quotes a follower of Meissonnier, whose master preferred 'le goût de *Borromini* au goût ennuyeux de l'antique, il s'étoit par là rapproché de nous; car le *Borromini* a rendu à l'Italie le même service que nous avons rendu à la France, en y introduisant une architecture gaie et indépendante de toutes les règles de ce que l'on appelloit anciennement le bon goût' (... preferred the style of Borromini to the monotonous antique style, thereby coming close to our own view; for Borromini has rendered Italy the same service that we have rendered France, by introducing a lively architecture independent of all the rules of what used to be called good taste). *Mercure de France*, February 1755, pp. 148ff.

11 Laugier, *op. cit.*, p. 3.

12 Winckelmann discusses the Greek temples at Agrigentum in *Anmerkungen über die Baukunst der alten Tempel zu Girgenti in Sicilien*, 1759, relying on drawings of them made by the Scottish architect Robert Mylne in 1757. His reference to Paestum occurs in *Anmerkungen über die Baukunst der Alten*, published in Leipzig in 1762 but written in 1760.

13 For the text and circumstances of Piranesi's polemical *Lettere di Giustificazione scritte a Milord*

Charlemont see J. Wilton-Ely (ed.), *Giovanni Battista Piranesi: The Polemical Works*, Farnborough, 1972.

14 Piranesi's début in the Graeco-Roman controversy with *Della Magnificenza* and the nature of his subsequent publications are discussed in R. Wittkower, 'Piranesi's "Parere su l'Architettura"', *Journal of the Warburg Institute*, II, 1938–9, pp. 147ff. For the texts concerned and their background see Wilton-Ely, *op. cit.*

15 Piranesi in a letter to Robert Mylne, 11 November 1760, mentions that: 'My work "On the Magnificence of Architecture of the Romans" has been finished some time since.... The Antiquities of Greece, brought to light by Mr Le Roy ... contributed to its enlargement.' Quoted in C. Gotch, 'The Missing Years of Robert Mylne', *Architectural Review*, CXXX, September 1951, p. 182.

16 Ramsay's anonymous dialogue was subsequently published under his name in a collection of essays, *The Investigator*, London, 1762. See A. Smart, *The Life and Art of Allan Ramsay*, London, 1952, pp. 86, 90–93. Ramsay in a letter to Sir Alexander Dick, 31 January 1762, claims: 'My dialogue of Taste has become remarkable by a large folio which it has given rise to by Piranesi at Rome, and of which some copies are already come to London by land.' *Curiosities of a Scots Charta Chest*, ed. Mrs Atholl Forbes, Edinburgh, 1897, p. 199, quoted in Smart, *op. cit.*, p. 91.

17 G. L. Bianconi, *Opere* II, Milan, 1802, pp. 127–40. Among those said to have assisted Piranesi were Mons. Bottari, Father Contucci, Mons. Riminaldi, Clemente Orlandi and the Abbé Pirmei. It is evident from surviving manuscript notes for a later work, the *Diverse Maniere*, that Piranesi was fully capable of formulating his own ideas even if he relied on erudite help for literary authorities and quotations.

18 Mario Guarnacci had worked in Rome until 1757 and had been in the service of Cardinal Carlo Rezzonico, the future Clement XIII. His *Origini Italiche, o siano memorie istorice-Etrusche* was eventually published in Lucca between 1767 and 1772.

19 Vico's principles of historical enquiry were first published in Latin in 1720–22, reappearing in Italian as the *Scienza Nuova* in 1725. A rewritten version, published in 1730, was revised in the 3rd edition shortly after Vico's death in 1744. Piranesi may also have been familiar with *De antiquissima Italorum sapientia*, 1710, in which Vico showed the survival of certain Etruscan words in Latin. The probable influence of Vico upon Piranesi is discussed by Maurizio Calvesi in the exhibition catalogue *Giovanni Battista e Francesco Piranesi*, Calcografia Nazionale, Rome, 1967–8, pp. 8–10, and in the edition (with A. Monferini) of H. Focillon, *Giovanni Battista Piranesi*, Bologna, 1967, pp. viii ff.

20 J. G. Legrand, *Nouvelles de l'estampe*, no. 5, 1969, p. 207 (translation from J. Scott, *Piranesi*, London and New York, 1975, p. 174).

21 The first surviving reference to the future *Ichnographia* of the Campus Martius occurs in

June 1755 when, according to a letter to James Adam, Piranesi 'threatens' to dedicate it to Robert as part of the proposed *Antichità Romane* (J. Fleming, *Robert Adam and his Circle in Edinburgh and London*, London and New York, 1962, p. 354). By September Robert Adam had persuaded the artist to issue the map separately (Fleming, *op. cit.*), and Piranesi in 1756 refers in the *Antichità* (Vol. I, p. 40) to the 'grande Iconografia di Roma antica che sto in procinto di dare alla luce' (great *Ichnographia* of ancient Rome which I am about to publish). Before leaving Rome in April 1757, Adam visited Piranesi's studio to find that he was etching the dedication plate of this map (Fleming, *op. cit.*, p. 231).

22 R. Wood and J. Dawkins, *The Ruins of Palmyra*, 1753.

23 Piranesi's survey of Hadrian's Villa would have been greatly facilitated by the publication of Pirro Ligorio's map of the site as *Ichnographia Villae Tiburtinae Adriani Cesaris a Pyrro Ligorio et Francesco Continio*, in *Pianta della Villa Tiburtina di Adriano Cesare*, Rome 1751.

24 An analysis of the planning patterns of the *Ichnographia* appears in V. Fasolo, 'Il "Campo Marzio" di G. B. Piranesi', *Quaderni dell'Istituto di Storia dell'Architettura*, Rome, no. 15, 1956, p. 13.

25 As quoted from the translation by S. Powell of the *Anmerkungen über die Baukunst der Alten*, Leipzig, 1762, in D. Irwin (ed.), *Winckelmann, Writings on Art*, London, 1972, p. 87.

26 'Sebbene ciò di che io piuttosto temer dubbio, si è, che non sembrino inventate a capriccio, più che prese dal vero, alcune cose di questa delineazione del Campo; le quali se taluno confronta coll'antica maniera di architettare, comprenderà, che molto da essa si discostano, e s'avvicinano all'usanza de' nostri tempi. Ma chiunque egli sia, prima di condannare alcuno d'impostura, osservi di grazia l'antica pianta di Roma ... osservi le antiche ville del Lazio, quella d'Adriano in Tivoli, le terme, i sepolcri, e gli altri edifizi di Roma, che rimangono in ispezie poi fuori di porta Capena: non ritroverà inventate più cose dai moderni, che dagli antichi contra le più rigide leggi dell'architettura. O derivi pertanto dalla natura e condizione delle arti, che quando sono giunte al sommo, vanno a poco a poco in decadenza e in rovina, o così porti l'indole degli uomini, che nelle professioni ancora reputansi lecita qualsisia cosa; non è da maravigliarsi, se troviamo eziando dagli architetti antichi usate quelle cose, che nelle fabbriche nostrali talvolta biasimiamo.'

27 Contrary to this constructive interpretation of Piranesi's *Ichnographia*, see the view put forward in M. Tafuri, 'G. B. Piranesi: l'architettura come "utopia negativa"', *Angelus Novus*, no. 20, June 1971, pp. 102ff.; idem, *Progetto e Utopia. Architettura e sviluppo capitalistico*, Bari, 1973, pp. 16ff.

28 For a discussion of the problems arising over dating the ten additional fantasies in the *Opere Varie*, see M. Calvesi and A. Monferini, *op. cit.*, pp. 293–4.

29 The problems of Piranesi's artistic and in-tellectual development contributing to the *Osservazioni* and its supporting texts are discussed in R. Wittkower, *op. cit.*, and more recently reconsidered in J. Wilton-Ely, 'Vision and Design: Piranesi's "fantasia" and the Graeco-Roman controversy' in *Les actes du colloque 'Piranèse et les Français: 1740–1790'* (1976), Académie de France à Rome (in press).

30 Although not illustrated in the *Parere*, James Adam's British order, involving a capital with lion, unicorn and royal insignia for a projected parliament building in Westminster, was shown to Piranesi in April 1762 during the Scot's visit to Rome. (See Fleming, *op. cit.*, pp. 305–6). Piranesi in fact attributes the design to Robert although the capital features prominently in Batoni's portrait of James, painted in Rome during 1763.

31 *Diverse Maniere d'adornare i Cammini*, p. 12.

32 *Ibid.*, p. 33.

V The Fever of the Imagination

1 Thomas De Quincey, *Confessions of an English Opium Eater*, first published in the *London Magazine*, 1821. The quotation is taken from the modern edition, ed. A. Hayter, Harmondsworth, 1971, pp. 105–6.

2 Although the literature on the *Carceri* is considerable, among the most significant contributions are: A. Huxley and J. Adhémar, *Prisons*, London, 1949 (the interpretative essay by Huxley has been reprinted with minor changes as 'Variations on the Prisons' in *Themes and Variations*, London and New York, 1950, pp. 192ff.); U. Vogt-Göknil, *Giovanni Battista Piranesi: Carceri*, Zürich, 1958; P. M. Sekler, 'Giovanni Battista Piranesi's "Carceri" etchings and related drawings', *Art Quarterly*, Detroit Institute of Arts, XXV, 1962, pp. 331ff.; M. Calvesi's introduction to the Italian edition of H. Focillon, *Giovanni Battista Piranesi*, Bologna, 1967, pp. xi ff.; S. Gavuzzo-Stewart, 'Nota sulle Carceri Piranesiane', *L'Arte*, 15–16, 1972, pp. 57ff.; P. Hofer, *The Prisons (Le Carceri) of G. B. Piranesi*, New York, 1973; M. Praz, *G. B. Piranesi: Le Carceri*, Milan, 1976; M. Tafuri, 'Giovan Battista Piranesi. L'utopie négative dans l'architecture', *L'Architecture d'aujourd'hui*, no. 184, March-April 1976.

3 The effect of opium upon certain writers and artists, including Piranesi, is discussed in A. Hayter, *Opium and the Romantic Imagination*, London, 1968. For another recent interpretation of the *Carceri* as products of drug-induced hallucinations see K. Clark, *The Romantic Rebellion*, London, 1973.

4 The respective prices of Piranesi's works available in 1757, as stated in the Barberini copy of the *Antichità Romane* in the Vatican Library; cf. Gavuzzo-Stewart, *op. cit.*, p. 57. By the early 1760s, when the reworked plates of the *Carceri*, with two extra ones, were published under Piranesi's name, they were priced at 20 *paoli* a set.

5 See Vogt-Göknil, *op. cit.*, and Sekler, *op. cit.*

6 For antecedents to the *Carceri* in early eighteenth-century theatre designs of prison interiors, see Sekler, *op. cit.*, p. 341, fig. 16; P. Murray, *Piranesi and the grandeur of ancient Rome*, London, 1971, p. 25, figs 24, 25; Gavuzzo-Stewart, *op. cit.*, pp. 57–8, figs 2, 3, 6, 7; C. Bertelli, 'Le parlanti rovine', *Grafica*, Calcografia Nazionale, Rome, II, 1976, pp. 90ff., figs 80, 101, 104, 105.

7 The drawing is discussed in H. Thomas, *The Drawings of Piranesi*, London and New York, 1954, pp. 41–2, no. 18, and was first connected with *Carceri*, pl. XI in Sekler, *op. cit.*, p. 342.

8 The drawing for pl. VIII in the Kunsthalle, Hamburg, is discussed in Thomas, *op. cit.*, p. 37, no. 4, and that for pl. XII in the Biblioteca Nacional, Madrid, in Sekler, *op cit.*, p. 341, fig. 18.

9 See Thomas, *op. cit.*, p. 38, no. 8.

10 See Thomas, *op. cit.*, pp. 38–9, no. 9.

11 In the frontispiece to the earliest known edition of the *Carceri*, c. 1745, Piranesi spelt the publisher's name in Venetian dialect as 'Buzard', but corrected it to 'Bouchard' when the plates were republished in the *Magnificenze de Roma* in 1751.

12 One of the most recent and thorough discussions concerning the dating of the second edition of the Carceri is found in Focillon, *op. cit.*, pp. 282ff.

13 See A. Robison, 'Giovanni Battista Piranesi: prolegomena to the Princeton Collections', *Princeton Library Chronicle*, XXXI, no. 3, Spring 1970, pp. 172–5.

14 See Calvesi's introduction to Focillon, *op. cit.*, pp. xvii–xviii, and Gavuzzo-Stewart, *op. cit.*, pp. 60–72.

15 The complete phrase, *Ad terrorem increscentis audaciae*, from which the inscription is taken, comes from Livy, I, 33. See Calvesi, *op cit.*, p. xvii.

16 The inscription is a paraphrase of a passage from Livy, I, 26. See Calvesi, *op. cit.*, p. xvii, and Gavuzzo-Stewart, *op. cit.*, p. 72.

17 For a discussion of the use made by Piranesi of Tacitus, *Annals*, XVI, see Gavuzzo-Stewart, *op. cit.*, pp. 60–61.

18 The Desprez *Prison* fantasy is discussed in *First Annual Report to the Fellows of the Pierpont Morgan Library*, New York, 1950, p. 54, and the exhibition catalogue *Piranèse et les Francais: 1740–1790*, Académie de France à Rome, 1976, pp. 130–31 (64).

19 W. Beckford, *Dreams, Waking Thoughts and Incidents*, printed in 1783 but suppressed on the eve of publication. Its first subsequent publication was in 1891 (London), from which the quotation is taken.

20 The *Prison façade* of Delafosse is discussed in the exhibition catalogue *Piranèse et les Francais: 1740–1790*, p. 109 (51).

21 Sir Reginald Blomfield was among the first to recognize the impact of Piranesi's vision upon

Newgate: 'It was . . . the *Carceri* that inspired the younger Dance to design Newgate, those visions of a peculiar hell that for once stimulated a merely mechanical practitioner to scale heights inaccessible to all but men of genius' ('Some Italian Draughtsmen, and Piranesi' in *Architectural Drawing and Draughtsmen*, London, 1912, p. 70). See also *idem*, 'The Architect of Newgate' in *Studies in Architecture*, London, 1905, p. 87. Later commentators have tended to play down the influence. For instance, Sir John Summerson considers that 'It is tempting – perhaps a little too tempting – to associate the giant drama of Newgate at once with Piranesi and especially with the *Carceri*. . . . Very likely there is a connection of mood, but it accounts for nothing in the composition or detail of the building, except possibly the macabre festooning of chains over the doorways' (*Architecture in Britain, 1530–1830*, Harmondsworth, 1969 (5th ed.), p. 274). A similar opinion is expressed in H. D. Kalman, 'Newgate Prison', *Architectural History*, XII, 1969, p. 55.

VI Freedom in Design

1 J. Wilton-Ely, 'A bust of Piranesi by Nollekens', *Burlington Magazine*, CXVIII, August 1976, pp. 593–5.

2 Clement XIII exempted Piranesi from paying tax on the paper required for this sumptuous publication.

3 Among the background details of Piranesi's portrait of Clement XIII, etched by Domenico Cunego, appear a pair of highly ornate column bases from the Baptistery of Constantine, illustrated in pl. IX of *Della Magnificenza*.

4 For Piranesi's work as a practising architect, especially with regard to the Aventine commission, see W. Körte, 'Giovanni Battista Piranesi als praktischer Architekt', *Zeitschrift für Kunstgeschichte*, II, 1933, pp. 16ff., and R. Wittkower, 'Piranesi as Architect' in *Studies in the Italian Baroque*, London, 1975, pp. 247ff.

5 Piranesi's design and the iconographic programme of the Aventine commission are discussed at length in J. Wilton-Ely, 'Piranesian symbols on the Aventine', *Apollo*, CIII, March 1976, pp. 214ff.

6 The Avery account book consists of 384 pages in quarto, bound in vellum, containing 762 entries concerning the work directed by Pelosini. It records a total cost of 10,947.29½ *scudi* and was endorsed by Piranesi on 10 April 1767. See Wittkower, *op. cit.*, p. 250. A contemporary account of Piranesi's Aventine work in progress is given in *Diario Ordinario di Roma*, no. 7497, 20 July 1765.

7 The history of the priory of the Knights of Malta on the Aventine and of the church in particular is summarized in Renzo U. Montini, *S. Maria del Priorato*, Rome, 1959, which also contains a full bibliography of previous publications relating to the subject.

8 Körte, *op. cit.*, p. 29.

9 Piranesi singles out Ligorio's Casino di Pio V for qualified praise in the *Diverse Maniere*, pp. 3–4.

10 The inscription is as follows: JOHANNES BAPTISTA REZZONICO/ SS. DOMINI NOSTRI CLEMENTIS. PP. XIII/ FRATRIS FILIUS AC MAGNUS PRIOR UT LOCI MAIESTATEM AUGERET AREAM HANC LAXANDAM CURAVIT/ A.P.C.N./MDCCLXV.

11 The working drawings for the piazza reliefs are discussed in F. Stampfle, 'An unknown group of drawings by G. B. Piranesi', *Art Bulletin*, XXX, no. 2, June 1948, p. 133, nos. 53 and 54. They belong to a distinct group of 133 by, or connected with, Piranesi, probably gathered direct from his studio.

12 For the Capitoline friezes – a key source for the Aventine programme – see H. Stuart Jones (ed.), *Catalogue of the Ancient Sculpture in the Municipal Collections of Rome – Sculpture of the Museo Capitolino*, Oxford, 1912, pp. 258ff., nos. 99, 100, 102, 104, 105 and 107, pls. 61–2. The original function and location of these six fragments are uncertain, but some at least of them are believed to have been at S. Lorenzo fuori le Mura before being recorded in the Palazzo dei Conservatori in the mid-sixteenth century.

13 The early history of the Aventine is discussed in B. B. Lugari, 'L'Aventino e le origini pagane e cristiane di Roma', *Dissertazioni della Pontif. Accad. di Archeol.*, s. II. VI, Rome, 1896; A. Merlin, *L'Aventin dans l'antiquité*, Bibliothèque des Ecoles d'Athènes et de Rome, fasc. 97, Paris, 1906; A. Boëthius and J. Ward-Perkins, *Etruscan and Roman Architecture*, Harmondsworth, 1970.

14 For the *Armilustrium* and the probable site of the ceremony on the Aventine see J. W. Crous, 'Florentiner Waffenpfeiler und Armilustrium', *Mitteilungen des deutschen archäologischen Instituts, Römische Abteilung*, 48, 1933, pp. 1ff.

15 *Della Magnificenza* pl. XIII. In the *Diverse Maniere* (p. 12) Piranesi refers to these antique capitals as outstanding examples of stylized forms taken from nature.

16 Wittkower, *op. cit.*; *idem*, 'S. Maria della Salute' in *Studies in the Italian Baroque*, pp. 125ff.

17 The drawing is discussed in Stampfle, *op. cit.*, p. 133, no. 50.

18 For this sketch, which was acquired by the Pierpont Morgan Library subsequently to the group referred to in note 11, see J. Bean and F. Stampfle, *Drawings from New York Collections, III: The Eighteenth Century*, New York, 1971, p. 94.

19 For the Berlin sketch see Marianne Fischer, 'Piranesis radiertes Oeuvre und die zugehörigen Entwürfe in der Kunstbibliothek', *Berliner Museen*, N.F.XVI, Heft 2, 1966, pp. 17ff.

20 Apart from certain formal resemblances between the Aventine altar and the monument to the right of the *Circus* fantasy, Piranesi anticipates another feature with the triple-sword ram attached to a sarcophagus in the middle foreground in this plate in the *Antichità*.

21 For this drawing see Stampfle, *op. cit.*, p. 133, no. 51.

22 For Righi's monument to Balestra and the circumstances of the quarrel at the Accademia di San Luca involving Piranesi, see C. Bertelli, 'Un progetto per Poets' Corner e una picca all'Accademia', *Grafica*, Calcografia Nazionale, Rome, II, pp. 117–120, repr. fig. 125.

23 The nature and extent of the Lateran commission are discussed in the exhibition catalogue *Giovanni Battista Piranesi: Drawings and Etchings at Columbia University*, New York, 1972. Prior to the discovery of these drawings, a detailed examination of the other evidence relating to Piranesi's designs appeared in M. F. Fischer, 'Die Umbaupläne des Giovanni Battista Piranesi für den Chor von S. Giovanni in Laterano', *Münchner Jahrbuch der bildenden Kunst*, XIX, 1968, pp. 207ff.

24 A drawing by Borromini showing a projected plan for the east end of S. Carlo al Corso, remarkably close to certain of Piranesi's Lateran solutions, is reproduced in P. Portoghesi, *The Rome of Borromini*, Rome, 1967, fig. CXXVII.

25 'Sa Sainteté, voulant orner la basilique de Saint-Jean-de-Latran d'un maître-autel qui réponde à la magnificence de cette église, elle a ordonné sieur Piranesi, célèbre architecte-sculpteur, de composer un dessein propre à l'exécution de ce projet. . . .' (His Holiness, wishing to adorn the basilica of S. Giovanni in Laterano with a high altar corresponding to the magnificence of the church, has commissioned Master Piranesi, the celebrated architect and sculptor, to produce a suitable design. . . .) A. de Montaiglon, *Correspondance des Directeurs de l'Académie de France à Rome*, XI, Paris, 1901, S.489, no. 5696: 'Nouvelles de Rome'.

26 All the drawings are discussed and reproduced in the catalogue, *Giovanni Battista Piranesi: Drawings and Etchings at Columbia University*.

27 Piranesi's intention to complete Borromini's scheme in the spirit of the master is borne out by inscriptions on two of the three studio designs for the *baldacchino* and altar. Pl. XXI is denoted *sul gusto del Boromino* and pl. XXIII *su le stile del Boromino*.

28 A detailed account of Piranesi's investiture ceremony is given in *Diario Ordinario di Roma*, 15 October 1766.

29 The Minneapolis table is discussed in F. B. J. Watson, 'A Side Table by Piranesi', *Minneapolis Institute of Arts Bulletin*, LIV, 1965, pp. 19ff.

30 See W. Rieder, 'Piranesi's "Diverse Maniere"', *Burlington Magazine*, CXV, May 1973, pp. 309ff.

31 See Stampfle, *op. cit.*, p. 139, no. 106; H. Thomas, *The Drawings of Piranesi*, London and New York, 1954, pp. 52–3, no. 49.

32 For the influence of furniture excavated at Herculaneum and Pompeii on European eighteenth-century design see the exhibition catalogue, *The Age of Neo-Classicism*, Burlington House, London, 1972, *passim*.

33 See Jones, *op. cit.*, pp. 258–9, no. 99.

34 See Fischer, 'Piranesis radiertes Oeuvre'.

35 See Stampfle, *op. cit.*, p. 134, no. 63.

36 Sir W. Hamilton's letter to Piranesi from Naples, 3 October 1767 (now in the Pierpont Morgan Library), acknowledges receipt of proofs of certain plates later published in the *Diverse Maniere*.

37 Among the motifs of the Berlin sheet (see Fischer, 'Piranesis radiertes Oeuvre') associated with Piranesi's furniture designs later published in the *Diverse Maniere* are an *acerra*, or ceremonial incense box, with three clawed feet, which appears in relief to either side of the chimneypiece in pl. 187: H. Focillon, *Giovanni Battista Piranesi, essai de catalogue raisonné de son oeuvre*, Paris, 1918, no. 883. Other motifs are associated with the two chimneypiece designs: Focillon nos. 871 and 901. On the verso of the sheet is a study for the title page to the *Lapides Capitolini*, dedicated to Clement XIII and published in 1762.

38 Information kindly communicated by Mr Brinsley Ford.

39 See W. Rieder, 'Piranesi at Gorhambury', *Burlington Magazine*, CXVII, September 1975, pp. 582ff.

40 See Stampfle, *op. cit.*, p. 138, no. 97; Thomas, *op. cit.* p. 52, no. 48.

41 This letter is quoted from J. H. Jesse (ed.), *George Selwyn and his Contemporaries*, London, 1882, p. 312.

42 For a discussion of Egyptian taste in European art see N. Pevsner and S. Lang, 'The Egyptian Revival', in Pevsner, *Studies in Art, Architecture and Design*, London, 1968, I, pp. 213ff.; and for Piranesi's conception and pioneering use of it, see Wittkower, 'Piranesi and Eighteenth-century Egyptomania' in *Studies in the Italian Baroque*, pp. 259ff.

43 See L. Salerno, *Piazza di Spagna*, Rome, 1967, *passim*.

44 According to Piranesi's letter to Hollis, now at the Society of Antiquaries and attached to their copy of the *Diverse Maniere*: 'Vederete in quest'Opera usato cio che peranche in questo genere non era conosciuto. L'Architettura Egiziana, per la prima volta apparisce; la prima volta, dico, perchè in ora il mondo ha sempre creduto non esservi altro che piramidi, guglie, e giganti, escludendo non esservi parti sufficienti per adornare e sostenere questo sistema d'architettura.' (You will see employed in this work something hitherto unknown in the genre. Egyptian architecture appears here for the first time; the first time, because until now the world has always believed that there was nothing in Egypt but pyramids, obelisks and colossi, and that this system of architecture had insufficient elements to adorn and sustain it.) As quoted in Pevsner and Lang, *op. cit.*, p. 216.

45 Among Piranesi's likely published sources were the travel book by F. L. Norden (*Travels in Nubia and Egypt*, 1755) and the antiquarian works by Montfauçon and Caylus.

46 B. Ford (ed.), 'The memoirs of Thomas Jones', *Walpole Society*, XXXII, 1946–8: Dec. 1776.

47 See note 37.

48 *Diverse Maniere*, p. 15.

49 Piranesi's attitude towards design is compared with the more conventional approach of Vanvitelli in J. Wilton-Ely, 'The relationship between Giambattista Piranesi and Luigi Vanvitelli in eighteenth-century architectural theory and practice', *Atti del Congresso Vanvitelliano (1973)*, Naples (in press).

50 James Barry's letter to Burke of 8 April 1769 is published in J. Barry, *Works*, London, 1809, I, pp. 160–61.

51 From the 'Advertisement' of Horace Walpole, *Anecdotes of Painting in England*, London, 1786 (4th ed.), IV, p. 398.

VII The Closing Years

1 According to Legrand (*Nouvelles de l'estampe*, no. 5, 1969, p. 214), among those who restored antiquities for Piranesi were Cardelli, Jacquietti and Franzoni. In addition to these, who also worked for the Vatican Museums, Piranesi used the services of his associate Cavaceppi, who established a prosperous business of his own as featured in the two volumes *Raccolta di Antiche Statue restaurate da Bartolomeo Cavaceppi*, Rome, 1768–72. See also A. Michaelis, *Ancient Marbles in Great Britain*, Cambridge, 1882, *passim*.

2 For the dealing activities of Cavaceppi, see Michaelis, *op. cit.*; for those of Thomas Jenkins see also Michaelis, *op. cit.*; T. Ashby, 'Thomas Jenkins in Rome', *Papers of the British School at Rome*, VI, 1913, pp. 487ff.; S. Rowland Pierce, 'Thomas Jenkins in Rome', *Antiquaries' Journal*, XLV, 1965, pt II, pp. 200ff.; B. Ford, 'Thomas Jenkins: Banker, Dealer and Unofficial English Agent', *Apollo*, XCIX, June 1974, pp. 416ff.; for those of Gavin Hamilton see Michaelis, *op. cit.*; A. H. Smith, 'Gavin Hamilton's letters to Charles Townley', *Journal of Hellenic Studies*, XXI, 1901, pp. 306ff.

3 S. Howard, 'An antiquarian hand-list and the beginnings of the Pio-Clementino', *Eighteenth Century Studies*, University of California at Davis, VII, no. 1, Autumn 1973, pp. 40ff. On this sheet among the Vatican Ferrajoli MSS. occurs *Cavalier Piranesi, accanto il portone Tomati in strada felice*. In the Status Animarum MSS., S. Andrea delle Fratte, 1761–78, is listed *G. B. Piranesi venezo, incis, 40, Pal. Tomati via Felice*.

4 Smith, *op. cit.*, pp. 307ff.

5 D. Stillman, 'Chimney-pieces for the English Market. A thriving business in late eighteenth-century Rome', *Art Bulletin*, LIX, no. 1, March 1977, pp. 85–94.

6 The Thorpe letters are mainly in the muniment room of Hook Manor, Donhead St Andrew, Wiltshire, and some of them are at Ugbrooke Park, Devon. Information kindly communicated by Mr Howard Colvin, to whom the author is indebted for the various references made.

7 A. Rowan, 'Wedderburn Castle, Berwickshire', *Country Life*, 8 August 1974, p. 356.

8 W. Rieder, 'Piranesi at Gorhambury', *Burlington Magazine*, CXVII, September 1975, pp. 582ff.

9 For the activities of James Byres see J. Fleming, *Connoisseur Year Book*, 1959, pp. 24–7; B. Ford, 'James Byres: Principal Antiquarian for the English Visitors to Rome', *Apollo*, XCIX, June 1974, pp. 446.

10 Rieder, *op. cit.*, p. 586, *n.* 21. The two vases purchased by the Walters from Piranesi are illustrated in the *Vasi*: H. Focillon, *Giovanni Battista Piranesi, essai de catalogue raisonné de son oeuvre*, Paris, 1918, no. 675(?) and no. 690.

11 For the Warwick vase see Michaelis, *op. cit.*, pp. 663–4. Three of the *Vasi* plates are devoted to it: Focillon, *op. cit.*, nos. 602–4.

12 A. Geffroy, 'Essai sur la formation des collections d'antiques de la Suède', *Revue Archaeologique*, XXIX, 1896, p. 27; E. Kjellberg, 'Piranesis antiksamling i Nationalmuseum', *Nationalmusei Årsbok*, 2, 1920, p. 159. In Francesco Piranesi's list of items sold to Stockholm, compiled in 1793 and published in the preceding article, the Monument of Augustus Urbanus appears as no. 20 with restoration by Malatesta.

13 P. Gusman, *La Villa Impériale de Tibur*, Paris, 1904, pp. 29, 253–7.

14 Gusman, *op. cit.*, pp. 256–7; M. McCarthy, 'Sir Roger Newdigate and Piranesi', *Burlington Magazine*, CXIV, July 1972, pp. 466ff.

15 F. de Clarac, *Musée de Sculpture Antique et Moderne*, Paris, 1841, ii, pt 1, pp. 411–12.

16 D. Stillman, 'Robert Adam and Piranesi', *Essays in the History of Architecture presented to Rudolf Wittkower* (ed. D. Fraser), London and New York, 1967, pp. 197ff.

17 J. Fleming, *Robert Adam and his Circle in Edinburgh and London*, London and New York, 1962, p. 258.

18 T. J. McCormick and J. Fleming, 'A Ruin Room by Clérisseau', *Connoisseur*, CXLIX, 1962, pp. 239ff; T. J. McCormick, 'An unknown collection of drawings by C. L. Clérisseau', *Journal of the Society of Architectural Historians*, XX, 1963, pp. 125–6, repr. fig. 9.

19 Vol. II of *The Works in Architecture*, containing Piranesi's four plates of Syon, first appeared in five instalments before being published in one volume in 1779.

20 *Parere su l'Architettura*, p. 13.

21 *The Works in Architecture of Robert and James Adam* (ed. R. Oresko), London and New York, 1975, p. 46.

22 For a discussion of the development of Adam's chimneypiece designs see Stillman, 'Robert Adam and Piranesi', pp. 303ff.

23 E. Harris, *The Furniture of Robert Adam*, London, 1963, p. 102; C. Musgrave, *Adam and Hepplewhite Furniture*, London and New York, 1966, p. 210; M. Tomlin, *Catalogue of Adam*

Period Furniture, Victoria and Albert Museum, London, 1972, p. 106.

24 Stillman, 'Robert Adam and Piranesi', p. 203; *idem, The Decorative Works of Robert Adam*, London and New York, 1966, pp. 59–60, 75–6.

25 For the context of Delafosse and Neufforge in the Louis XVI style, see S. Eriksen, *Early Neo-Classicism in France*, London, 1974, pp. 170, 207.

26 Delafosse's chimneypiece design is discussed in the exhibition catalogue *Piranèse et les Français: 1740–1790*, Académie de France à Rome, 1976, p. 113 (54E).

27 For the design of the andirons see R.P. Wunder, 'Bagatelle and two drawings by Bélanger in the Cooper Union', *Connoisseur*, CXLVIII, 1961, pp. 171ff., fig. 2; and for the commode see J. Stern, *A l'ombre de Sophie Arnould, François-Joseph Bélanger, Architecte des Menus-Plaisirs*, Paris, 1930, I, repr. opp. p. 60.

28 G. Schéfer, 'Giovanni Battista Piranesi, un rénovateur de l'art décoratif', *Les Arts*, April 1913, pp. 18ff.

29 H. Thomas, *The Drawings of Piranesi*, London and New York, 1954, pp. 24–5, 57–8; *idem*, 'Piranesi und Pompeii', *Kunstmuseets Årsskrift*, 1952–5, pp. 13–28.

30 Thomas, *The Drawings of Piranesi*, p. 25.

31 *Ibid.*, pp. 22–4, 55–7.

32 S. Lang, 'The early publications of the Temples at Paestum', *Journal of the Warburg and Courtauld Institutes*, XIII, January–June 1950, pp. 48ff.; S. Lang and N. Pevsner, 'The Doric Revival', in Pevsner, *Studies in Art, Architecture and Design*, London, 1968, I, pp. 200–201; J.M. Crook, *The Greek Revival: Neo-Classical Attitudes in British Architecture, 1760–1870*, London, 1972, *passim*; M. McCarthy, 'Documents on the Greek Revival in Architecture', *Burlington Magazine*, CXIV, November 1972, pp. 760ff.

33 For Angelini's statue see J. Wilton-Ely, 'A bust of Piranesi by Nollekens', *Burlington Magazine*, CXVIII, August 1976, pp. 593–5.

34 C. Pietrangeli, 'Sull'iconografia di Giovanni Battista Piranesi', *Bollettino dei Musei Comunali di Roma*, an. 1, 1954, nos. 3–4, pp. 40ff.

35 For the life and works of Francesco Piranesi see exhibition catalogue *Giovanni Battista e Francesco Piranesi*, Calcografia Nazionale, Rome, 1967–8, *passim*.

36 Geffroy, *op. cit.*, pp. 1ff.; Kjellberg, *op. cit.*, pp. 115ff.

37 Legrand, *Nouvelles de l'estampe, op. cit.*, pp. 191ff.

38 See N. Pevsner, 'Goethe and Architecture', *Studies in Art, Architecture and Design*, pp. 165–73. The quotation is taken from Goethe, *Italian Journey, 1786–1788* (translation of the *Italienische Reise* by W.H. Auden and E. Mayer), London, 1962, p. 304.

39 M. Binney, 'Great Packington Church', *Country Life*, 8 July 1971, pp. 110ff. The Doric columns, although undoubtedly inspired by Piranesi, were taken from illustrations of the order from the Temple of Neptune in Thomas Major's *Ruines de Paestum*, 1768.

40 Specific borrowings by Ledoux from Piranesi's *Ichnographia* are examined in O. Reutersvärd, *The neo-classic temple of virility and the buildings with a phallic-shaped ground plan*, University of Lund, Sweden, 1971, pp. 10ff.

41 For the influence of Piranesi on Ledoux's *barrières* see J. Wilton-Ely, 'Vision and Design: Piranesi's "fantasia" and the Graeco-Roman controversy', *Les actes du colloque 'Piranèse et les Français: 1740–1790'* (1976), Académie de France à Rome (in press).

42 J.-M. Pérouse de Montclos, *Etienne-Louis Boullée, 1728–1799: de l'architecture classique à l'architecture révolutionnaire*, Paris, 1969, p. 178.

43 'That men, unacquainted with the remains of Ancient Buildings, should indulge in licentious and whimsical combinations is not a matter of surprise, but that a man, who had passed all his life in the bosom of Classic Art, and in the contemplation of the majestic ruins of Ancient Rome, observing their sublime and grand combinations, a man who had given innumerable examples how truly he felt the value of the noble Simplicity of those buildings, that such a man, with such examples before his eyes, should have mistaken Confusion for Intricacy, and undefined lines and forms for Classical Variety, is scarcely to be believed; yet such was Piranesi.' J. Soane, *Lectures on Architecture* (ed. A.T. Bolton), London, 1929, p. 131.

44 For the uncertain circumstances relating to Soane's acquisition of the fifteen Paestum drawings by Piranesi see McCarthy, *op. cit.*, p. 766. One of the two Piranesi *capricci* bought from the Adam sale by Soane is discussed and illustrated by Thomas, *op. cit.*, p. 47, fig. 36.

45 C. Proudfoot and D. Watkin, 'The furniture of C.H. Tatham', *Country Life*, 8 June 1972, pp. 1481ff.

46 *Ibid.*, p. 1482.

47 D. Watkin, *Thomas Hope (1769–1831) and the Neo-classical Idea*, London, 1968, pp. 114–18, 210–11.

48 The extent of Piranesi's influence upon the Louis XVI and Empire styles is discussed in a review of H. Mayor, *Piranesi*, and the ensuing correspondence in the *Times Literary Supplement*, February–July 1953, pp. 100, 413, 445, 461, 477 and 493.

49 F. Mancini, *Scenografia italiana dal Rinascimento all'età romantica*, Milan, 1966.

50 Robert's painting is discussed in the exhibition catalogue *The Eye of Jefferson*, National Gallery of Art, Washington D.C., 1976, pp. 169–170 (281).

51 Apart from possessing a strong affinity with Piranesi's vision, Turner used the *Carceri* as the basis for a couple of lecture diagrams. See exhibition catalogue *J. M. W. Turner*, Royal Academy, London, 1975, p. 181 (B54 b & c).

52 J. Summerson, 'J. M. Gandy' in *Heavenly Mansions and other essays on architecture*, London, 1949, and New York, 1950.

53 Martin painted *Belshazzar's Feast* in 1821 and after its highly successful exhibition at the British Institution published mezzotints of it in 1826 and 1832. See C. Johnstone, *John Martin*, London and New York, 1974, p. 37.

54 Quoted in Johnstone, *op. cit.*

55 The influence of Piranesi upon the early Romantics in England is examined in J. Andersen, 'Giant Dreams: Piranesi's influence in England', *English Miscellany*, 3, Rome, 1952, pp. 49ff. For a discussion of the French Romantic writers' attitude towards Piranesi see M. Yourcenar, 'Le cerveau noir de Piranèse', *Sous bénéfice d'inventaire*, Paris, 1962, and L. Keller, *Piranèse et les romantiques français: Le mythe des escaliers en spirale*, Paris, 1966.

56 Victor Hugo, *Les rayons et les ombres*, Paris, 1839, XIII.

57 According to G. L. Bianconi in his 'Elogio storico del cavaliere Giambattista Piranesi', *Opere* II, Milan, 1802, pp. 133–4: 'Oh how different is *the design from the actual execution of the building!* The work turned out to be overloaded with ornaments which, even though taken from antiquity, were not in harmony with one another. The church of the Priorato will certainly please many, as it must above all have pleased Piranesi who always regarded it as a masterpiece, but it wouldn't have pleased either Vitruvius or Palladio if they returned to Rome.' Francesco Milizia classified the Aventine buildings among those works which provoked such disgust 'that their designers are not worthy of mention': *Roma nelle belle arti del disegno*, Bassano, 1787, p. 197.

58 Legrand, *Nouvelles de l'estampe, op. cit.*, p. 222.

VEDUTE DI ROMA

Captions on page 297

VEDVTE DI ROMA DISEGNATE ED INCISE DA GIAMBATTISTA PIRANESI ARCHITETTO VENEZIANO

Veduta della Basilica e Piazza di S. Pietro in Vaticano

1. Palazzo Pontificio, fabricato da Sisto V.
2. Scala Regia, Architettura di Bramante Lazzari, e
dipinta da Raffaele d'Urbino.
3. Guglia eretta da Sisto V.
4. Veduta tutta di un pezzo di monte Orientale.

Veduta interna della Basilica di S. Pietro in Vaticano.

Spaccato interno della Basilica di S. Paolo fuori delle Mura, eretta da Costantino Magno, divisa in cinque Navate co' sua Crociata. Ottanta Colonne di marmo arreggevenate di varie colonne temporali, dall'ordine di Adriano Imperatore, sostengono le Navate separando, ed ornandizzasi, interno la Crociata, interno alla quale come interno li Stati delle maggior Colonnari, Altre Colonne di erugidio sono spario per la Crociata, interno alle quale si Stati delle maggior li restanti di tutti i Romani Pontefici Romani con altri Pitture antiche già quasi consumate dal tempo. Il Parlamento delle Navate è formato di troti pezzi di marmo, le restanti Statue, di alte Edifici antichi consumamente divoti, et vivono.

Veduta della Basilica di S. Giovanni Laterano

1 Cappella fabbricata da Clemente XII. Corsini.   4 Guglia Egiziana giacente   Architettura di Alessandro Galilei.
2 Palazzo fabbricato da Sisto V con Conser.   5 Mura della Città
3 Scala Santa   Piranesi del Sc.

Veduta della Basilica di S.ᵃ Maria Maggiore con le due Fabbriche laterali di detta Basilica

1. Colonna antica del Tempio della Pace
   quivi eretta da Paolo V.
2. Ospitale di S. Antonio Abate.

La Facciata di mezzo Architettura del Cav. Ferdinando Fuga.
Piranesi Del. Sculp.

Veduta della Piazza del Popolo

Veduta della Piazza di Monte Cavallo

1. Palazzo Pontificio
2. Palazzo della Famiglia Pontificia
3. Statue Colossali rappresentanti Alessandro, che doma il Bucefalo
4. Quartiere de' Soldati, e Scuderia Pontificia
5. Palazzo Rospigliosi

opere di Prassitele, e Fidia Scultori Greci

Piranesi del. et sculp.

1. S. Agnese
2. Palazzo Pamfili
3. Fontana con Guglia Egiziaca archit.o di Bernini

Veduta di Piazza Navona

a le rovine del Circo Agonale

4   S. Giacomo de Spagnoli.   28.
5   Fontana Architettura di Michelangelo.
Piranesi del. sc.
Presso l'autore a Strada Felice nel Palazzo Tomati vicino alla Trinità de monti.

10

Veduta della Piazza della Rotonda

1 Pantheon fabbricato da Marc'Agrippa oggi S. Maria ad Martyres   3 Fontana
2 Fontana con Guglia Egizia architettura di Filippo Barigioni   4 Palazzo Crescenzi

Veduta della vasta Fontana di Trevi anticamente detta l'Acqua Vergine.
Architettura di Nicola Salvi.

Piranesi del Scolp

Veduta del Sepolcro di Cajo Cestio

1. Porta S. Paolo
2. Mura di Roma

Piranesi del.me

Veduta del Romano Campidoglio con Scalinata che và alla Chiesa d'Aracéli

Arch. Vetturai di Michelangelo Bonaroti

1. Palazzo del Senato Romano
2. Piazza ove si governano le Pittore anticke
3. Palazzo ove risiede il Governo, e Pittore
4. Palazzo equestre di Marco Aurelio di metallo Corintio

5. Statue Colossali antiche di Castore, e Polluce
6. Trofei di Mario
7. Colonna milliaria aurea
8. Leoncello di marmo Egizio

Piranesi Architetto Fecit

14

Veduta di Campo Vaccino

Veduta degli avanzi di due Triclinij che appartenevano alla Casa aurea di Nerone, presi erroneamente per i Tempio del Sole, e della Luna, e d'Iside, e Serapide. 1. Avanzo del Triclinio a uso dell'estate.   2. Avanzo dell'altro
a uso dell'inverno.   Questi rimangono nel Giardino de' PP. di S. Francesca Romana in Campo Vaccino.

1. *Bucca fatta scavare da Sisto V, con recinto di muro, o Scala che discende al piano della Colonna.*

Colonna Trajana

2. *Chiesa del Nome di Maria.*
3. *Palazzo Bonelli.*

Piranesi fecit

1. Palazzo Ghigi
2. Piazza Colonna

Colonna Antonina

3. Strada del Corso

Veduta dell' Arco di Costantino, e dell' Anfiteatro Flavio detto il Colosseo.

1 Meta Sudante
2 Radice del Palatino

3 Vestigie delle Terme di Tito
4 Radice dell' Esquilino

Piranesi Architetto

VEDUTA DELL' ESTERNO DELLA GRAN BASILICA DI S. PIETRO IN VATICANO. Architettura di Michelagnolo Buonarota. Questa pianta in parte sopra i fondamenti del Circo Neroniano. 1 Luogo ove si lavorano i musaici di S. Pietro. 2 Sagrestia. viciene, a quella vicinità del terreno, a piedi l'Obelisco che era si vide nella Piazza di S. Pietro, e fuori e cadeva sulla Spina del Circo Nerone 4. Monte Vaticano. 5 Avanzi di Colonne di Granito e marmo. Parte, il quale rappresenta. 3 Ivi, gran Cupola, nella cima della quale vi vi la Palla di metallo. dentro cui si capisono, circa venti persone. A Abitazioni domestiche de' Sisto V. Prezzo Scudro ed una Felice nel pogium Roma viene alla Venuta da mezza.

1. *Fontana detta la Barcaccia, Architettura del Cav. Bernino.* 2. *Scalinata,*
da condursi sul monte Pincio. 3. *Chiesa col Monastero della SS. Trinità de' monti*
Uffiziata dai Frati Minimi di S. Francesco di Paola della nazione Francese. 4. *Strada*
del Babuino che va alla Piazza del Popolo.

Veduta di Piazza di Spagna.

Presso l'Autore a Strada Felice nel palazzo Tomati vicino alla Trinità de' monti.

Veduta del Porto di Ripetta.

1. S.Girolamo de Schiavoni.　2. Dogana di Ripetta.　3. Colonne, o mete, nelle quali sono segnate le maggiori escrescenze del Tevere.　4. Palazzo del Principe Borghese.　5. Stalle dello Messo Principe.　6. Palazzo della sua Famiglia.　7. Collegio Clementino.

Piranesi Architetto fec.

22

23

TEATRO DI MARCELLO.

Questo fù fabricato da Augusto, e dedicato a Marcello suo Nipote.   Pianori Architetto.
1. Palazzo Orsini ristaurato da Baldassarre da Siena Architetto.   2. Capella di S. Maria in Campitelli.
Presso l'Autore a strada Felice nel Palazzo Tomati vicino alla Trinità de monti.

TEMPIO DI BACCO

Ogni S.Costanza fuori delle Mura. 1. Colonne n.º 24 d'Giro antiche. 4. Candelieri antichi di marmo. 5. Pitture moderne e Urna
nite che regiono il Tempio. 2. Mosaici antichi. 3. Finestre di Porfido tutta d'un pezzo lunga pal. 11. alta p.º 8 e largo. e. lle p.º 5.

Regnes Architetto fec.

Veduta del Sito, ov'era l'antico Foro Romano.

Veduta della Curia Ostilia.

VEDUTA DEGLI AVANZI DEL TEMPIO DELLA PACE.

Veduta del Tempio della Fortuna virile.

Piranesi Architetto fec.

1. S. Lorenzo in Miranda di Speziali

Veduta del Tempio di Antonino e Faustina in Campo Vaccino.

Questa fu eretta da Sisto V. nella Piazza di S.Gio.Laterano.
1. Palazzo fabricato da Sisto V. ora Conservatorio di Zitelle.

2. Scala Santa.
3. Rovine di Acquedotti antichi.

Piranesi Architetto fec.

OBELISCO EGIZIO

31

Arco di Settimio Severo.

33

Veduta dell'Atrio del Portico di Ottavia.

1. S. Angelo in Pescaria. 2. Interno dell'Atrio
3. Tavoloni di marmo, che coprivano l'Atrio, sopra

colonne, le quali si spezze in piede un pezzo di marmo,
intagliato di un'Aquila in basso rilievo. 4. Pitture moderne.

Veduta interna dell' Atrio del Portico di Ottavia

Questa fu fabbricata sulle rovine della Curia di
Antonino Pio nel suo Foro.
1. Avanzo di Colonne rimaste, oggi mezzo
   interrate nella nuova Fabbrica.
2. Architrave antico ristorato.
3. Cornicione, ed Ordine Attico nuovamente rifatto.

4. Abitazione moderna.
5. Collegio Bergamasco.
6. Quartiere di Soldati.
7. Strada chiusa al Corso.

Veduta della Dogana di Terra a Piazza di Pietra.

Piranesi Architetto.

Veduta dell'avanzo del Castello, che avanza una porzione dell'acqua Giulia dal condotto principale, parte ne diffondeva in una magnifica Fontana che si era aderente, e decorata da M.Agrippa frà gli altri ornamenti de Trofei d'Augusto che nel 1714 si vedeva nel Campidoglio, e parte ne tramandava per via di Portici sul Monte Celio. a Porzione di barbacani refatta dai moderni. 3 Diramazioni dette epoca del Castello, la quali romandavano l'acqua nella fontana, e per il Celio Muri, e legno moderni. 4 Villa Palombara moderna 5 Villa Palombara moderna. I luogo dove si fecero tutti i detti Trofei.

VEDUTA del Mausoleo d'Elio Adriano (ora chiamato Castello S. Angelo). A Avanzo del Mausoleo antico. B Coperture moderna di mattoni sopra l'antico Mausoleo. C Rocchi di Artiglieria collocata nel Corridore, che gira all'intorno. D Loggia diumerale, opposta alla Facciata di dentro del Castello. E Carceri per le persone riguardevoli. F Archivio. G Magazzini. H Angolo di mezzdi. I Baluardi di mezzi. K Corridore fabbricato sopra l'ordine delle stele; che si fece aprire da Urbano VIII. Quello Corridore s'estinue da gran numero i Fabbricati e del Palazzo Vaticano sino dentro al Mausoleo. L Ponte levatore del Corridore. M Polveriera. N Cordonata la quale porta sopra l'Terrapieno. O Recinto di Mura, e Baluardi, che serrando il Mausoleo. P Armeria. Q Abitazioni per gli Ufficiali, e Soldati. R Albera Polveriera.

Presso l'Autore a Strada Felice vicino alla Trinità de' Monti.

Piranesi Archit. dis. ed inc.

Veduta della Basilica di S. Paolo fuor delle mura, eretta da Costantino Magno. 1. Laterali rustici della Basilica che dimostrano l'opera esterna del detto Imperadore. 2. Ornamenti, Musaici, e finestre fatti dai successori Cesari, e ristaurati da' Sommi Pontefici. 3. Portico ultimamente aggiuntovi sotto il Pontificato di Benedetto XIII. 4. Porta finta 5. Parte Settentrionale della Basilica verso Roma, e Monti sotto de' quali è uno degl' ingressi delle Catacombe degli antichi Cristiani.

Piranesi F.

Veduta della Facciata di dietro della Basilica di S. Maria Maggiore.

Veduta della Facciata della Basilica di S. Croce in Gerusalemme

Giovani Batista Piranesi Architetto dis dine

1. *Monastero de Monaci Cisterciensi* 2. *Muro moderno, fabbricato sulle rovine dell'Anfiteatro Castrense.* 3. *Avanti del Tempio della Speranza Vecchia.*

Veduta del Castello dell'Acqua Paola sul Monte Aureo

Veduta del Palazzo fabbricato sul Quirinale per le Segreterie de Brevi e della Sacra Consulta
Architettura del Cavalier Ferdinando Fuga

1 Corpo di Guardia de' Cavaleggieri. 2 Corpo di Guardia de' Corazzieri. 3 Palazzo Apostolico. 5 Monastero e Chiesa di 3 Palazzo del Sig.r Principe Rospigliosi.
4 Corpo di Guardia de' Soldati Rossi. S.ta Maria Maddalena. Gio Battista Piranesi Architetto dis e inc
7 Porta Pia sulle mura Urbane

42

43

VEDUTA nella Via del Corso, DEL PALAZZO DELL'ACCADEMIA istituita da LUIGI XIV. RE DI FRANCIA per i Nazionali Francesi studiosi della Pittura, Scultura, e Architettura; colla liberal permissione al Pubblico di eser-
citarvisi in tali arti per il comodo della esposizione quotidiana del Nudo, e dei Modelli delle più rare Statue ed altri segni della Romana Magnificenza, si antichi, che moderni.   1. Stanze ove sono esposti i modelli della Colonna Trajana, Statue Eque-
stri, Pedestri, Rustiche, e Bassirilievi.   2. Stanze per l'esposizione del Nudo.   3. Appartamento Regio ornato parimente di Modelli.   4. Appartamento del Signor Direttore.   5. Palazzo Panfilj.   6. Via del Corso.   7. Porta del Popolo.
Gio. Batta Piranesi Architetto dis. e inc.

44

Veduta del Palazzo Odescalchi

1. *Palazzo Colonna.* 2. *Basilica de' SS. XII. Apostoli.* 3. *Convento de' PP. Serviti di S. Marcello.* 6. *Piazza de' SS. Apostoli.*
2. *Convento de' PP. Minor. Conventuali.* 4. *Palazzo Muti.* 5. *Convento de' PP. Serviti di S. Marcello.*
Piano d'autore. *Strada Felice nel palazzo Tomati vicino alla Trinità de' monti.* *Ses. Bass. Piranesi deli. F.*

Veduta del Porto di Ripa Grande

1. Dogana grande. 2. Dogana del pesce. 3. Arsenale. 4. Granari dell' Annona. 5. Avanzi di una delle più dell' antico Ponte Sublicio, già il Licone, e rifatto po-
3. Ospizio Apostolico di S.Michele, e Casa degl' Invalidi, e educazione nelle arti seia di pietra da Emilio, e ristorato dai Cesari. 7. Avanzi delle Saline antiche.
e correzione de' Fanciulli, e di condanna delle Donne delinquenti. 8. Avanzi di muri de' tempi bassi falsamente supposti del detto Ponte Sublicio.

Presso l'autore a Strada Felice nel palazzo Tomati vicino alla Trinità de' monti. Apresi due paoli.

Veduta del Ponte Salario

Veduta degli avanzi del **Foro di Nerva**

95

Veduta del Tempio di Giove Tonante

Veduta del Tempio di Cibele a Piazza della Bocca della Verità

Veduta del Tempio di Bacco, inoggi Chiesa di S. Urbano, distante due miglia da Roma, fuori della Porta di S. Sebastiano. Esso e'il più intero di questa, forma che sia rimaso a Roma, stconsi noltri. La sua Aratti governati di nell'esterno che nell'interno. ECTIAL- AIONYCOY- AΠΡΟΝΙΑΝΟC-ΙΣΡΟΦΑΝΤΗC: Ara di Bacco, Aproniano Sacerdote. 1. Muri fra gl'Intercolonnj del Pronao, e la delli peranche nel Pronao colla iscrizione impiegaren per lo stesso fine. 3. Avanza dell' antica cura dell' Editton. 2. Chiari delle catene di ferro impiegaten per lo stesso fine. 3. Avanza dell' antica cura dell' Editton. Pani da la ligne VIII per riparan la revina del Tem.

Gio. Batt. Piranesi Arch. F.

51
50

Veduta dell' Arco di Tito

Edificio eretto a questo Imperadore dopo la di lui morte in memoria della distruzione di Gerosolima, e vengase parte de suoi ornamenti. A Bassirilievi indi . . . *maggior parte della* . . . . *stesso Cesare espressa in un' Aquila che le scolleva al Cielo. C Orti Farnesiani* . . . . *D Chiesa di S. Sebastiane. E Rovine della Casa Augustana sul Palatino* . . . . *canti il di lui trionfo: adornati colle spoglie del Tempio di Salomone. B Apoteosi della* . . . . . . *G. Strada che conduce a S. Bonaventura*

Presso l'autore a Strada Felice vicino alla Trinità de' Monti. A paoli due e mezzo. Gio: Batta Piranesi Architetto disegnò e incise

Veduta della Basilica di S.Lorenzo fuor delle mura

1. Via Tiburtina

Piranesi F.

Veduta del Castello dell'Acqua Felice
presso le Terme Diocleziane.   2 Chiesa di S.Maria, della Vittoria

Veduta sul Monte Quirinale del Palazzo dell'Eccellentissima Casa Barberini, Architettura del Cav.r Bernino

55

Veduta del Campidoglio di fianco

Piramide di C. Cestio

Veduta dell' Anfiteatro Flavio, detto il Colosseo

Veduta della Basilica di S. Sebastiano fuori delle mura di Roma su la via Appia

M·AGRIPPA·L·F·COS·TERTIVM·FECIT

Veduta del Pantheon d'Agrippa oggi Chiesa di S. Maria ad Martyres

Veduta del tempio della Sibilla in Tivoli

61

ALTRA VEDUTA DEL TEMPIO DELLA SIBILLA IN TIVOLI

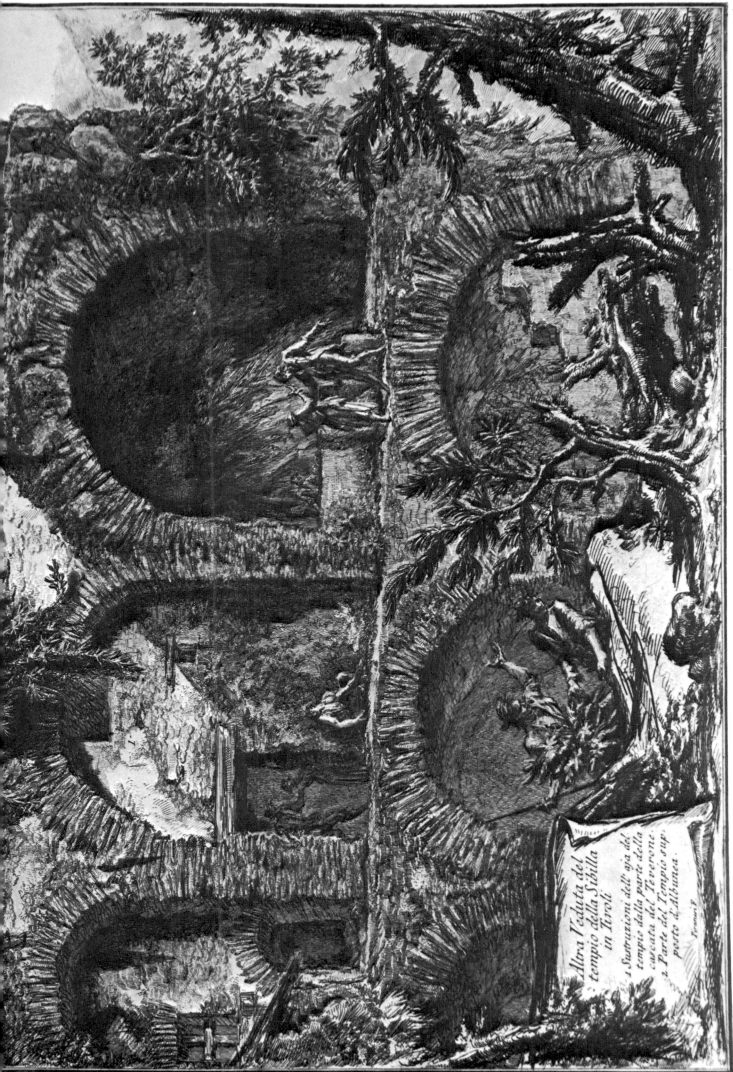

Altra Veduta del
tempio della Sibilla
in Tivoli

1 Sustruzioni dell' già del
tempio dalla parte della
caduta del Teverone.
2 Parte del Tempio sup.-
posto d'Albunea.

Piranesi f.

Veduta del Ponte Molle sul Tevere due miglia lontan da Roma

Avanzi della Villa di Mecenate
a Tivoli costruita di travertini
a opera incerta

A Capitello il sede rimaste interio
B Avanzi dintonaco dipinto a minio
Piranesi F

Veduta delle due Chiese, l'una detta¹ della ⌐
presso³ la Colonna Tra┐

Piranesi F.

na di Loreto l'altra 2 del Nome di Maria
q. Salita al monte Quirinale

Si vende presso l'autore a paoli due e mezzo

Veduta del Ponte Lugano su l'Aniene
nella via Tiburtina risarcito ne' tempi bassi
A Sepolcro della famiglia Plauzia

Veduta del Tempio, detto della Tosse
su la Via Tiburtina, un miglio vicino a Tivoli
Piranesi fece e inc.

Veduta interna del Tempio della Tosse [...] costruito di
mattoni e di tufi li Muri de' quali erano state rivestite le pareti in tempo delli

Tempio antico volgarmente detto della Salute
su la via d'Albano, cinque miglia lontan da Roma. l'opera con tutt'i suoi
ornamenti è di terra cotta, e'l capitello è composito, a differenza di tr.gli altri.

A Veduta del Sepolcro di Prisone Licinicano e l'antica via appia, oltre qui acquidott di ferre di mezza via di Albano: è vi lavori e un di terra cetto B.Sepolcro della famiglia Cornelia, quindetto, de' suoi ornamenti. C.Omic di altri antichi Sepolcri

Veduta del Tempio ottangolare di Minerva Medica
A già era ironicamente ornato di marmi, B di musaici bianchi, ed esteriormente
coperto di stucco C Resno d'altre edifizi congiunto posteriormente col Tempio.

VEDVTA DELLA CASCATA DI TIVOLI

Rovine delle Terme Antoniniane

Rovina del Nettuno sia della gran sala
delle terme Antoniniane

Veduta interna dell'antico Tempio di Bacco in oggi Chiesa di S. Urbano due miglia distante da Roma fuori di porta S. Sebastiano. Le pareti interiori di questo Tempio sono le uniche, che conservano l'antica loro Architettura, benche spogliate in parte di suoi ornamenti di Stucco. A Pitture à tempo bassi. B Avanzi di antichi Profoli di stucco. C Avanzi di Lacunari di Stucco parimente antichi. D Altare moderno. E Ara antica di Bacco. F Scala per la quale si scende ad una stanza sotterranea. Cavalier Piranesi dieg. ed inc.

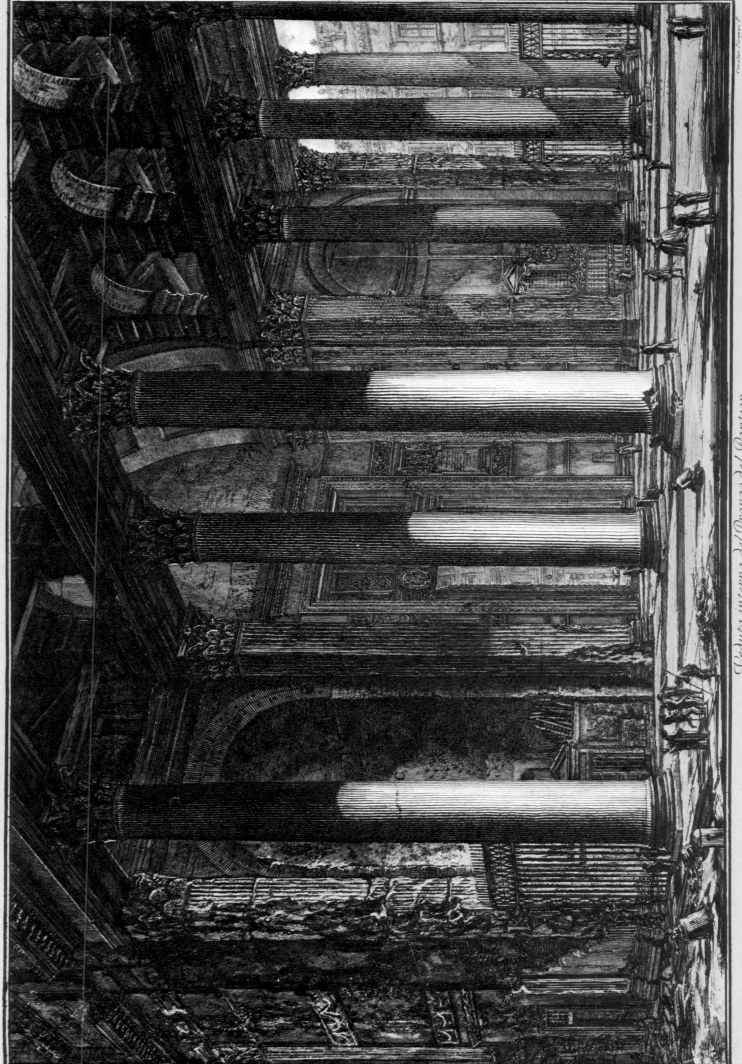

Veduta interna del Pronao del Panteon

Sostenuto da sedici colonne di granito, sodo i pezzi, grosse di diametro palmi 6 6 alte palmi 63 8. A Pilastri architravi, l'aggetto della porta composti di gran macigni di marmo greco. B Lacunari di legname anticamente di bronzo, tolta via da Urbano VIII e fatti rifondere per formare la confessione di S. Pietro in Vaticano. C Macigni dove erano collocate statue di Agrippa quali erano incrostati di marmo greco. D'Archi di Agrippa quali erano incrostati d'marmo greco. D'Archi da altre furono levate le lastre di marmo greco per adornare il Museo Sagro nel Vaticano. E Memorie di Urbano VIII F Porta di bronzo trasportata da altro edifizio antico, e in parte nuovamente ristaurata nel detto anno 1757. G Interno del Tempio che nel tempo di Benedetto XIV l'anno 1757

Cavalier Piranesi F.

Altra veduta interna della Villa di Mecenate in Tivoli
A Stanze publiche. B Cave ne' quali erano le teste delle
trasature di felci, quali servivano anticamente per uso di abitazione.
Cavalier Piranesi inc.

Veduta interna del Panteon. Questo tempio, fabbricato da M. Agrippa, è di forma rotonda, la quanto à suo diametro. Il primo ordine è tutto intorno. Le stelle, Nome principale sono di gialli come le due della Tribuna guati, nate, sono state una cupola della premura dove situate sono. Le colonne ... di ricom con, di marmi, del Piano da verde. Il secondo ordine è ... di marmi, ... di profess, ... di septembre, le ... vengono nelle di M. Pantheon. M. Panch numerat numero, che le salemat di situali, come, si crede, il presente. L'altar maggiore con ... ambedue ancora il pavimento composte di avalli, di enamel, et profess.

Veduta interna della Basilica di
S. Maria Maggiore

Veduta interna della Basilica
di S. Giovanni Laterano 230

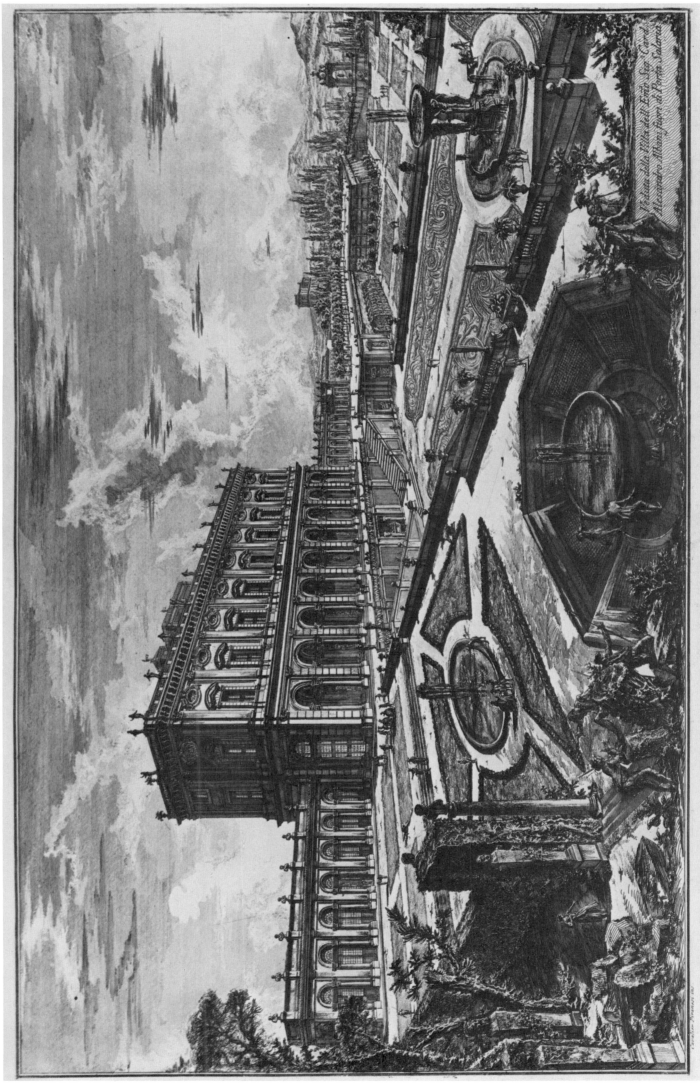

Avanzi del Tempio del Dio Canopo nella Villa Adriana in Tivoli. A. Nicchie, e fontane che vano rimanendo di tartaro. B. Volta ch' era ricoperta di mosaico bumbi e d'altri colori. C. Le pareti. C. erano rimessate d'opera di marmo. D. altre ch' erano di questi tempio d'ornamento di conserve d'acqua e di natazioni. Da tali contrassegni credesi ch'eesi adornare e contenere il Dio Nettuno. D. Due gran massigni caduti dalla Volta.

Veduta del Tempio di Ercole nella Città di Cora, dieci miglia lontano da Velletri

Cavalier Piranesi delin. e inc.

Rovine d'una Galleria
di Statue nella Villa Adriana à Tivoli

Veduta degli avanzi del Castro Pretorio nella Villa Adriana a Tivoli

VEDVTA DEGL'AVANZI
DEL FORO DI NERVA

VEDVTA DELL'ARCO DI COSTANTINO

SENATVS
POPVLVSQVE ROMANVS
DIVO TITO DIVI VESPASIANI F
VESPASIANO AVGVSTO

Veduta dell'Arco di Tito
1 Villa Farnese. 2 Avanzi del Tempio stato di
Giove Statore. 3 Monte Capitolino. 4 Rovine
del Tempio detto della Pace. Piranesi F.

Veduta dell' Arco di
Settimio Severo

Vaccino

8. *Avanzi del Tablino della Casa Aurea di Nerone volgarmente detti il Tempio della Pace.*

9. *Tempio di Romolo e Remo in oggi Chiesa de SS. Cosmo e Damiano.*
10. *Tempio di Antonino e Faustina.*

11. *Tazza antica di granito di un sol pezzo situata nel luogo dove una volta era il lago Curzio.*

Cavalier Piranesi del e inc.

Veduta della gran Piazza e Basilica di S. Pietro situata ove era anticamente il Circo e gl' Orti di Cajo e Nerone nella Valle Vaticana.

Veduta interna della Basilica di
S. Pietro in Vaticano vicino alla Tribuna

Veduta della Piazza di Monte Cavallo
1 *Palazzo Pontificio.* 2 *Strada che conduce a Porta Pia*
3 *Palazzo della Consulta.* 4 *Statue Colossali di*
Prasitele, e Fidia. 5 *Palazzi della Famiglia Pontificia*

Veduta in prospettiva della gran Fontana dell'Acqua Vergine detta di Trevi Architettura di Nicola Salvi

VEDVTA DELLA
VILLA ESTENSE
IN TIVOLI

Veduta del Palazzo
Farnese

Veduta di Piazza Navona sopra le rovine del Circo Agonale

Veduta del Tempio, detto
della Concordia
A des. A Vittore Greca

Altra Veduta degli avanzi del Pro=
nao del Tempio della Concordia.

Veduta della Piazza del Campidoglio

Avanzi di gran Sala appartenente al Castro Pretorio nel la Villa Adriana in Tivoli.
A. Tribunale ornato di nicchie.

Veduta degli avanzi superiori
delle Terme di Diocleziano
in S. Maria degli Angeli

Cavalier Piranesi

Veduta degli avanzi superiori delle Terme di Diocleziano

116

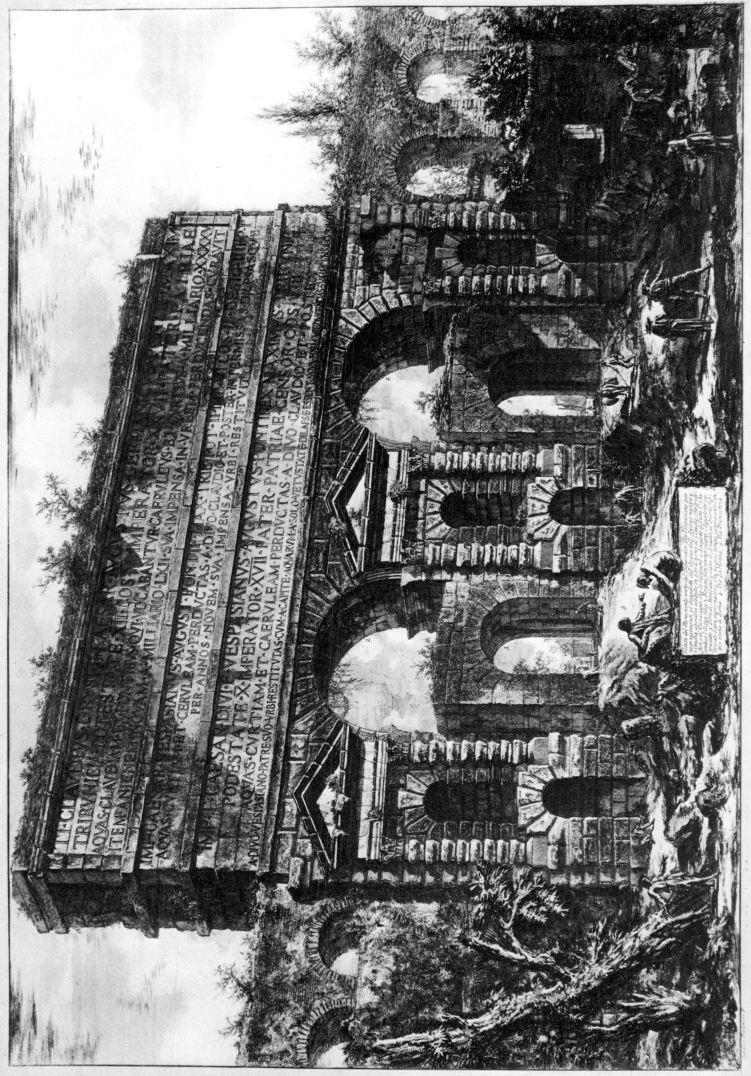

Veduta dell'insigne Basilica Vaticana coll'ampio Portico, e Piazza adiacente

CRISTO · SALVATORI · IN · HONOREM · S · IVDAE · ET · IVE · VANG

VEDUTA DELLE TERME DI TITO

VEDUTA delle antiche sostruzioni, fatte da Tarquinio Superbo dette il Bel Lido, e come altri erette da Marco Agrippa a tempi B Tempio di Cibele, o come altri d'Ercole, il quale ora situato nell'antico Foro Boario. C Avanzi delle antiche
Augusti, in occasione, ch'Egli, fece repurgare tutte le Cloache, fino al Tevere. A Sbocco della Cloaca Massima al medesimo Fiume. D Monistero e Chiesa di S. Alessio. Saline.
E Priorato della Sacra Religione di Malta.

125

VEDUTA degli Avanzi delle Fabbriche del Secondo
Piano delle Terme, di Tito.
A. Prime Piena. B. Avanzi del Teatro, che piantava
il 109

VEDUTA DEL PALAZZO STOPANI
Architettura di Raffaele d' Urbino.
i Disegn del Cav.   da Piranesi F.

VEDUTA in... *terna della Chiesa della Madonna degli Angioli, detta della Certosa che anticam. era la principal Sala delle Terme di Diocleziano. E stata nuova-mente abbellita...* &c.

Avanzi d'un antico Sepolcro oggi detto la Conocchia, che si vede poco lungi dalla Porta di Capua per andare a Napoli.
Questo Sepolcro non si sa a qual Famiglia abbia
potuto appartenere, stante che gli è stata tolta la sua antica Iscrizione, come vedesi.

VEDUTA degli Avanzi della Circon ferenza delle antiche Fabbriche di una delle Piazze della Villa Adriana, vogadi chiamata Piazza d'oro

INTERNO del Tempio d' i Canope nella Villa Adriana.
A Sito dovevano anticamente delle Fontane. B Ponte rustico coperto
negli Eterni fatti nel 1771. C Antica Mostra... In Roma R...

VEDVTA DELL'ARCO
DI BENEVENTO NEL
REGNO DI NAPOLI

Veduta interna del Pantheon volgarmente detto la Rotonda

CARCERI D'INVENZIONE

CARCERI
INVENZIONE
G BATTISTA
PIRANESI
ARCHITE
VENE

I

III

IV

V

VII

VIII

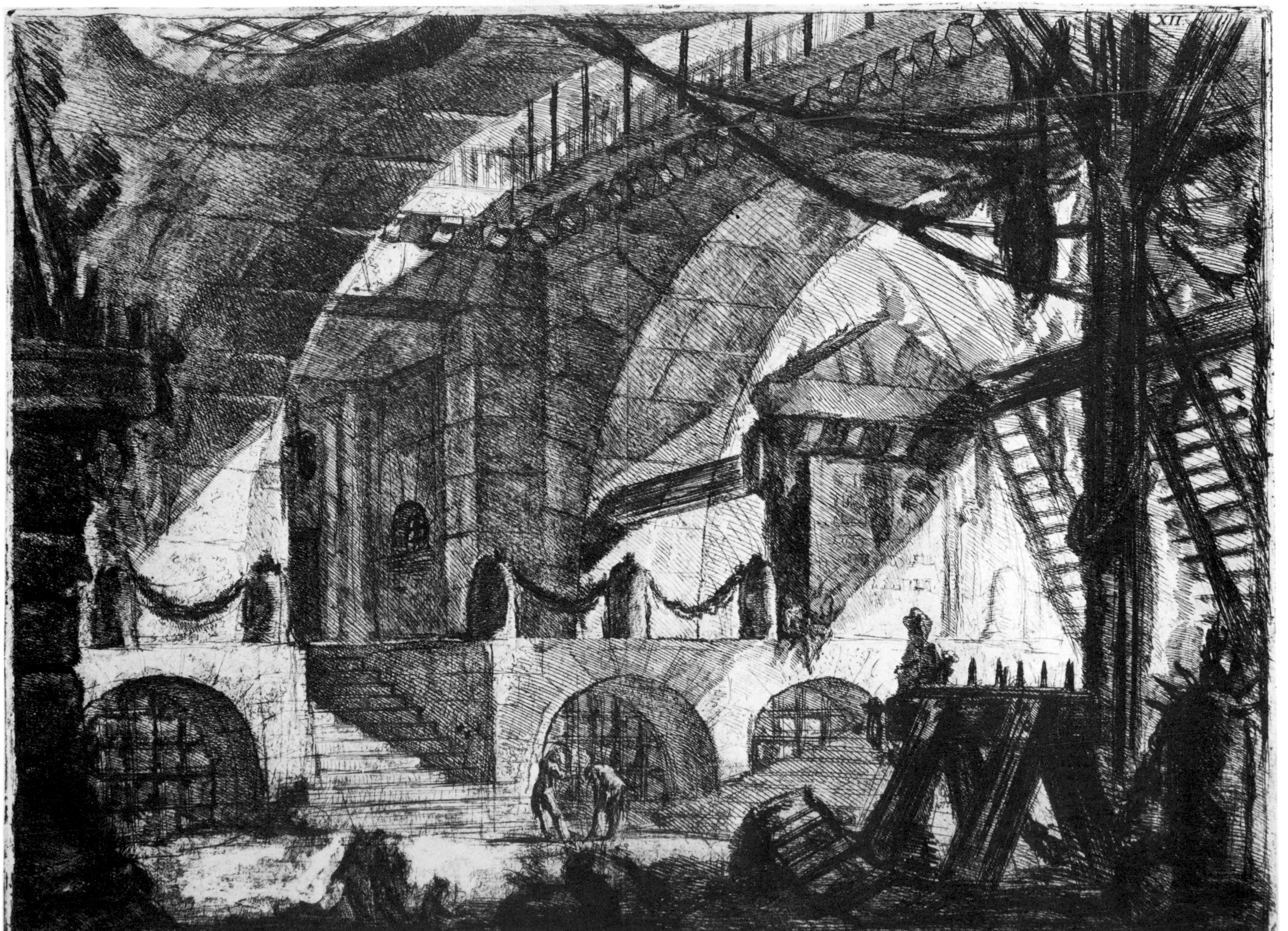
XII.

Vedute di Roma

The order of the plates used here follows that which the latest research indicates was Piranesi's order of composition. This is in many cases different from the order hitherto accepted and for the benefit of those who wish to refer to older publications the plate numbers used by Arthur M. Hind are given in brackets after each title.

Select Bibliography

Piranesi's own publications

1743   *Prima Parte di Architetture e Prospettive*

c. 1745   *Grotteschi*
Invenzioni capric di Carceri

1745   Plates published by Fausto Amidei in *Varie Vedute di Roma Antica e Moderna* (several of them being of an earlier date)

c. 1748 (or earlier)—1778   *Vedute di Roma*

1748   *Antichità Romane de' Tempi della Repubblica e de' Primi Imperatori*

c. 1750   *Opere Varie di Architettura, Prospettiva, Groteschi, Antichità* (reprint of *Prima Parte*, except for one plate, with additions, plus the *Grotteschi*)

1750   *Camere Sepolcrali degli Antichi Romani le quali esistono dentro e di fuori di Roma*

1751   *Le Magnificenze di Roma* (composite publication by Giovanni Bouchard containing a selection of the early plates of the *Vedute di Roma*)

1753   *I Trofei di Ottaviano Augusto*

1756   *Le Antichità Romane*

1757   *Lettere di Giustificazione scritte a Milord Charlemont*

c. 1760   *Carceri d'Invenzione* (reworking of *Invenzioni capric di Carceri* with two additional plates)

1761   *Della Magnificenza ed Architettura de' Romani*
Catologo delle Opere (subsequently revised in many states)
Le Rovine del Castello dell'Acqua Giulia

1762   *Lapides Capitolini*
Descrizione e Disegno dell'Emissario del Lago Albano
Di due Spelonche ornate dagli Antichi alla Riva del Lago Albano
Il Campo Marzio dell'Antica Roma

1764   *Antichità di Albano e di Castelgandolfo*
Antichità di Cora
Raccolta di Alcuni Disegni del . . . Guercino

1765   *Osservazioni sopra la lettre de M. Mariette*, accompanied by *Parere su l'Architettura* and *Della Introduzione e del Progresso delle belle arti in Europa de' tempi antichi*

after 1765   *Alcune Vedute di Archi Trionfali* (reprint of *Antichità Romane de' Tempi della Repubblica e de' Primi Imperatori*)

1769   *Diverse Maniere d'adornare i Cammini*

1774–9   *Trofeo o sia Magnifica Colonna Coclide*

c. 1774   *Pianta di Roma e del Campo Marzio*

1778   *Vasi, Candelabri, Cippi, Sarcofagi . . .*
Différentes vues de trois grands édifices qui subsistent encore dans le milieu de l'ancienne ville de Pesto

Posthumous publications issued by Francesco Piranesi

1781   *Pianta delle fabbriche esistenti nella Villa Adriana*

1791   *Dimostrazione dell'Emissario del Lago Fucino*

1804–7   *Les antiquités de la Grande Grèce*

Biographical sources and early publications

G. L. Bianconi, 'Elogio storico del Cavaliere Giambattista Piranesi celebre antiquario, ed incisore di Roma', *Antologia Romana* nos. 34–6, February-March 1779 (reprinted in *idem*, *Opere* II, Milan, 1802, pp. 127–40).
J. G. Legrand, 'Notice sur la vie et les ouvrages de J. B. Piranesi . . . Rédigée sur les notes et les pièces communiquées par ses fils, les compagnons et les continuateurs de ses nombreux travaux' [Paris, 1799], Paris, Bib. Nat. MSS. nouv. acq. fr. 5968 (printed inaccurately in G. Morazzoni, . *Giovanni Battista Piranesi: notizie biografiche*, Milan, n.d. [1921]; reprinted in *Nouvelles de l'estampe*, no. 5, 1969, pp. 191ff.).
Calcographie des Piranesi frères, *Oeuvres de Jean-Baptiste et de François Piranesi qui se vendent chez les Auteurs, à Paris rue de l'Université, Dépôt des Machines no. 296*, Paris, 1800.
P. Biagi, *Sull'incisione e sul Piranesi*, Venice, 1820.
J. Kennedy (?), 'Life of the Chevalier Giovanni Battista Piranesi', *Library of the Fine Arts or Repertory of Painting, Sculpture, Architecture, and Engraving*, II, no. 7, London, August 1831, pp. 8–13 : supposedly based on a MS. life written by one of Piranesi's sons, which has since disappeared.

Books

Académie de France à Rome, *Les actes du colloque 'Piranèse et les Français : 1740–1790'* (1976), Villa Medici, Rome (in press).
R. Bacou, *Piranèse: gravures et dessins*, Paris, 1974 (published in English as *Piranesi: Etchings and Drawings*, London, 1975).

Calcografia Nazionale, Rome, *Grafica*, II, 1976: special issue dedicated to Piranesi with catalogue by T. V. Salamon and articles by C. Bertelli.
Columbia University, New York, *Piranesi Drawings and Etchings at the Avery Architectural Library, Columbia University, New York: The Arthur M. Sackler Collection* (catalogues of the drawings by D. Nyberg and of the etchings by H. Mitchell), 1975.
H. Corfiato, *Piranesi Compositions*, London, 1951.
G. Cressedi, *Un Manoscritto derivato dalle 'Antichità' del Piranesi (Vaticano Latino, 8091)*, Rome, 1975.
E. L. Ferrari, *Giovanni Battista Piranesi en la Biblioteca Nacional: Estudio Preliminar y Catálogo*, Madrid, 1936.
H. Focillon, *Giovanni Battista Piranesi, 1720–1778*, Paris, 1918 (new ed. Paris, 1963; published in Italian as *Giovanni Battista Piranesi* (ed. M. Calvesi and A. Monferini), Bologna, 1967).
——, *Giovanni Battista Piranesi, essai de catalogue raisonné de son oeuvre*, Paris, 1918.
M.-P. Fouchet, *Jean Baptiste Piranesi : Les prisons imaginaires*, Paris, 1970.
A. Giesecke, *Giovanni Battista Piranesi* (Meister der Graphik, VI), Leipzig, 1911.
F. Hermanin, *Giambattista Piranesi, Architetto ed Incisore*, Turin, 1915 (2nd ed. Rome, 1922).
——, L. Volpicelli and C. A. Petrucci, *Giambattista Piranesi: Carceri d'Invenzione*, Rome, 1966.
A. M. Hind, *Giovanni Battista Piranesi: A Critical Study with a List of his Published Works and Detailed Catalogues of the Prisons and the Views of Rome*, London, 1922 (reprinted 1968).
P. Hofer, *The Prisons (Le Carceri) by Giovanni Battista Piranesi*, New York, 1973.
A. Huxley and J. Adhémar, *Prisons*, London, 1949.
L. Keller, *Piranèse et les romantiques français : Le mythe des escaliers en spirale*, Paris, 1966.
H. Levit, *G. B. Piranesi : Views of Rome, then and now*, New York, 1976.
V. Mariani, *Studiando Piranesi*, Rome, 1938.
A. Hyatt Mayor, *Giovanni Battista Piranesi*, New York, 1952.
G. Morazzoni, *Giovan Battista Piranesi, Architetto ed Incisore, 1720–1778*, Rome, 1921.
A. Muñoz, *G. B. Piranesi, con prospetto bibliografico e un indice di tutte le opere incise*, Rome, 1920.
P. Murray, *Piranesi and the grandeur of ancient Rome*, London, 1971.
R. Pane, *L'Acquaforte di G. B. Piranesi*, Naples, 1938.
G. B. Piranesi, *Die frühen Ansichtenwerke: I, Varie Vedute di Roma, 1748; II, Alcune Vedute di Archi Trionfali, 1765*, Uhl Verlag, Unterschneidheim, 1974 (a modern reprint of Piranesi's two early suites of *vedute*).
——, *Il Campo Marzio dell'Antica Roma, 1762*, Florence, 1972 (a modern reprint with an introduction by F. Borsi and an appendix

containing the official inventory of Piranesi's possessions at his death in 1778).

——, *Die Tempelruinen von Paestum*, Uhl Verlag, Unterschneidheim, 1973 (a modern reprint of the *Différentes vues ... de Pesto*).

M. Praz, *G. B. Piranesi: Le Carceri*, Milan, 1975.

—— and L. Jannattoni, *G. B. Piranesi. Magnificenza di Roma*, Milan, 1961.

A. Samuel, *Piranesi*, London, 1910.

J. Scott, *Piranesi*, London and New York, 1975.

R. Sturgis, *The Etchings of Piranesi*, New York, 1905.

H. Thomas, *The Drawings of Giovanni Battista Piranesi*, London and New York, 1954.

U. Vogt-Göknil, *Giovanni Battista Piranesi: Carceri*, Zürich, 1958.

H. Volkmann, *Giovanni Baptista Piranesi, Architekt und Graphiker*, Berlin, 1965.

J. Wilton-Ely (ed.), *Giovanni Battista Piranesi: The Polemical Works*, Farnborough, 1972: includes reprints of *Lettere di Giustificazione, Della Magnificenza, Parere* and *Diverse Maniere*.

Catalogues of principal exhibitions

Auckland (New Zealand), City Art Gallery, *Giovanni Battista Piranesi, 1720–1778* (ed. R. Fraser), 1963.

Benevento, Museo del Sannio, *Omaggio a Piranesi: Mostra antologica* (ed. E. Galasso), 1968.

Berlin, Kupferstichkabinett und Sammlung der Zeichnungen, Staatliche Museen zu Berlin, *Rom in Ansichten von Giovanni Battista Piranesi* (ed. H. Ebert and R. Kroll), 1970.

Bologna, Palazzo di Re Enzo, *Incisioni di G. B. Piranesi* (ed. M. Catelli-Isola, A. Mezzetti and S. Zamboni), 1963.

Geneva, Musée d'Art et d'Histoire, *Giovanni Battista Piranesi* (ed. E. Rossier), 1969.

Hamburg, Kunsthalle, *Piranesi-Ausstellung*, 1970.

Hanover, Kestner-Museum, *Giovanni Battista Piranesi: Vedute di Roma* (ed. C. Mosel), 1964.

Leningrad, Hermitage Museum, *G. B. Piranesi* (ed. I. S. Grigor'eva), 1959.

London, British Museum, *Giovanni Battista Piranesi: his Predecessors and his Heritage* (ed. E. Croft-Murray), 1968.

——, P. & D. Colnaghi & Co. Ltd., *Etchings by Giovanni Battista Piranesi, 1720–1778* (ed. K. Mayer-Haunton), 1973–4.

New York, Pierpont Morgan Library, *Giovanni Battista Piranesi: Drawings* (ed. F. Stampfle), 1949.

——, Avery Architectural Library, Columbia University, *Giovanni Battista Piranesi: Drawings and Etchings at Columbia University* (ed. D. Nyberg), 1972.

Northampton (Massachussetts), Smith College Museum of Art, *Piranesi* (ed. R. O. Parks), 1961, with the following contributions: P. Hofer, 'Piranesi as Book Illustrator', pp. 81–87; K. Lehmann, 'Piranesi as Interpreter of Roman Architecture', pp. 88–98; R. Wittkower, 'Piranesi as Architect', pp. 99–110.

Paris, Bibliothèque Nationale, *Piranèse* (ed. J. Adhémar and Mme Bonéfant), 1962.

Prague, Národní Galerie, *Piranesi* (ed. J. Wittlichová), 1972.

Princeton, University Library, *Giovanni Battista Piranesi* (ed. A. Robison), 1971.

Rome, Calcografia Nazionale, *Giovanni Battista e Francesco Piranesi* (ed. M. Calvesi), 1967–8.

——, Académie de France à Rome, Villa Medici (and Dijon and Paris), *Piranèse et les Français: 1740–1790* (ed. A. Chastel and G. Brunel with P. Arizzoli, G. Erouart, J.-F. Méjanès, M. Mosser, W. Oechslin and M. Roland-Michel), 1976.

Turin, Galleria Civica d'Arte Moderna, *G. B. Piranesi: Acqueforti e Disegni* (ed. F. Salamon), 1961–2.

Warsaw, University Library, *Giovanni Battista Piranesi, 1720–1778* (ed. W. Juszczak and E. Budzinska), 1967.

Articles

J. Andersen, 'Giant Dreams: Piranesi's influence in England', *English Miscellany*, Rome, III, 1952, pp. 49–60.

E. Bier, 'Vasi – Piranesi', *Maso Finiguerra*, III, 1938, pp. 1ff.

A. Bovero, 'Rivendo Piranesi', *Emporium*, LXVIII, no. 135, 1962, pp. 7–12.

H. Brauer, 'Giovanni Battista Piranesi verwirklicht einen Traum: Eine Zeichnung zum St Basilius-Altar in Sta Maria del Priorato', *Miscellanea Bibliotechae Hertzianae*, 1961, pp. 474–7.

M. Catelli-Isola, 'Interpretazione di G. B. Piranesi', *L'Urbe*, XXV, no. 3, 1962, pp. 1–5.

S. Chamberlain, 'The Triumphal Arches of Piranesi', *Print Collector's Quarterly*, XXIV, no. 1, 1937, pp. 62–79.

L. Cochetti, 'L'opera teorica di Piranesi', *Commentari*, VI, 1955, pp. 35–49.

E. Di Castro, 'Giovanni Battista Piranesi e i mobili del Settecento romano', *L'Urbe*, XXIV, no. 2, 1961, pp. 23–8.

L. Donati, 'Piranesiana', *Maso Finiguerra*, III, 1938, pp. 206–13; IV, 1939, pp. 121–3; V, 1940, pp. 261–70.

——, 'Giovanni Battista Piranesi e Lord Charlemont', *English Miscellany*, Rome, I, 1950, pp. 231–42.

——, 'Una ignota stampa postuma del Piranesi', *Strenna dei Romanisti*, 1953, pp. 121–3.

J. Erichsen, 'Eine Zeichnung zu Piranesis "Prima Parte"', *Pantheon*, XXXIV, no. 3, 1976, pp. 212–16.

V. Fasolo, 'Il "Campo Marzio" di G. B. Piranesi', *Quaderni dell'Istituto di Storia dell'Architettura*, XV, 1956, pp. 1–14.

M. E. Fischer, 'Die Umbaupläne des Giovanni Battista Piranesi für den Chor von S. Giovanni in Laterano', *Münchner Jahrbuch der bildenden Kunst*, XIX, 1968, pp. 207–28.

M. Fischer, 'Piranesis radiertes Oeuvre und die zugehörigen Entwürfe in der Kunstbibliothek', *Berliner Museen*, XVI, no. 2, 1966, pp. 17–24.

A. Geffroy, 'Essai sur la formation des collections d'antiques de la Suède', *Revue Archéologique*, XXIX, 1896, pp. 1ff: discusses the contents of Piranesi's *museo* as sold to Gustav III. See also Kjellberg.

A. Giesecke, entries 'Francesco Piranesi' and 'Giovanni Battista Piranesi' in Thieme-Becker, *Allgemeines Lexikon der bildenden Künstler*, Leipzig, 1933, XXVII, pp. 79–83.

G. Guillaume-Coirier, 'Archéologie et imagination: les représentations du tombeau de Bibulus de Pollaiuolo à Piranèse', *Gazette des Beaux-Arts*, LXXXI, April 1973, pp. 215–26.

J. Harris, 'Le Geay, Piranesi and International Neo-Classicism in Rome, 1740–1750' in *Essays in the History of Architecture presented to Rudolf Wittkower* (ed. D. Fraser), London and New York, 1967, pp. 189–96.

A. M. Hind, 'G. B. Piranesi and his Carceri', *Burlington Magazine*, XIX, May 1911, pp. 81ff.

——, 'G. B. Piranesi: some further notes, and a list of his works', *Burlington Magazine*, XXIV, December 1913, pp. 135–8; XXV, January 1914, pp. 187–203; February 1914, pp. 262–4.

K. Kassirer, 'Piranesi disegnatore di figure', *Roma*,

Rivista di Studi e di Vita Romana, II, 1924, pp. 180–81.

E. Kaufmann, 'Piranesi, Algarotti and Lodoli: a Controversy in XVIIIth-century Venice', *Gazette des Beaux-Arts*, XLVI, 1955, pp. 21–8.

F. Kimball, 'Piranesi, Algarotti and Lodoli' in *Essays in Honour of Hans Tietze*, New York, 1958, pp. 309–16.

E. Kjellberg, 'Piranesis antiksamling i Nationalmuseum', *Nationalmusei Årsbok*, Stockholm, 2, 1920, pp. 115ff: contains a catalogue of the contents of Piranesi's *museo* as sold to Gustav III. See also Geffroy.

W. Körte, 'Giovanni Battista Piranesi als praktischer Architekt', *Zeitschrift für Kunstgeschichte*, II, 1933, pp. 16–33.

W. Kroenig, 'Storia di una veduta di Roma', *Bollettino d'Arte*, ser. 5, LVII, nos. 3–4, 1972, pp. 165–98.

J. Lopez-Rey, 'Las Cárceles de Piranesi, los Prisioneros de Goya' in *Scritti di Storia dell'Arte in onore di Lionello Venturi*, Rome, 1956, II, pp. 111–16.

M. McCarthy, 'Sir Roger Newdigate and Piranesi', *Burlington Magazine*, CXIV, July 1972, pp. 466–72.

V. Mariani, 'Giambattista Piranesi', *Capitolium*, IX, no. 1, 1933, pp. 23–4.

A. Hyatt Mayor, 'Piranesi', *Bulletin of the Metropolitan Museum of Art*, XXXIII, no. 12, 1938, pp. 279–84.

——, 'Two Piranesi drawings in the Gilmor Collection', *The Baltimore Museum of Art News*, XX, no. 1, 1956, pp. 1–2.

M. G. Messina, 'Teoria dell'architettura in Giovanbattista Piranesi: L'affermazione dell'eclettismo', *Controspazio*, VI, 1971, pp. 20–28.

B. Molajoli, 'Piranesi Architetto', *Bollettino del Centro Internazionale di Architettura 'Andrea Palladio'*, 1963, pp. 212–14.

A. Mongan, 'Una fantasia architettonica di Giovanni Battista Piranesi', *Arte Veneta*, IV, 1951, pp. 176–7.

R. E. Moore, 'The art of Piranesi: looking backward into the future' in *Changing taste in eighteenth-century art and literature*, William Andrews Clark Memorial Library, Los Angeles University, California, 1972, pp. 3–40.

R. Mormone, 'Una lettera del Vanvitelli al Piranesi', *Bollettino di Storia dell'Arte* (Salerno), II, 1952, pp. 89–92.

K. T. Parker, 'G. B. Piranesi', *Old Master Drawings*, X, no. 38, September 1935, p. 27; XII, no. 48, March 1938, pp. 54–5.

A. Petrucci, entry 'Giambattista Piranesi' in *Enciclopedia italiana di scienze, lettere ed arti*, Rome, 1935, XXVII, pp. 353–7.

C. A. Petrucci, 'L'incisione del Settecento a Roma e i Piranesi', *Atti dell'Accademia nazionale di S. Luca*, Rome, new series, III, 1957–8, pp. 105–8.

C. Pietrangeli, 'Sull'iconografia di G. B. Piranesi', *Bollettino dei Musei Comunali di Roma*, I, nos. 3–4, 1954, pp. 40–43.

——, 'La Sala Nuova di Don Abbondio Rezzonico', *Capitolium*, XXXVIII, 1963, pp. 244–6.

G. Poulet, 'Piranèse et les poètes romantiques français', *La Nouvelle Revue Française*, XIII, no. 160, April 1966, pp. 660–71; XIV, no. 161, May 1966, pp. 849–62.

W. Rieder, 'Piranesi's "Diverse Maniere"', *Burlington Magazine*, CXV, May 1973, pp. 309–17.

——, 'Piranesi at Gorhambury', *Burlington Magazine*, CXVII, September 1975, pp. 582–91.

A. Robison, 'Giovanni Battista Piranesi: prolegomena to the Princeton Collections', *Princeton*

University Library Chronicle, XXXI, no. 3, Spring 1970, pp. 165–206.

——, 'The "Vedute di Roma" of Giovanni Battista Piranesi: Notes towards a revision of Hind's catalogue', *Nouvelles de l'estampe*, no. 4, 1970, pp. 180–98.

——, 'Piranesi's Ship on Wheels', *Master Drawings*, XI, 1973, pp. 389–92.

J. Rosenberg, 'Two Piranesi Drawings', *Old Master Drawings*, X, no. 37, June 1935, pp. 9–10.

F. Salamon, 'G. B. Piranesi', *Goya*, LXVI, May–June 1965, pp.365–75.

T. V. Salamon, 'Giovanni Battista Piranesi: A catalogue', *The Print Collector* XXIX, nos. 14–15, September–December 1975, pp. 4–52.

S. Sawicka, 'Fantaisies architectoniques de G. B. Piranesi', *Arte Veneta*, XVI, 1962, pp. 190–94.

G. Schéfer, 'Piranesi, un rénovateur de l'art décoratif', *Les Arts*, XI, no. 128, August 1912, pp. 26–32; XII, no. 136, April 1913, pp. 18–25.

P. M. Sekler, 'Giovanni Battista Piranesi's "Carceri" etchings and related drawings', *Art Quarterly*, Detroit Institute of Arts, XXV, no. 4, 1962, pp. 331–65.

F. Stampfle, 'An unknown group of drawings by G. B. Piranesi', *Art Bulletin*, XXX, no. 2, June 1948, pp. 122–41.

S. Gavuzzo Stewart, 'Nota sulle Carceri Piranesiane', *L'Arte*, XV–XVI, 1972, pp. 57ff.

D. Stillman, 'Robert Adam and Piranesi' in *Essays in the History of Architecture presented to Rudolf Wittkower* (ed. D. Fraser), London and New York, 1967, pp. 197–206.

M. Tafuri, 'Giovan Battista Piranesi: l'utopie négative dans l'architecture', *L'architecture d'aujourd'hui*, no. 184, March 1976, pp. 93–108.

H. Thomas, 'Piranesi and Pompeii', *Kunstmuseets Årsskrift*, Copenhagen, 1952–5, pp. 13–28.

——, 'De tekenningen van Piranesi in het Museum Boymans', *Bulletin Museum Boymans*, VIII, 1957, pp. 10–20.

I. Vitali, 'Le quattro "Lettere di Giustificazione" di Piranesi', *Belvedere*, VI, 1924, pp. 29–33.

F. J. B. Watson, 'A side table by Piranesi: a masterpiece of neo-classic furniture', *Minneapolis Institute of Arts Bulletin*, LIV, 1965, pp. 19–29.

J. Wilton-Ely, 'Piranesian symbols on the Aventine', *Apollo*, CIII, March 1976, pp. 214–27 (republished in *Annales de l'Ordre Souverain Militaire de Malte*, XXXIV, nos. 1–2, January–June 1976, pp. 8–23).

——, 'A bust of Piranesi by Nollekens', *Burlington Magazine*, CXVIII, August 1976, pp. 593–95.

——, 'The relationship between Giambattista Piranesi and Luigi Vanvitelli in eighteenth-century architectural theory and practice' in *Atti del Congresso Vanvitelliano (1973)* (in press).

——, 'Vision and Design: Piranesi's "Fantasia" and the Graeco-Roman Controversy', *Les actes du colloque 'Piranèse et les Français: 1740–1790 (1976)*, Académie de France à Rome (in press).

R. Wittkower, 'Piranesi's "Parere su l'Architettura"', *Journal of the Warburg Institute*, II, 1938–9, pp. 147–58 (republished as 'Piranesi's Architectural Creed' in *Studies in the Italian Baroque* (ed. M. Wittkower), London, 1975, pp. 235–46).

——, 'Piranesi as Architect' (see exhibition catalogue Northampton, Smith College Museum of Art; republished in *Studies in the Italian Baroque*, op. cit., pp. 247–58).

——, 'Piranesi and Eighteenth-century Egyptomania' in *Studies in the Italian Baroque, op. cit.*, pp. 260–73.

M. Yourcenar, 'Le cerveau noir de Piranèse' in *Sous bénéfice d'inventaire*, Paris, 1962 (reprinted in an abbreviated form as 'Les prisons imaginaires de Piranèse', *La Nouvelle Revue Française*, IX, no. 67, January 1961, pp. 63–78).

S. Zamboni, 'Il percorso di Giovanni Battista Piranesi', *Arte Antica e Moderna*, XXV, 1964, pp. 66–85.

G. Zucchini, 'Un disegno del Piranesi', *Il Commune di Bologna*, XXI, no. 8, 1934, pp. 28–9.

Photographic Credits

Index

Italic numerals refer to plates
Ved. plus a numeral refers to the *Vedute di Roma*